Practical Information Security Management

A Complete Guide to Planning and Implementation

Tony Campbell

Apress®

Practical Information Security Management: A Complete Guide to Planning and Implementation

Tony Campbell
Burns Beach
Australia

ISBN-13 (pbk): 978-1-4842-1684-2   ISBN-13 (electronic): 978-1-4842-1685-9
DOI 10.1007/978-1-4842-1685-9

Library of Congress Control Number: 2016960737

Managing Director: Welmoed Spahr
Acquisitions Editor: Susan McDermott
Developmental Editor: Matt Moodie
Technical Reviewer: Nigel Hardy, Tristan Bennett
Editorial Board: Steve Anglin, Pramila Balen, Laura Berendson, Aaron Black, Louise Corrigan, Jonathan Gennick, Robert Hutchinson, Celestin Suresh John, Nikhil Karkal, James Markham, Susan McDermott, Matthew Moodie, Natalie Pao, Gwenan Spearing
Coordinating Editor: Rita Fernando
Copy Editor: Kim Burton-Weisman
Compositor: SPi Global
Indexer: SPi Global
Cover image: Designed by Hurca - Freepik.com

Distributed to the book trade worldwide by Springer Science+Business Media New York, 233 Spring Street, 6th Floor, New York, NY 10013. Phone 1-800-SPRINGER, fax (201) 348-4505, e-mail orders-ny@springer-sbm.com, or visit www.springer.com. Apress Media, LLC is a California LLC and the sole member (owner) is Springer Science + Business Media Finance Inc (SSBM Finance Inc). SSBM Finance Inc is a Delaware corporation.

For information on translations, please e-mail rights@apress.com, or visit www.apress.com.

Apress and friends of ED books may be purchased in bulk for academic, corporate, or promotional use. eBook versions and licenses are also available for most titles. For more information, reference our Special Bulk Sales–eBook Licensing web page at www.apress.com/bulk-sales.

Any source code or other supplementary materials referenced by the author in this text is available to readers at www.apress.com. For detailed information about how to locate your book's source code, go to www.apress.com/source-code/.

Printed on acid-free paper

"I saw the angel in the marble and carved until I set him free."

—Michelangelo

This book is dedicated to the two people in my life that inspire me the most.
For Sharon and Lara: set your angels free.

Contents at a Glance

Contents

About the Author

Tony Campbell has been in and around the cyber security industry for over 25 years with the early part of his career providing consultancy services to the UK government in security architecture and security management. Prior to moving to Perth in 2013, Tony was Chief Security Architect on a large UK Ministry of Defence ICT programme and managed a team of enterprise security architects. Since moving to Australia, Tony has provided strategic security consultancy to a variety of local government agencies and developed ISO 27001 security management systems for a number of government and private organisations.
Tony now works for Kinetic IT, a successful AustralianIT managed services provider, where he works as their Principal Security Consultant. Tony also writes for the Australian Security Magazine and you can read his weekly blog on IT News's website: http://www.itnews.com.au/author/tony-campbell-747578.

About the Technical Reviewers

 **Nigel Hardy** is Security Services State Lead for Australia's largest telecommunications company, with a focus on delivering information security and risk management services to their many clients. He has worked with companies ranging from start-ups, to many of the Fortune Global 500, and has spent the last 20 years working across the ICT and security industries to help address challenges and improve security posture.

He has been successful in providing security leadership at all levels, and has presented at various security conferences and forums globally, provided subject matter expertise to law enforcement during cybersecurity incident investigations, and is supporting the Australian government's cybersecurity initiatives both locally and nationally.

His technical background enables him to engage at all levels within a business, and he is just as likely to be found performing penetration testing and research, as he is to be in the boardroom discussing how a vulnerability may impact business continuity.

Nigel is currently working on security operations and incident response processes, and researching vulnerabilities and vulnerability management within the industrial control systems environment.

Tristan Bennett has over a decade of experience within the IT industry in numerous security roles for both government and private entities across Australia. Mostly working in operational roles he has been involved in implementing a wide range of security technologies tailored to address customers concerns.

His current role has seen him take on the lead technical position in establishing a security operations center in Western Australia, which now provides security monitoring and oversight for a number of private and public organizations.

Acknowledgments

The acknowledgements section of a book can sometimes read like a celebrity speech at an award ceremony. They thank everyone that has ever contributed to their career development, all the way from their parents to their pets. Another factor is that acknowledgements are rarely read by anyone other than the author and the people being acknowledged, oftentimes because the author has told them about the mention. What I'll try and do here is something a little different, since I have too many people to thanks and the things I'd like to thank them for may be directly unrelated to the topic of cybersecurity but have contributed to my own perspectives. I grew up in Northern Ireland during the 1970s, which as anyone with an ounce of world history knowledge will know, was a particularly troubled time for the province. As a young lad trying to find my way in life, I quickly had to learn which parts of Belfast city were off limits to the likes of me, based on the intangibles of religion, the school I went to and the color of scarf I wore. I also learned to read situations well and quickly assess the clientele in pubs so that I could predict any trouble before it escalated, which it often did. So, from the moment I ventured out on my own as a naïve schoolboy, I was programmed to assess physical risks that had the potential to lead to harm or even death in pretty much every situation I found myself in. You might ask yourself what this has to do with information security. That's easy, I was technically minded and certainly spent a lot of time building electronics projects, and programming computers (I had a ZX Spectrum), so coupling that mindset with an innate capability to assess risks, falling into a security career was almost destined. When I finally left Northern Ireland in 1989, I moved to a job in England, working for the UK Meteorological Office, where I became a C and Fortran programmer. However, my love was in systems and administration, as well as network architecture, so I ditched the programming life for a sys admin job, which is where things turned around. System administration was awesome back then—we were the guys with all the power. When we finally replaced all of our old DEC equipment with Windows NT 4.0, I finally realized that security was the job for me. I moved from Meteorological Office to a Ministry of Defence contractor and from there started working directly on highly-classified military systems. I was in my element as a security administrator, but always seemed to end up inheriting a team of wannabe security guys that I had to mentor. This was always fun, but came with some frustrations that what I considered obvious from a risk perception point of view seemed hard for these guys to grasp. I had no problem in teaching concepts and methodologies to these guys, but what I noticed was that it took a significant amount of time for people to just get it. What I had forgotten was that my time was served watching my back on the streets of Belfast, which had programmed me in a way that was alien these mainlanders, who didn't have to think twice about answering a question such as, "What school did you go to?" In Belfast, the wrong answer to that question could result in your kneecaps being smashed with a tire iron. So security, for me, became a calling and no matter what kind of role or project I took on, I always covered the security viewpoint. Security became my career and when it was possible to be classified as a security professional, I was there in line for the badge, and I've never looked back. To me it's been a calling in life that I have no found, coupled with my other calling, writing, so the opportunity to fuse these two passions together into this book was an exciting prospect. Security is all about risk assessment, management, and ensuring you've done enough but no too much, since too much security will stop you from doing the things you want to do.

But let's get back to the point of my life story. I could personally reach out and thank dozens upon dozens of people who have been with me on my personal journey, but there are a few who need special mention, those who taught me about risk assessment, contingency planning and writing and self-critique, to whom I am eternally grateful. My grandfather Davy taught me to question and consider people's motives and to not take anything for granted. George Purvis taught me self-control and Pete Day taught me to consider and plan for contingencies. My mum and dad taught me unconditional love and respect for my elders, while my colleagues and friends taught me how to deal with life. All of these mentors have helped me through to today, where I can now consider myself lucky enough to be in an industry that I adore, in a country that I love and working with people that I respect. I really must acknowledge my biggest critic, Sharon, who keeps my head level and my ego in check. Lara is just cool, say no more on that.

My technical reviewers on this book have been awesome. Nigel Hardy is one of the finest information security consultants, managers, and friends I could have in the industry, and he certainly pulls no punches. Tristan Bennett is the best operational security guy I have ever had the pleasure of meeting. Without these two guys being critical of my work and helping me deliver a complete overview of information security management, this book would not have been as complete as it is. Finally, thanks to the Apress team, Rita, Susan, and Matt, who have helped get me to the end of this project without any lasting battle scars (at least, none that won't heal given time and therapy).

If I've missed anyone that deserved a specific mention, sorry, it wasn't intentional. I thank you all.

Introduction

I wrote this book because I saw the need. As someone who's been in this game for such a very long time, I felt somewhat obliged to help those who want to get started. I often get asked how you get started in a career in infosec. People ask if they should switch over from a management role, or maybe a technical job, or maybe they work in corporate risk and compliance and want to go deeper into the cybersecurity side of things. I've been having these conversations with increasingly regularity, but I noticed that the line of questioning always ends up looking at why they think they want a security career? What is it about this weird and often frustrating field that has piqued their interest?

I now believe that you need to have a passion for this business to make it a success. I also believe that there are people who are already in security who just don't get it, while there are countless people not in security that really could and should be. The passion I speak of comes from an innate personal trait that many of us are born with, compelling us to rip stuff apart to see how it works. It's this same innate ability that drives the best security guys to look beyond the surface of systems, processes, and people, to see the weaknesses and vulnerabilities that leave them exposed to attack.

Note   I've taken 20 years of experience, academic theory, along with real-world experience and distilled it into a practical guide that shows you the ropes. You can use this as a textbook that you reference as you work, not contradicting anything you will need to learn should you want to pursue academic studies at college or university, or if you intend to shoot for some of the most valued and recognized industry certifications, such as CISSP, SABSA, CISM, or CISMP.

This book looks at just one of the myriad career paths you could opt for if you want to get started in security: *information security manager* (ISM). It's a truism that being an ISM is no easy ride. Information security management is a tough subject to master and there are dozens of standards and guidelines that explain *what* you need to do to secure your organization, without explaining *how* to do it.

The reality is that all of these standards and guidelines are useful, but without context, you're left scratching your head (or whatever it is you scratch in times of trouble), wondering how it applies to you and the systems and information that you protect. This textbook bridges some of the gaps between the *what* and the *how* of information security, offering ISMs some practical advice on developing skills and competencies in this complicated and often-infuriating discipline.

What You Will Learn

- The practical aspects of being an effective information security manager

- How to strike the right balance between cost and risk

- How to take security policies and standards and make them work in reality

- How to leverage complex security functions, such as digital forensics, incident response, and security architecture

As I said, I've aimed this book primarily at newly appointed *information security managers* or anyone who is already in a security role but fancies their chances as an ISM. That being said, I've also gone wide in coverage so that this can be as useful a reference as possible even for experienced ISMs and security engineers who are interested expanding their knowledge.

Let's start with a short history to put this in perspective.

Somewhere in Time

Over half a century ago, US Defense Advanced Research Projects Agency (DARPA) scientist, J.C.R. Licklider, had an absurd idea. He proposed the wild notion of a so-called *Galactic Network*. The concept was simple: a ubiquitous, global internetwork of computers that anyone could use to access information and programs in real time.

Licklider's vision foreshadowed the Internet that we now take for granted every day, however, back then, the notion was more like science fiction than fact, but with persistence, Licklider's dream became a reality. Over the next ten years, DARPA developed a plethora of standards and technologies that would laid the foundation of the global internetwork we use today. Devices such as *interface message processors* linked together to form the backbone of a distributed network—the mesh network—that soon became recognized as ARPANET.

When scientists connected the first two nodes to ARPANET in 1969, they demonstrated host-to-host message transfer from UCLA's Network Measurement Center to the Stanford Research Institute (SRI), serving the simple purpose of proving Licklider's vision was not just a pipedream.

The US Department of Defense had already developed the *Transmission Control Protocol/Internet Protocol* (TCP/IP) in the early 1970s; however, they did not adopt it until later that decade.

By 1985, ARPANET was still only providing government and research services. However, increasing pressure to extend its reach into commercial and academic sectors accelerated plans to grow over the next five years. By 1990, ARPANET was decommissioned and the Internet was born.

■ **Note**   Due to the illegal actions of some phreakers, the term *phreaker* became quickly associated only illegality. Phreakers were, in the eyes of the media, all criminals, whether they were simply hanging out on AT&T's network or acting with criminal intent. Today, we see the same issues with terminology, where modern media uses *hacker* to define anyone acting illegally on computer systems and networks. Like phreaker, hacker described someone with natural talent and aptitude for tinkering with and learning about computers. However, the media now labels anyone acting with criminal or malicious intent as a hacker, so it is now dangerous to refer to yourself as a hacker if you are acting with good intentions.

You might ask yourself what the point of this history lesson is—fair question, given this book is about information security management. However, remembering that timeline of development of the Internet, let us now jump sideways onto a different timeline and track a different historical course that brings us to today's understanding of where security is.

During the late 1950s and early 1960s, AT&T's management learned of the existence of an underground group of technology geeks, known as *phone phreakers*. The phreakers were accessing AT&T's telephone network without permission, sometimes for their own gain, such as those using custom tone-generators, dubbed as *blue boxes*, to obtain free calls. In 1964, AT&T started monitoring their exchanges, trying to catch and prosecute the phreakers who were stealing calls. This audit program ran for six long years, with no more than 200 viable convictions to show for all their efforts. What's interesting is that the majority of phreakers were nothing more than interested hobbyists and geeks, all with a love of technology and a yearning to explore the mysteries of the telephone network.

Computer security has been around for as long as networks and computers, since the innate nature of humankind is to look for ways to turn systems and tools against us. Just like every society-changing evolution throughout history, the global community has today come to rely, almost ubiquitously, on the interconnectedness of all things. We have built connectivity into our businesses and homes, but more so we are not connecting all sorts of things that previously were autonomous. Fridges are ordering food for themselves. Microwave ovens are reaching out to the Internet to acquire cooking times for the meals we are preparing rather than you having to work these out yourself. We are even using fast ordering technologies, such as Amazon Dash Buttons, to order replacement products directly from its online shop.

▨ **Note** German chemist Martin Klaproth discovered uranium in 1789. In 1932, James Chadwick discovered the neutron, while experiments by John Cockcroft and Ernest Walton showed that transformations were possible through atomic bombardment. It wasn't until 1939 that a German team of physicists, led by Niels Bohr, proved that the astounding amount of energy released from splitting the atom was as much as 200 million electron volts. This kicked off research right across the world into harnessing that energy to provide potentially infinite power. Six years later, scientists were turning this society-changing science into the most devastating weapon of our time, dropping it on two Japanese cities and killing hundreds of thousands of innocent civilians.

When systems are initially conceived, it's rare that the consideration of how they might be misused is at the fore of the inventor's mind. Normally, the imagination of science fiction writers yields the most insight into how systems turn against their creators. Think of all those science fiction stories that have become Hollywood blockbusters over the years.

- *Do Androids Dream of Electric Sheep?*. This Philip K. Dick novel was turned into the movie *Blade Runner*. It tells the story of synthetically created humans (a.k.a the *replicants*) that disobey their orders and return to Earth, causing trouble as they go.

- *The Terminator*. This 1984 movie tells the story of a post-apocalyptic future where the robots have turned against their masters to take over the world.

- *Frankenstein*. Mary Wollstonecraft Shelley's 1823 novel is probably the most famous and most reproduced story about a scientific creation turning against its master.

While we've digressed somewhat from computer security, the point I'm making is that we have recognized for some time that science and technology can be used for good or ill. However, the technology itself is impartial to how it's used—it just does what it's predisposed to do. It's humans and their innate nature of attacking one another and taking from one another that causes the problems. Our computer systems and networks are no exception. Coupled with the copious number of vulnerabilities, bugs and design flaws we hear of every day, affecting the systems we use to access our bank accounts, plays games, run our businesses and orchestrate military conflicts, it's little wonder that those that wish us harm use these weaknesses to attack us.

It was not long ago that a bank heist involved rushing into a branch with a couple of double-barreled shotguns and taking physical cash from the vault. This was highly dangerous for the criminals and very risky for all concerned.

In today's globally interconnected banking world, it's a different story: billions of dollars go missing every single year, channeled back into organized crime, carried out by threat groups who no longer use guns but instead use keyboards.

The Subliminal Verses

This book is split up into 14 chapters, taking you on a journey through the initial assessment of an information security program within your organization, to career management, hiring of an infosec team, designing a career development plan and implementing your security mission within the context of your organization's business and technical strategy. The latter half of the book, from Chapter 7 onward looks at specific areas of protection, starting with information, and then looks at people, premises, systems, and digital evidence, before looking at the security issues with modern cloud computing environments, industrial control systems and software, and systems development life cycles.

Chapter 1: Evolution of a Profession

Chapter one looks at the history of the information security profession and covers some of the basic career path choices open to people entering the professional, either coming in at the bottom through school and college, or through a sideways shift from a relevant background, where the switch is as much about a mindset change than learning new stuff. We'll also look at some of the key language and terminology you are likely to come across on your travels and explain some of the basic principles that we'll deal with in more detail later in the book.

Chapter 2: Threats and Vulnerabilities

The sophistication and capability of cybercriminals is greater today than it has ever been, with technically superior threat actors researching and developing insidious malware frameworks that allow them or their customers to break into their victims' systems, maintaining access, covering their tracks, evading countermeasures and siphoning gigabytes of confidential information off for sale on the black market. This chapter looks at the myriad threats and vulnerabilities that are affecting us every day, including those that are man-made and those that are naturally occurring threats that are often overlooked when considering information security.

Chapter 3: Introducing the Security Manager

In Chapter 3, we dive into the role of information security manager and look at what they have to do on a day-to-day basis. We also focus on how information security managers can manage the skills and competencies of their team using a recognized skills framework and how professionalism within the security sector can be used to elevate all of our roles as security guys out of the traditional IT envelope into a profession all of its own. We will also look at some of the common myths and misconceptions related to professional training courses and academic courses and their bearing on your career development plans, closing off this chapter with a brief look at what an *information security management system* is.

Chapter 4: Information Security as a Business Function

Chapter 4 looks at how the information security manager can embed security as a function within the business, ensuring that we align all of the people, processes, and technology to security outcomes that support the business and its strategic imperatives. We will look at the traditional organizational structures we see every day in business, looking at how to layer security into these structures to ensure that we cover all aspects of risk, not just those related to cyber. This chapter takes a deeper look at risk management, business continuity management and enterprise architecture, explaining the part security plays in each of these business functions. This chapter closes with a brief explanation of how security can integrate with facilities management, before we go into a lot more details in Chapter 9, which discusses protection of premises.

Chapter 5: Information Security Implementation

Information security implementation goes into more details on how the information security manager can integrate the functions of the security team with the functions provided by the rest of the organization, such as risk management, architecture and software development. Most importantly, this chapter looks at the concept of security requirements as opposed to security controls, showing you how to elicit security requirements at the project initiation stage to ensure that threats, vulnerabilities, and risks are dealt with by design rather than as an afterthought.

Chapter 6: Standards Frameworks Guidelines and Legislation

As the basis of everything we do in security, especially when operating in the role of *information security manager*, we need to justify what we impose on the business from the perspective of risk reduction. In a world where threats and vulnerabilities affect what we do each day, there are now myriad standards, frameworks, guidelines and national legislation that drive what we have to do to meet certain industry or legal requirements. Chapter 6 looks at a variety of international standards and guidelines that affect our organizations, assessing their value to you as an information security manager as well as their value to the industry in general.

Chapter 7: Protection of Information

Information is the lifeblood of modern businesses, no matter whether they trade in travel insurance, government secrets, building, and construction or further education—information sits at the heart of making these businesses work. Chapter 7 looks at how we can establish systems to help protect the vitally important information within our organizations, taking into account the sensitivity of the data and the access control systems we can employ to ensure that only those that need to access get it.

Chapter 8: Protection of People

In business, our people are one of our most valuable assets. However, they can also be our biggest weakness, given the innate human fallibility, which is exactly what attackers using social engineering target. Chapter 8 looks at some of the threats and vulnerabilities organizations face through employment of staff, as well as some of the mechanisms we can use to protect ourselves from these kinds of attack. We'll look at security clearance, auditing, and monitoring, coupled with security awareness training, as means to bolster this inherently vulnerable aspect of our organization.

Chapter 9: Protection of Premises

Our offices, field sites, and datacenters can all be weak points within our operations where attacks can take place. In Chapter 9 we look at the physical security measures we can take to defend our castles, including the primary considerations the information security manager should have when working alongside the experts in the facilities management team, the business executive and law enforcement to help protect our physical environments.

Chapter 10: Protection of Systems

Chapter 10 is the most technical chapter in this book. It looks at some of the technical design patterns and technical controls that the information security manager needs to know about within enterprise architectures, ensuring a reasonable baseline of security knowledge can be added to any security manager's arsenal. This will help information security managers when they have conversations with technical teams, such as network engineers, Windows operation systems specialists and database administrators, ensuring the information security manager can speak their language while translating technical risks into meaningful security controls.

Chapter 11: Protection of Evidence

Digital evidence is extremely important in todays connected world and not a single police investigation goes in that doesn't have some kind of electronic footprint, be that from a laptop, tablet, mobile phone, GPS device or games console. The impact of social media and cloud computing is also disrupting the traditional approach to investigating crimes, since much of the data produced on smartphone now resides on cloud-based systems rather than on the device itself. Chapter 11 looks at some of the considerations that information security managers need to take when evaluating the need to collect irrefutable digital evidence from the systems the workforce use every day.

Chapter 12: Cloud Computing Security

One of the most disruptive changes to corporate IT and the traditional approach to managing IT on your own premises is that of *cloud computing*. However, cloud computing comes with its own issues and risks, something that the information security manager needs to be acutely aware of. Chapter 12 looks at some of the issues we face in cloud computing environments and how we can mitigate these in the context of expediency for the business while remaining in control of our information's security.

Chapter 13: Protection of Operational Technology

Operational technology is the most recent term to describe the systems we use to run physical processes within our businesses. These might be the controllers used in automated manufacturing plants, the software that controls valves and pressure systems in water distribution networks, or the technology that sits behind the cooling systems in nuclear reactors, each of which could be the target of a cyberattack. Chapter 13 looks at how information security managers need to understand their OT environment and apply some of the same risk mitigation strategies used for the rest of the business in this highly critical yet overlooked aspect of information security.

Chapter 14: Secure Systems Development

Chapter 14 looks at some of the issues that businesses face when software developers do not use secure-coding practices to create line-of-business applications. However, it's not just about coding—this chapter focuses on the creation of a security development process that encompasses requirements management, security testing and systems patching to build a life cycle management capability that ensure that information security is considered as a core deliverable from every team within the business.

Finally, Wear the Hat!

All that remains for me to say is that the information security business is without doubt the most exciting and challenging business you can work in.

If you've started this journey, count yourself lucky as you've got a long road ahead of you, but it will be filled with adventures like you may never have imagined, into places that are sometimes scary but will certainly leave you with stories for the grandchildren that other aspects of business may not.

Our industry has evolved from a subgenre of IT into what's now a stand-alone profession all of its own, freeing itself from the shackles of the organizational constraints of the CIO as it moves into the boardroom as a primary concern of the chief executive.

I truly hope you get as much enjoyment and value out of reading this book as I have from writing it and I hope your information security adventure is as exciting and rewarding as mine has been.

If you want to be an infosec guy, start by wearing the hat.

—Tony Campbell
tony@infosecskills.com

CHAPTER 1

■ ■ ■

Evolution of a Profession

Information security is one of the most exciting industries in which to work. However, to get to grips with this diverse and challenging profession, it is important to understand how it evolved over the past few decades into what it is today and become familiar with the language the experts in this field use to communicate.

Thirty or forty years ago, when information technology was in its infancy, the concept of hiring dedicated *IT security* personnel was almost unheard of. Instead, the most knowledgeable and skilled systems architects, administrators and programmers were mobilized in a crisis and had to cope with whatever was thrown at them.

As recently as the late 1990s, there still were not well-defined roles in non-technical businesses. Instead, the information security function was bolted on to other job roles, such as operations manager, system administrator, network administrator, and even quality manager (depending on the focus).

Nevertheless, on March 26, 1999, everything changed. One highly publicized global event helped accelerate the acceptance that security was no longer a backroom activity and needed consideration at the highest levels of the boardroom. The media called it *Melissa*. It was in fact a mass-mailing macro virus that propagated at frightening speed across the connected world, leveraging a weakness in Microsoft Outlook that allowed it to send infected documents to the first 50 entries in each infected user's address book.

Melissa infected hundreds of thousands of computers within a matter of days, rapidly spreading around the world. The virus struck with such ferocity that companies' Exchange servers were overwhelmed with traffic; in some cases, leaving them without email for weeks while technicians eradicated the threat.

What this highlighted was that the world wasn't quite ready to deal with incidents of this magnitude. The limited number of security guys we had to rely on needed help, support and guidance on how to fix not only the technical issues, but how to work with managers, how to work with vendors, external business continuity advisors, media and communications teams and even legal teams to address the damage from a computer based attack. Furthermore, it became apparent that it was not a matter of pushing teams harder to fix these problems, but that businesses needed someone who really understood the threats, vulnerabilities, and risks to the organization and could conceive ways of addressing them that considered the entire problem, not just the technical aspects. And so, our profession was formed.

THE PENALTY FOR MISCHIEF

On December 10, 1999, David Smith of Aberdeen, New Jersey, pleaded guilty and was sentenced to ten years' imprisonment for releasing Melissa on the newsgroup called alt.sex. He enticed Usenet users to open the malicious payload, suggesting that it contained the usernames and passwords of dozens of pornography sites. The investigation took a few months and included multiple law enforcement organizations, across multiple countries, and saw collaboration between academia and industry to close the case. Smith served 20 months in prison and he was fined $5,000 in damages.

© Tony Campbell 2016
T. Campbell, *Practical Information Security Management*, DOI 10.1007/978-1-4842-1685-9_1

Over the next few years, malware and hacking was rife with new breaches hitting the headlines on a regular basis. Information security was no longer seen as just an ICT issue; instead, it had found its way into the top levels of management and even into political rhetoric. A new breed of security threats was keeping business executives awake at night, as criminal gangs entered the threat landscape along with an arsenal of new cyberweaponry used for stealing money and identities.

Adware and spyware were both on the rise, and as mainstream media got an inkling that security made good headlines, names like Code Red, Nimda, Slammer, and Conficker appeared on the front pages of the newspapers.

Today, threat and vulnerability researchers routinely create media-friendly names for malware and vulnerabilities, creating fantastic headlines that instill panic against the underlying backdrop of *cyberwar* and *cyberterrorism*. Terms such as *cyberespionage, cyberintruders, cyberstalking*, and *cyberbullying* are in the news every week and the information security industry has now accepted the word *cyber* to mean anything to do with security (at least from a public perception perspective). The reality is that *cyber* is a very polarizing term. There are dozens of C-level executives who the term really resonates with, while an equivalent number despise it and have banned its use in their organizations.

BLAME THE MEDIA

Media outlets are perpetuating the tradition in the security research community of dubbing malware and vulnerabilities with high-impact names, with some of the best we've seen over the past few years; names like Zeus, CryptoLocker, Heartbleed, Shellshock, POODLE, and Reaper are all designed for one thing and one thing only: to strike excitement and fear in the hearts of news teams and the public.

Phishing and *spear phishing* are two techniques that are commonly used to begin a security breach. Criminals use this simple, yet incredibly effective technique to convince victims to follow links to malware-ridden websites or to open infected email attachments, so beginning the events that lead to the next big headline.

Identity fraud, credit card fraud and healthcare data breaches have accelerated at pace as massive caches of data are routinely traded on underground websites. Individual records fetch anything from $1 to $100, depending on the kind of record. You will regularly hear about zero-day attacks, anti-forensics toolkits, rootkits, IPS and AV evasion systems, click fraud, hacks-for-hire, Anonymous, the Hacking Team, the Impact Team, advanced persistent threats, and nation-state actors. These are alongside high-profile attacks, such as the successful breaches of Sony, Target, Ashley Madison, and the US Office of Personnel Management by hackers over the last few years.

ASHLEY MADISON DATA BREACH

On July 12, 2015, Avid Life Media (ALM) employees went to work as usual (ALM is the parent company of the Ashley Madison online infidelity website). However, as they logged into their workstations they were greeted by a message that read as follows:

We are the Impact Team. We have taken over all systems in your entire office and production domains, all customer information databases, source code repositories, financial records, and emails. Shutting down AM and EM [Established Men] will cost you, but non-compliance will cost you more: We will release all customer records, profiles … and matching credit card details … Avid Life Media will be liable for fraud and extreme harm to millions of users.

This warning was accompanied by the rock anthem "Thunderstruck" by the legendary rock band AC/DC.

After being contacted by the Impact Team, a week later, reporter Brian Krebs broke the story on his blog (http://krebsonsecurity.com/2015/07/online-cheating-site-ashleymadison-hacked/), quickly making this hack one of the most publicly discussed data breaches of all time. One month passed and all went quiet. However, seemingly ignoring the warning from the Impact Team, Ashley Madison executives and subscribers were dismayed when all 37 million of their user records were released to the public. The aftermath of this attack has seen countless lawsuits, celebrity shaming, outing of business leaders, divorce proceedings, as well as scandals affecting all levels of governments around the world. Unfortunately, a small number of users were so dismayed about their infidelity being disclosed that they felt they had no option but to end their lives. This tragic end may not have been the goal of the Impact Team, but impact is what they created and the hurt will be felt all over the world for years to come.

Being an information security professional is now one of the hardest jobs in an organization. But why is that? Because we need to find ways of increasing the costs to an attacker, whilst comprehensively managing our risks, based on an understanding of our threats (of which there are many). We need to be technical experts, risk managers, business continuity experts, facilitators, managers, and fantastic communicators to do this job properly, and to top it all, if we are doing our job well, our communications to the business will continually raise awareness and help develop an ongoing security culture. But when the shit hits the fan, we're the guys who are blamed.

On the other side of the fence, the bad guys take as long as they need to plan their attacks, methodically scanning each and every one of our systems for the single chink in the armor that will let them in. Maybe not today; maybe not tomorrow, but invariably soon, defenses will seem worthless and all the long hours worked to defend the castle will seem entirely wasted. This is the unfortunate reality and inevitability of working in security; while it's exciting, exhilarating, and often demoralizing, there is one constant you can always depend on—you'll never be bored. So, let's get started on this amazing journey to becoming an information security professional.

What's in a Name?

You'll find references to *computer security* as far back as the 1960s. The earliest mentions are mostly from a government and military perspective, with *computer security* primarily referring to the measures taken by administrators and programmers to protect these military systems. Nevertheless, back then the majority of attacks resulted in nothing more than service degradation and hackers played the game for bragging rights rather than profit.

If you were to liken the IT industry to a three-ring circus, computer security was a sideshow; the unicycling monkey of the IT world. It was staffed by the geekiest, socially awkward technical geniuses who no one really wanted to see, but they were still there in the shadows doing their thing, because they had to be. The focus of security was to configure the technical measures in hardware and software to keep out script kiddies and make sure that systems kept running without the phreakers and hackers stealing precious bandwidth.

Over the next four decades, the world shifted. The adoption of ubiquitous home and enterprise computing saw security professionals dedicate more focus to the information they were protecting. From a metaphorical perspective, security refocused its lens from technology to information, allowing the security experts to consider management systems and processes that they'd never considered before.

This shift away from technology to a more holistic viewpoint of business saw computer security rebranded to *information security*.

Information security has been used ever since, and security guys are proud to call themselves *information security* professionals. For this reason, information security is the most commonly used name for what we do. However, a new term appeared a decade ago: *information assurance*.

Since information can exist in many forms and threats can originate from outside the scope of ICT systems, information assurance was used to describe an even more holistic approach to security that included physical measures, business continuity, policy, standards, and law.

ORIGINS OF "CYBER"

Cyber has become a ubiquitous prefix in today's media that means anything concerned with Internet privacy or security. It's rare that a day goes by without hearing or reading about cyberwar, cyberattacks, cybersecurity, cyberbullying, and cybersafety. But where did this peculiar prefix come from? The first evidence of usage (aside from the Greek root meaning *governing*) dates back to the 1940s, when mathematician, Norbert Weiner wrote about *cybernetics* as computer systems that could one day run on feedback and be self-governing. During the 1980s, the term was prepended to any word to make it sound futuristic or cutting-edge, replacing the less cool terms, digital. In the 1990s, cyber developed an entirely new meaning as cybersex arrived on the scene, referring to virtually making out (among other things) with your partner in dial-up IRCs and online forums. As the years trundled by and the concept of cybersex was largely replaced with online pornography and dating sites, the term was taken back by the government and the military started referring to the next shift in warfare paradigms being into battleground of cyber. And with cyberwarfare, came cybersecurity, cyberattacks, and cyberintelligence. Today, *cyber* can pretty much be appended to anything you like, but the media has focused its use primarily on the security industry, hence we have all become cybersecurity professionals, whether we like it or not.

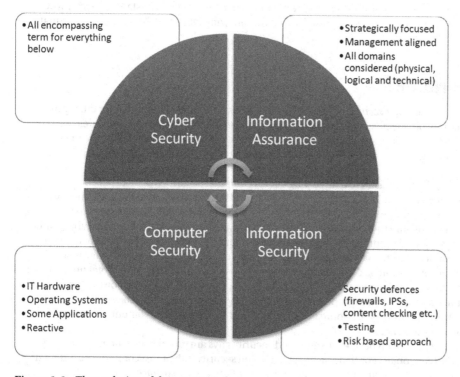

Figure 1-1. The evolution of the security industry

Information assurance was originally used by the government in the United States and in the United Kingdom to include the management of information in all of these other forms. As part of the information assurance management system, it included ancillary services such as forensic readiness planning, security management, and risk management, along with strategy, law, policy, and training.

Interestingly, while this term never got much traction outside of government circles, the remit of *information security* has expanded to cover these areas. Therefore, today when we refer to *information security*, there is an expectation that it means the same core set of principles covered by information assurance.

There is yet another term that needs explaining. To make life easier for the US military, they adopted *cyber* to denote any aspect of warfare that has an electronic component within the scope of a modern military campaign. In essence, it refers to the exploitation of electronic measures for military effect. For example, *cyberwarfare* denotes any element of warfare that has an electronic component. In an isolated military context, this usage makes sense, as it allows policy makers to build doctrine on the rules of engagement in *cyberspace*. I honestly don't mind the term *cybersecurity* as long as it's properly used. If the meaning remains focused on all technical aspects of operational security, it's hard to go far wrong. If nothing else, at least the use of cyber now has the public interested in the work that we security professionals do, and if you call yourself a *cybersecurity professional*, people can relate to it.

As a final note in our stroll through this industry, there is one additional term to get familiar with. *Infosec* is the simple contraction of *information security* and is most widely used within the industry to save time in writing the words out in full. Everything from academic papers to magazine articles, and from books to online media substitutes the term *infosec* for information security. We are infosec professionals and we use our infosec skills to solve infosec problems.

The Language of Security

Like any field of study, security has a unique set of terms and TLAs (three-letter acronyms) that you must become familiar with to succeed. You need to be able to relate to and understand the context of a range of processes, standards, technologies, and functions to communicate with your peers. You also need to understand how to translate this unique parlance into business boardroom language so that everyone else can understand you.

■ **Tip** Most of the terminology used in *information security* is taken from a variety of international standards documents: ISO/IEC 27000:2014—Overview and vocabulary; ISO/IEC 27001:2013—Information security management system; ISO/IEC 27005:2011—Information security risk management; ISO Guide 73:2009—Risk management; ISO/IEC 31000—Risk management—Principles and guidelines.

CIA

There are three special security properties—sometimes referred to as the *three tenets of security*—that are fundamentally at the heart of everything we do. Every risk you mitigate and every control you implement is from the perspective of one or more of these properties. Figure 1-2 shows the relationship between *confidentiality*, *integrity*, and *availability* and how they apply to every asset we protect.

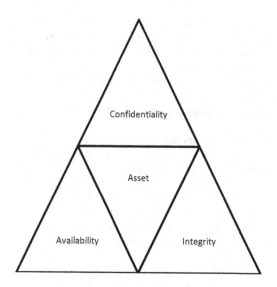

Figure 1-2. *CIA: Three tenets of information security*

Information security provides measures to protect these properties, so when you design solutions to improve the security of your organization, you analyze threats that affect these. Controls are implemented to protect these security properties and some controls can be physical while others are technical or process oriented depending on how you want to solve the problem. Just remember the mantra, "people, process, and technology" as you progress on your information security journey and you won't go far wrong. For example, you might install two-factor authentication (covered in detail later in the book) to protect a sensitive computer system as it implements stronger identification and authentication of users. However, the security manager could achieve the same outcome by isolating the computer system within a physically secure building, and providing separate keys to anyone who needs access. These controls achieve the same outcome from the perspective of protecting the systems and their information. However, do they meet the requirements of the business? An isolated computer system only works when all of the users are within the same geographical area. If some users are in another state or country, this clearly isn't a good solution.

Confidentiality

The first of the three tenets to look at is *confidentiality*. ISO/IEC 27000:2012 defines this as where "Information is not made available or disclosed to unauthorized individuals and entities or processes."

By upholding the confidentiality of a secret government document, you make sure that it isn't read by a foreign national that could use it for espionage. In essence, if something is secret, it stays secret. Our job as information security professionals is to assist in preventing the intentional and unintentional disclosure of sensitive information to unauthorized persons.

A loss of confidentiality can occur in many ways, such as through the intentional release by someone who has legitimate access, such as a trusted (but not trustworthy) employee or systems administrator. This could have a negative effect on the company's share price and damage any competitive edge they might have in the market. This might have a knock on effect on profits for years to come. By understanding the threats to your organization, security managers can implement technical, physical, and process controls that restrict access to those with a *need to know*. Limiting access to users with the need to know is one of the primary principles in designing computer systems that handle sensitive information. The majority of operating systems have features that can authenticate users and only permit users with appropriate authorization from gaining access to information assets. Information should be classified to help you understand its value; that way you can invest an appropriate amount of money in protecting what's important while not overprotecting what is considered lesser in value. This is why governments will mark documents with classifications, such as CONFIDENTIAL, SECRET, and TOP SECRET, as these give the document an intrinsic value, and if that document is lost, the impact can be determined. Loss of a CONFIDENTIAL document, while damaging or embarrassing, won't be quite as harmful as the loss or public release of a TOP SECRET document. You can use a variety of controls to protect confidential information, such as encryption, identification, and authorization, and authentication to ensure that only authorized people can access protected information.

HILLARY CLINTON'S PERSONAL EMAIL SAGA

Hillary Clinton faced a variety of allegations relating to her use of a private email server during her time as the secretary of state. This came to light in 2015 when she was first accused of using an email system that a State Department inspector found was not approved and wasn't compliant with US government rules. After the protracted FBI investigation concluded, it was suggested that there was no "reasonable prosecutor" that would be used to bring a criminal case against Mrs. Clinton. However, the report suggested that both Clinton and her aides were "extremely careless" in their actions. The detail of this investigation shows just how easy it is to think you are doing something clever, while jeopardizing not only yourself, but potentially your entire organization. Mrs. Clinton used the server she'd set up in her own home town of Chappaqua, New York, for all of her email correspondence, both work-related and personal, during her tenure as Secretary of State.

While this may seem like an innocuous and innocent mistake, where no one was harmed, the fact that a third-party actor, believed to be either the Russian or Chinese government, tried to hack the system shows how at-risk this kind of behavior puts what could be sensitive government information.

Clinton's excuse for this err in judgement was that her own email system was more convenient and that she preferred to use just one email address on her smartphone.

Since Mrs. Clinton was on the verge of becoming the Democratic presidential nominee, this controversy served only to tarnish her reputation and cast doubt over her eligibility.

As it turned out, the FBI didn't recommend criminal charges against Clinton for this incident, but FBI Director James Comey said her actions were "extremely careless," while criticizing the agency she worked for having a slapdash approach to handling classified material.

Let's look at some examples to put this in context. If a potential employer got access to your Facebook, what might happen? The updates you routinely share with friends and family are not usually something that you'd share with a stranger, right? You might post pictures from a drunken night out, or you might make a flippant political comment, meant as a joke for the people that know you. However, if your Facebook security is compromised and your information loses the perceived confidentiality that you consider it should have, the HR department or hiring manager might see that information and prejudge you as a heavy drinker or a political activist and see you as too much of a risk. This loss of confidentiality leads to your not being invited for interview, yet in this case you might not even know this is the reason because there is no indication of the security breach.

The second example is a real example and dates back to June 2015. The Office of Personnel Management (OPM) is the US government department responsible for looking after the human resources aspects of government employees, including management and issuance of security clearances (using the Standard Form 86). The FBI released a statement accusing Chinese hackers of breaching OPM systems in what was classed a *massive cyberattack* that compromised the data of about 4 million current and former employees. Later investigation revealed this estimate to be a massively understated, with the reality being closer to 22 million records that were stolen. Each instance of the Standard Form 86 should be considered a social engineer's handbook for the individual concerned, as it contains all the information attackers would need to plan and execute an identity theft or role compromise, or even an espionage campaign. This is a massive, pervasive problem for the US government as the data breach includes details of intelligence operatives, high-ranking officials, and military staffs.

Integrity

The second of the three tenets to look at is *integrity*. ISO/IEC 27000:2012 defines integrity as "the property of accuracy and completeness of assets." Integrity is the principle of protecting information from changes, whether they are intentional, unauthorized, or accidental. Some kinds of information need to be correct and you need to be able to trust that it is accurate and hasn't been tampered with. Some information is used in critical (sometimes life-threatening,) decision making, such as when a physician gives you a blood transfusion. The doctor needs assurance that your blood type is really what it says on your chart. Maintaining integrity ensures the following:

- Unauthorized personnel or processes do not make modifications to data.

- Authorized personnel or processes do not make unauthorized modifications to information.

- Information is internally and externally consistent.

The following are a few examples where loss of integrity can have a negative impact:

- A student deliberately modifies his grades to pass instead of a fail an exam (negative for the institution but positive for the student).

- A payment is changed from $100 to $1,000 and that amount is debited from your bank account.

- A medical patient's blood group is modified on their hospital admission forms from O+ to A+.

As you can see from these examples, integrity is an important security property and in the case of the last example, if the patient was given blood type A+, it is a life threatening mistake.

Security controls such as cryptographic processes and segregation of duties can protect information integrity. More on this later in the book.

Availability

The last of our three tenets of security is *availability*. ISO/IEC 27000:2012 defines this as "the property of being accessible and usable upon demand by an authorized entity."

This ensures that users have reliable and timely access to the data and resources they need to do their job. Incidents such as denial of service attacks and disasters (such as floods or hurricanes) are the kinds of things that adversely affect availability. In essence, availability means making sure systems keep running and information stays accessible. This is probably the most straightforward of the three tenets to understand, but vitally important for businesses that rely on information being available when employees need it. Here are a few examples that show just how important availability can be:

- A maintenance company cuts through the main power supply to your datacenter, but you have no backup generator. Your systems are no longer available to your staff or customers.

- A hacker launches a denial of service (DOS) attack against your website and your users are no longer able to browse your inventory or checkout their purchases.

Depending on the nature of your business and the target of the attack, availability impacts your company's reputation and cash flow. Imagine how much money Amazon.com might lose if its online shopping systems were unavailable over the Black Friday shopping period?

Non-Repudiation

There is one additional property—called *non-repudiation*—that exists alongside the CIA triad and is equally as important to consider in a variety of special circumstances. ISO/IEC 27000:2012 defines non-repudiation as the "ability to prove the occurrence of a claimed event or action and its originating entities."

The nature of non-repudiation is more obscure than CIA and unless you come from a legal background, you may not have heard this term before. Non-repudiation is a guarantee that you can prove who initiated a communication. In essence, there is no way the sender can deny it came from them. Coupled with integrity, you can build a system that not only guarantees that what was received is what was sent, you can also prove that the sender really sent it. This means they have no way of later claiming it was forged or fabricated. If messages or transactions are disputed then identity can be challenged and legal outcomes jeopardized. Typically, a third party attests to proof where neither sender nor receiver can dispute the action. The following are real-world examples that show the context of usage for non-repudiation systems:

- Proving that a member of staff actually sent an email that was damaging to the company's reputation.

- Proving that an individual performed a transaction, such as ordering goods from the Internet.

- Proving an individual signed the mortgage deed for a house. A bank will insist you have a lawyer/notary witness the signing of a mortgage contract so that there can be no dispute that it was signed by you.

Threats and Vulnerabilities

ISO/IEC 27000:2012 defines a threat as "the potential cause of an unwanted incident, which may result in harm to a system or organization." Threats are any action or actor that may causes an unwanted consequence, such as a breach of confidentiality or loss of service.

To be considered a threat, an incident or violation doesn't have to occur. Your job is to identify that this threat might occur and use this knowledge in a process called *risk assessment*—more on this later.

Even if a threat is unrealistic, such as a meteorite crashing into the building or a volcano erupting under the data center, it's still a threat. However, the amount of effort you expend on a threat has to be commensurate with the probability of that threat actually happening—again, more on this later.

Some organizations differentiate between threat sources—those who wish the compromise to occur—and threat actors—those who carry out the attack. A threat source can influence or coerce a threat actor to initiate an attack on their behalf, such as the US Department of Defense, asking someone in a foreign government department to steal some information on their behalf. In some situations, the threat actor is the same entity as the threat source, such as dishonest employees who steal some information for their own financial gain. Some examples of threats (and threat actors) are included here, but I'm sure you can think of many more specific threats that you might have considered in the past:

- Earthquake

- Computer viruses

- An aircraft crashing into a datacenter

- Flood

- Spies

- Competitors

- Journalists

■ **Note**   Threat modelling is a process used by security professionals to determine who potential threat actors are, what their means, motivation, and intent are, and how they might attempt to breach a system or organization. This helps to clarify the relationships between threat actors, threats, and threat scenarios. The process follows a structured approach to all aspects of security and helps teams address the most significant threats. For more information, you can learn about threat modeling on Microsoft's website at `https://msdn.microsoft.com/en-us/library/ff648644.aspx`.

Vulnerability is defined in ISO/IEC 27000:2012 as "a weakness of an asset or control that can be exploited by one or more threats." The presence of a vulnerability is not what causes harm to a system or compromises information. It's the relationship between a threat and a vulnerability that leads to harm since the threat actor needs to be aware of and exploit the vulnerability for an attack to be successful. Without a vulnerability, it doesn't matter how dangerous a threat is, it will never be able to attack the target.

Vulnerabilities exist in many forms and affect almost any kind of system. The following list shows that they are not limited to computer systems:

- Management processes and procedures

- People

- Buildings

- Information systems

- Hardware, software, and communications equipment

- Third parties

- Cryptographic systems

Risk and Consequence

The management of information risk is at the heart of everything we do in information security management. Risk is defined in ISO/IEC 31000 as "the effect of uncertainty on objectives." It might not have occurred to you before that risk can have both positive and negative effects on business objectives: a deviation from what is expected could well be a positive shift. This means that some risks result in good outcomes, even if it is somewhat unexpected, such as when the stock market unexpectedly moves in your favor.

In the context of information security, the risk is the outcome the business faces when a threat exploits a vulnerability to successfully attack a target that you are defending. This leads to some kind of deviation from the current state for your organization. Some examples of risks are as follows:

- Loss of intellectual property, leading to your business losing competitive advantage.

- Damage to brand reputation, leading to customers leaving your service.

- Loss of revenue, leading to redundancies and liquidation.

- Costs for remediation and cleanup of virus infection.

- Injury to staff.

- Loss of faith from investors and stock price crash.

Information security risk management is the process for assessing the risks your organization faces that are related to the management and protection of information. What's pertinent is that the majority of big businesses and government departments are heavily reliant on information for decision support and service management. This means that information security is now a critical component of the corporate risk management function, something that is often ignored in smaller businesses where this is less readily accepted.

Your job as the information security manager is to act as the glue between all areas of the business where security is a concern and to make sure that the risks to the business are well understood, not just by the technical teams but also by risk managers, operations managers, system administrators, marketing teams, sales teams, and the corporate board. You may not be the most popular person when you tell your CEO she is exposed to a possible million-dollar risk with a likelihood of almost certain in the next 24 months, but if this is the case and you present the evidence in a way that the CEO understands, she'll get it and give you the budget you need to protect her business. This process is called *information risk management*, and fixing the problem with technical, process or physical security controls is called *risk mitigation*.

If risk is the effect of uncertainty on objectives, *consequence* refers to the outcome of the risk occurring. In information security, this is often referred to as *impact*; however, consequence is the term used in ISO/IEC 27000:2012, so it's certainly worth understanding that both terms mean the same thing and they can be used interchangeably. The official definition of consequence is documented in ISO/IEC 27000:2012 as the "outcome of an event affecting objectives."

To string all these terms together into a meaningful chain of events, the successful exploitation of a vulnerability by a threat or threat actor will result in the loss of confidentiality, integrity, or availability of an information asset. This compromise will have a business impact, which is the consequence the compromise has on the operation or efficiency of the organization. For example, if Amazon.com's website was to be taken down by hackers, they can't take orders and hence they will lose revenue for the entire time they are offline. This "hack" may also affect their reputation, as customers perceive them to be less secure than they once might have thought. The reality is that they are no more or less secure than before, and are more than likely working hard behind the scenes to fix the problem, so at that stage, they are in fact paying more attention to security than they were yesterday. However, security is a fickle and abstract concept, and as such, it's as much about management of perception as it is about management of technology, processes, and physical environments. When you estimate the consequences of a successful attack happening, you need to consider all angles: financial, intellectual property loss, reputational damage, and even employee and customer safety. If your business is military or law enforcement related, then there are possible consequences of loss of life to consider, in the same way that if you run a power station, a transport business, or some other business that has a direct safety concern. Cyberattacks are having an increasing impact in the real work, especially with the push toward the Internet of Things, where previously separate, autonomous devices and items are now being connected into the Internet, meaning they are all now potentially vulnerable to attack. Understanding all of these consequences is now a critical component of the information security management function in these businesses.

■ **Note** For the majority of this book, I'll use the term *impact* rather than *consequence*, simply because it's more commonly used in information security, even though the ISO standard refers to it as *consequence*. Both terms are equally valid.

Glossary of Useful Terms

Table 1-1 lists the key terms and definitions you'll need to know about on your journey as an information security manager. Most of these definitions can be found elsewhere in international standards, government publications, books and a variety of authoritative websites, however, I felt it useful to put them here in one place to give you a single reference that you can keep on your desk or ebook reader to help you in your work.

Table 1-1. *Glossary of Terminology Used in Information Security Management*

Term	Meaning
attack	Attempt to destroy, expose, alter, disable, steal or gain unauthorized access to or make unauthorized use of an asset
access control	Access to assets is authorized and restricted based on business and security requirements
accountability	Assignment of actions and decisions to an entity
attribute	Property or characteristic of an object that can be distinguished quantitatively or qualitatively by human or automated means
authentication	Provision of assurance that a claimed characteristic of an entity is correct
authenticity	Property that an entity is what it claims to be
availability	Property of being accessible and usable upon demand by an authorized entity
conformity	Fulfillment of a requirement
control	Means of managing risk, including policies, procedures, guidelines, practices or organizational structures, which can be of administrative, technical, management, or legal nature
control objective	Statement describing what is to be achieved as a result of implementing controls
corrective action	Action to eliminate the cause of a detected non-conformity or other undesirable situation
event	Occurrence or change of a particular set of circumstances
guideline	Description that clarifies what should be done and how, to achieve the objectives set out in policies
information security	Preservation of confidentiality, integrity and availability of information
information security event	Identified occurrence of a system, service or network state indicating a possible breach of information security policy or failure of safeguards, or a previously unknown situation that may be security relevant
information security incident	Single or a series of unwanted or unexpected information security events that have a significant probability of compromising business operations and threatening information security
information security incident management	Processes for detecting, reporting, assessing, responding to, dealing with, and learning from information security incidents
information security management system	Part of the overall management system, based on a business risk approach, to establish, implement, operate, monitor, review, maintain and improve information security Note: Often written as ISMS

(*continued*)

Table 1-1. (*continued*)

Term	Meaning
information system	Application, service, information technology asset, or any other information handling component
level of risk	Magnitude of a risk expressed in terms of the combination of consequences and their likelihood
likelihood	Chance of something happening
management	Coordinated activities to direct and control an organization
management system	Framework of guidelines, policies, procedures, processes and associated resources aimed at ensuring an organization meets its objectives
policy	Overall intention and direction as formally expressed by management
preventive action	Action to eliminate the cause of a potential non-conformity or other undesirable potential situation
procedure	Specified way to carry out an activity or a process
process	Set of interrelated or interacting activities which transforms inputs into outputs
record	Document stating results achieved or providing evidence of activities performed
reliability	Property of consistent intended behavior and results
residual risk	Risk remaining after risk treatment Note: Residual risk can contain unidentified risk. Residual risk can also be known as *retained risk.*
review	Activity undertaken to determine the suitability, adequacy and effectiveness of the subject matter to achieve established objectives
risk acceptance	Decision to accept a risk
risk analysis	Process to comprehend the nature of risk and to determine the level of risk Note: Risk analysis provides the basis for risk evaluation and decisions about risk treatment and includes estimation
risk assessment	Overall process of risk identification, risk analysis and risk evaluation
risk criteria	Terms of reference against which the significance of risk is evaluated Note: Risk criteria are based on organizational objectives, and external and internal context. Risk criteria can be derived from standards, laws, policies and other requirements.
risk evaluation	Process of comparing the results of risk analysis with risk criteria to determine whether the risk and/or its magnitude is acceptable or tolerable Note: Risk evaluation assists in the decision about risk treatment.
risk identification	Process of finding, recognizing and describing risks Note: Risk identification involves the identification of risk sources, events, their causes, and their potential consequences. Can include data, theoretical analysis, informed and expert opinions, and stakeholders' needs.
risk management	Coordinated activities to direct and control an organization with regard to risk

(*continued*)

Table 1-1. (*continued*)

Term	Meaning
risk treatment	Process to modify risk Note: Can involve risk avoidance, taking or increasing risk to pursue opportunities, removing risk sources, changing likelihood or impact, sharing risk with a third party or retaining risk.
stakeholder	Person or organization that can affect, be affected by, or perceive themselves to be affected by a decision or activity
statement of applicability	Documented statement describing the control objectives and controls that are relevant and applicable to the organization's ISMS
validation	Confirmation, through the provision of objective evidence, that the requirements for a specific intended use or application have been fulfilled
verification	Confirmation, through the provision of objective evidence, that specified requirements have been fulfilled Note: This could also be called *compliance testing*.
vulnerability	Weakness of an asset or control that can be exploited by one or more threats

CHAPTER 2

■ ■ ■

Threats and Vulnerabilities

Today, cybercriminals require no technical knowledge only a means to pay.

—Raj Samani, McAfee EMEA CTO

The sophistication and capability of cybercriminals is greater today than it has ever been, with technically superior threat actors researching and developing insidious malware frameworks that allow them or their customers to break into their victims' systems, maintaining access, covering their tracks, evading countermeasures and siphoning gigabytes of confidential information off for sale on the black market.

The term threat actor, as explained in the last chapter, refers to the individual or group responsible for posing the threat to our information or systems. Threat actors are motivated by the variety of causes they support, be that for revenge, political ends, terrorism, or plain old monetary gain. There are very few attacks perpetrated these days for the bragging rights of old, aside maybe from those researching security vulnerabilities to showcase them at the big international conventions, such as Black Hat.

Given the complexity of the modern computing environment, malware developers, and those researching vulnerabilities, are some of the most talented programmers out there. To discover a new vulnerability that can be used to launch a sophisticated, multi-payload, stealthy attack, then to build some malware that uses that vulnerability while evading antivirus software and avoiding detection by intrusion prevention systems, requires deep knowledge of computer code, operating systems architectures and even user behavior. Researchers spend many thousands of hours reverse engineering software executable to figure out how they work, and then model the program logic to look for oversights and errors that could potentially be exploited, so forcing the systems into a failure state. This can be subsequently used to escalate privileges, exfiltrate user data, and monitor user activity.

To further compound the problem faced by law enforcement, malware developers are now making their living creating weaponized versions of their wares, selling them on the open market (via special websites on the Tor darknet) to anyone who wants to attack their enemies. Crimeware marketplaces have emerged over the past few years, allowing sellers to offer their products and services for sale on platforms not unlike Amazon.com, where buyers purchase the raw exploit code, but they also get high-quality documentation, service-level guarantees, and technical support for 12 months. Practically any product or service offering you'd expect to get from a shrink-wrapped commercial software product or from a vendor, such as Microsoft, will be available on the black market, often with 100% satisfaction guaranteed. Who says there is no honor among thieves?

The information security posture of the cybercriminal underground is now so much more robust than legitimate enterprises and it's becoming harder and harder for law enforcement to shut these networks of crimeware down, let alone detect them. From the perspective of an information security manager, security budgets are extremely hard fought and all too easy to spend, while criminals are investing millions of dollars shoring up their end-to-end defenses.

© Tony Campbell 2016
T. Campbell, *Practical Information Security Management*, DOI 10.1007/978-1-4842-1685-9_2

Threats

Threats come from a variety of sources. Some are physical, such as floods and volcanoes, while others are digital, such as from hackers, criminals, disgruntled employees, or competitors. This section looks at the overall *threat landscape* (this term denotes the plethora of threats that potentially affect our information's confidentiality, integrity, and availability), the threat actors (the people that enact those threats) and the kinds of malware and weaponized code being used to perpetrate such attacks.

First, let's start with a look at modern cybercriminals and how they keep themselves hidden from law enforcement while pedaling their wares. These guys hang out in obscure, invitation-only bulletin boards and IRC channels, only accessible through multiple layers of network encryption, using online pseudonyms to trade anonymously in hard-to-trace currencies, such as Bitcoin, CloakCoin, ShadowCash, LEOCoin, AnonCoin, and Monero.

Some cybercriminals have no intention of hacking end-user systems; instead, they build malware services that are sold to anyone who wants to target a victim. Sometimes, multinational or state-based cybercriminals write and use their own malware, but this mode of operation is more commonly associated with government hacking, more often than not for the purposes of espionage rather than monetary gain.

THE OFFICE OF PERSONNEL MANAGEMENT

The United States Office of Personnel Management (OPM) is the agency responsible for the management of personnel records for all aspects of the United States federal government. It provides case management for the security clearance process and holds all of the data related to government employees requiring security clearances, up to and including TOP SECRET. Previously hit by at least three reported cyberattacks, in June 2015, the OPM announced another massive data breach with initial reports suggesting unknown hackers had stolen approximately four million government employee's personnel records, however, this turned out to be massively underestimated. It wasn't too long before the FBI reported that closer to 18 million records had been stolen, with the breach enacted over more than a month before being detected (it could have been even longer but this has not been divulged). By July 2015, further refinement of the magnitude of the breach was released in a press statement, where investigators put the final total of individual personnel records stolen to be 22.1 million current, former, and prospective US government employees, along with their family members. The majority of those affected — 21.5 million people — were included in the OPM's repository of security clearance files. At least 4.2 million employees were affected by the breach of a separate database that contained personnel records that included Social Security numbers, job assignments, and performance evaluations. Officials from the OPM reported that of those affected, 3.6 million had data in both systems—an overlap that accounts for the 22.1 million total.

Soon after, the director of the OPM, Katherine Archuleta, resigned from office. It has also come to light, since then, that over four million fingerprint records were also stolen in the data heist. This is particularly troublesome as fingerprints have become the standard biometric used by smartphone users since Apple introduced the fingerprint reader with the iPhone 6. Furthermore, this means that government agents working in foreign countries can be identified by their fingerprints, so hence their positions, even under a false identity, have been totally compromised.

Who Was Responsible?

The FBI has named the Chinese government as the most likely perpetrator of this hack. But why would the Chinese government want this data? With 22.1 million records containing all the person details of highly cleared United States government employees, including staffers working in the National Security Agency (NSA), the Central Intelligence Agency (CIA), the Federal Bureau of Investigation (FBI), and the Department of Defense (DoD), then the potential for espionage using this data is catastrophic. This hack will have a lasting impact on the US government and it may be a very long time (an entire lifetime) before the safety of all government employees can be guaranteed again.

To access these encrypted, hidden sites, users need to be savvy enough to install the Tor browser on their computers and drop off the grid with regards to their ISPs and those who might be tracking what they're up to. But what is Tor and how does it work?

Hiding in Plain Sight

Running a criminal enterprise on the standard Internet is much too dangerous for cybercriminals, especially given how easy it is for law enforcement to identify who does what through a combination of easily accessible vendor logs they acquire via readily signed subpoenas. For this reason, tech-savvy cybercriminals are conducting their affairs behind the veil of high-grade, government-class encryption, using a special computer network, known as Tor (The onion router). Tor gets its name from the concept of multiple layers of the onion, representing the layers of encryption the network offers those using the service. Each layer of onion skin further masks the user's activities from the eyes of anyone who might be snooping on their network traffic. For this reason, Tor has become the standard for the criminal fraternity accessing the Internet.

Anonymity is one of the most important attributes of the criminal's interaction with the Internet, as well as for a vast number of other kinds of legitimate users. There are many varied motivations that drive the need for anonymity online, with demographics such as journalists, government agencies (law enforcement and intelligence services) and citizens in countries where oppressive governments monitor and prosecute citizens for breaking online laws such as Russia and China. Tor protects the citizens of these oppressed countries from prosecution, persecution, jail, and even in some cases, the death sentence, so this is why it perpetuates. The website where users download Tor states: "Tor is free software and an open source network that helps you defend against traffic analysis, a form of network surveillance that threatens personal freedom and privacy, confidential business activities, and relationships, and state security."

These altruistic use cases look at Tor through the lens of defending the rights of individuals, as well as freedoms of speech and the right to privacy, all of which has been lost when we use the Internet today. Without Tor, each and every action we perform on the Internet is logged, monitored, analyzed, and monetized by marketing companies, ISPs, and governments for any number of purposes, all traceable back to you as an individual.

However, just like any tool, Tor can be used for nefarious purposes as well as for good: a chisel can be used to craft a beautiful sculpture as easily as it can be used as a murder weapon. Some pundits argue that Tor should be banned because it allows criminals to proliferate their nefarious activities; however, you need to compare this viewpoint with the same viewpoint related to mobile phones back in the 1990s. If the technology world adopted this attitude, the mobile phone would be banned simply because the narcotic industry and drug cartels operating in remote regions of the South American jungle were the biggest users of these services and effectively kick started this multi-billion-dollar industry. Just because mobile phones are used to assist in committing crimes does not make them an instrument of crime.

How Does Tor Work?

When you connect to the Tor network, you are leveraging a massive network of volunteer-owned and operated servers that protect the user's privacy and identity by "tunneling" the connection through many thousands of nodes. The initial traffic/request is encrypted multiple times, and then each hop separately decrypts just enough data to allow it to pass the message to the next hop. The encryption technology is of a high-grade, making it virtually impossible to break into and trace the whereabouts of the user. Since the user never makes a direct connection to the website or service, it's impossible to determine who they are, where they are based, and what their original IP address is. From the perspective of the target website, it might look like the user is in Brazil, while they are actually in an office in Moscow. Even if law enforcement could trace your connection back one or two hops, IP addresses will appear to be in Europe, Africa, and North America, all for the same Russian user. The paths taken by individual packets passing over the Tor network are random and encrypted, meaning external monitoring is very difficult and piecing together a full network stream is nigh-on impossible.

The fundamental concept of onion routing is not new, originally conceived in the mid-1990s by a team of scientists in the United States Naval Research Laboratory. The initial intent was to protect US intelligence communications over the Internet. Further research and prototyping was undertaken by the United States Defense Advanced Research Agency (DARPA) in 1997, and subsequently over the following decade, it evolved into what it is today, now funded by the Electronic Frontier Foundation (EFF) and managed by a Massachusetts-based nonprofit that has fully productized it, while continuing with the research and development started by DARPA.

The Tor client is installed on your computer as a local service and acts as a proxy passing your web browsing traffic to the encrypted Tor network. Once in the Tor network, your traffic traverses the thousands of network relays used to disguise your location and data. You can easily configure your web browser to pass traffic into the Tor network using your advanced networking options (basically pointing the proxy address at the local Tor service installed on your computer), or you can make use of a special pre-packaged Tor browser, built on a fully customized version of the Mozilla Firefox web browser. This is by far the easiest way to get started with Tor and is how most non-technical users access the deep web. Furthermore, any application that is SOCKS-aware can also be configured to use Tor, meaning you can build entire computer ecosystems that direct traffic into the encrypted Tor network, which could easily become the way special marketplaces spring up in the coming years for malware, crimeware, and illicit services and content.

When you start the Tor browser, it takes a few seconds to connect through the proxy before it opens what looks like a standard browser page (see Figure 2-1).

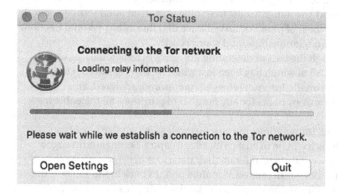

Figure 2-1. Connecting to the Tor network

Once your Tor browser has successfully connected to the Tor network, you can then proceed to test your IP address using button on the home page. This demonstrates that you are connected to the Tor network and your IP address is now different from the one provided by your IP, as shown in Figure 2-2.

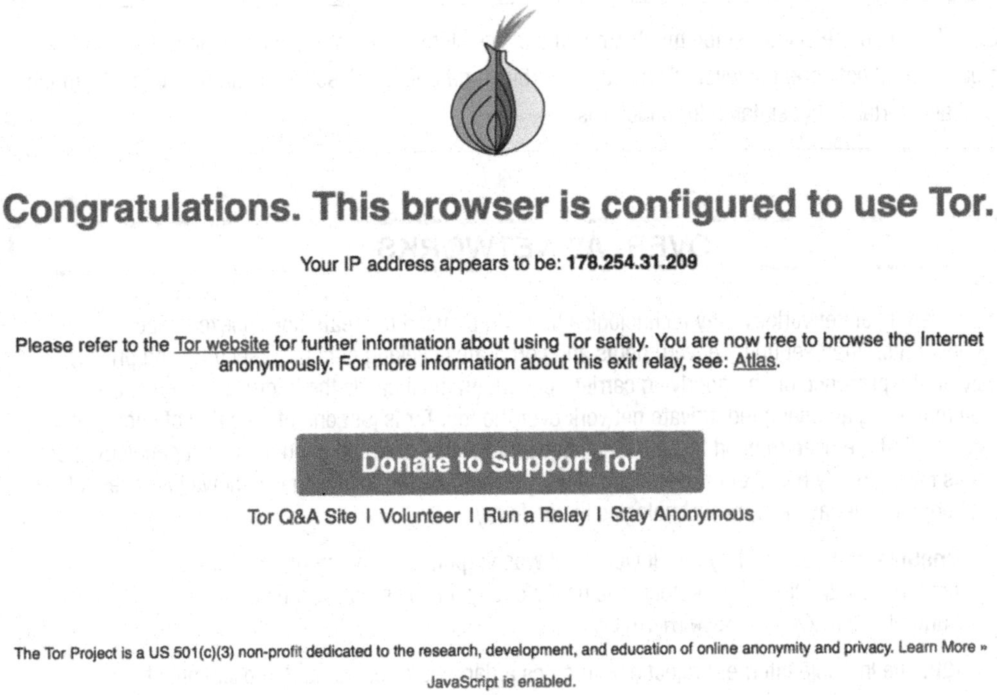

Congratulations. This browser is configured to use Tor.

Your IP address appears to be: **178.254.31.209**

Please refer to the Tor website for further information about using Tor safely. You are now free to browse the Internet anonymously. For more information about this exit relay, see: Atlas.

Donate to Support Tor

Tor Q&A Site I Volunteer I Run a Relay I Stay Anonymous

The Tor Project is a US 501(c)(3) non-profit dedicated to the research, development, and education of online anonymity and privacy. Learn More »

JavaScript is enabled.

Figure 2-2. *Once you are connected to the Tor network, go ahead and check that your IP address is different*

The Deep Web

The hidden network that exists within the Tor service is often referred to as the *deep web*. However, there are myriad other names it's been dubbed with over the years, such as the *dark web, darknet*, and the *dark market*. No matter what it's called, it operates much like the rest of the Internet, in terms of websites, file services, and web services, with one main difference: it's completely anonymous and unindexed (i.e., you can't find links to these services in Google, Yahoo!, or any other traditional search engine).

It contains a plethora of services, such as all of these criminal hacking and malware pedaling sites, and is the first port of call for researchers and counter-intelligence officers trying to keep ahead of what the cybercriminals are up to.

In effect, the deep web is a collection of connected systems that are protected using the encrypted overlay provided by Tor, which may appear at first glance to work much like the standard Internet, however, there is one main difference (from a user perspective) insomuch that sites are not indexed by standard search engines, such as Google. You'll not be able to find links to sites, such as the Silk Road, from a Google search; instead, you'll need to know how to get into the Tor network, and then you'll need to know the special .onion URL to find your way to that target site.

Navigating around the deep web can be complex, especially for those of you that are new to this kind of service, due to the lack of content indexing. The main thing to be aware of as someone new to this underground world is that most of the links you'll need are collected on a small number of wikis and bulletin boards, with the sole purpose of aggregating and categorizing these services into groups. If you are interested in taking a whistle-stop tour around the deep web, start by accessing The Hidden Wiki (http://kpvz7ki2v5agwt35.onion/wiki/index.php/Main_Page). This is a good jumping off place because it lists most of the underground categories you'd expect to find, from crimeware to hacking sites, along with links to illicit material, such as guns for sale, drugs on mail order, and all sorts of disturbing pornography.

■ **Caution**   I'd not advise spending too much time on this. It's all too easy to find yourself immersed in this intriguing underworld network; however, it's mostly disturbing and unfiltered, so tread carefully because much of it is illegal and certainly not suitable for under 18s.

OVERLAY NETWORKS

There is a variety of network overlay technologies that can be used to create non-indexed, hidden-access networks. Often set up by governments and corporates seeking enhanced security and privacy, they rely on the presence of an underlying carrier network (in most cases the Internet) for transport, and then managing an encrypted, private network over the top. Tor is just one of a myriad of encryption technologies that are used to build these overlay networks. Aside from the good old VPN technology that most of us have already heard of or even used in our businesses, the following list shows just a few of the most popular overlay network technologies in use today:

- **OneSwarm**: Developed by the University of Washington, OneSwarm offers a privacy-preserving P2P client that protects the user's anonymity by creating a distributed darknet. http://www.oneswarm.org/

- **I2P**: The Invisible Internet Project (I2P) creates a darknet for users (and applications) to securely send pseudonymous messages to each other. It provides features that include web surfing, chatting, blogging, and file transfers. https://geti2p.net/en/

- **Freenet**: A P2P platform that uses a distributed data store to store and transmit information, offering a range of software applications for publishing and communicating on the Internet without fear of censorship. https://freenetproject.org/

- **Tribler**: An open source distributed BitTorrent client that facilitates anonymous P2P communications. It is based on BitTorrent and uses an overlay network for content searching. https://www.tribler.org/

- **Zeronet**: Another distributed open source solution that builds an Internet-like network of P2P users. However, Zeronet is not anonymous by default, instead relying on users also using Tor to hide their IP addresses. http://zeronet.io/

There are dozens more of these technology solutions available—all you need to do is look—and there are more springing up all the time. The thing to remember when you are looking to set one up is be sure to follow the all the instructions and do your research on efficacy and usage, since some of these are better than others and are more suited to particular use cases than others. It's also worth noting that some of these "free" services have been known to include intentional backdoors, where the person responsible for the software has more nefarious purposes in mind.

As an aside, if you are an information security manager, it's worth looking for this kind of traffic on your own network as it may be an indicator that staff are accessing illegal or inappropriate content, or it could be an indicator of compromise since threat actors often use these networks to exfiltrate information from corporate networks.

Malware as a Service

This productizing of malware has led to a restructuring of the exploit marketplace, where hacking as-a-service (HaaS) is now the preferred delivery model. HaaS allows anyone who wants to dabble in cybercrime to get started, even if they have no technical skills at all. Hackers can simply license the malware they need from a developer, or hire the hacking group (by the hour) to launch attacks on their behalf. Obtaining the tools is also very easy. There are websites dedicated to selling malware developers' wares, where sellers offer tailored services specifically for the purposes of hacking the chosen target. This means the hacker can afflict any combination of negative outcomes on their target with little to no technical knowledge, for a very reasonable service fee.

To correct a common misuse of terminology, vulnerabilities are the design flaw or bugs in the system that allows threat actors to launch an attack, while an exploit is a weaponized tool designed to help make use of a vulnerability. Therefore, the exploits are sold on the black market as software tools, while the knowledge of vulnerabilities is also sold, especially if they are previously unknown. A previously unknown vulnerability that is pedaled on the black market, where the vendor is unaware of it, is known as a *zero-day vulnerability*. These fetch exceedingly high bounties, some being sold for as high as one million dollars.

A good analogy might be that a terrorist buys a vial of smallpox from a bioweapons supplier and releases it in the middle of New York City. The terrorist needs no medical knowledge to commit this act; instead all he or she needs is the motivation to enact the atrocity and the money to purchase the weapon. The bioweapons seller needs no motivation to commit the crime and has no gripe with the people of New York City; instead, their motivation is purely financial.

Investigators have even discovered malware that's been shrink-wrapped as if it's a commercial product, like Microsoft Office would be, with sales and marketing material, datasheets, brochures, and so forth advertising it for a specific purpose. "Perfect for penetrating financial systems," or, "Tailor your own denial of service attack: 100% guaranteed."

Packages are now available for a multitude of purposes, from stealing data from SQL and Oracle databases, or purloining credit card data and software source code, all the way through to holding victims' computers systems and data to ransom, as with the latest strains of cryptoware and ransomware.

RANSOMWARE

Ransomware is a kind of malware that works by limiting a user's access to his data by encrypting it in a way that makes it impossible to recover it without the decryption key. The type of encryption used by modern ransomware is high-strength public-key based, meaning there is no known method of reversing it. This means the user is effectively held to ransom until they pay the hacker for the decryption key. Since keys are custom generated for each infected computer, there is no way to crack the code or brute force the encryption, so the only way to get out of this situation is to either recover from a clean backup (if you are lucky) or pay the random.

What's interesting is that the ransom fee is usually quite small and manageable, in the ballpark of $250. That way, the crime is so small that most law-enforcement agencies cannot investigate it, and the majority of affected users will have enough money to pay up. The most recent ransomware iteration called CryptoWall, released into the wild by a Russian cybercrime gang, has been their most prolific malware to date, with reported earnings of over $325 million by the end of 2015 (http://www.coindesk.com/cryptowall-325-million-bitcoin-ransom/). Furthermore, some countries are blacklisted from CryptoWall damage (Eastern Europe mainly), suggesting the operators work from those regions, which also highlights that those nations are turning a blind eye to cybercrime activities as long as it does not negatively impact their own nation.

As an attacker, you can now select your preferred method of attack, along with the outcome you want to inflict on your victim, and have the malware designer customize and engineer it for your specific needs. Anything you want is available, with the only limitation being your imagination and the funds to pay for it. Furthermore, service offerings have now reached a new level of maturity as hackers offer completely customized cloud-based campaigns and guns for hire on online marketplaces, such as the notorious Silk Road. The income generated by these services also allows the creators to remain ahead of the antivirus companies, who are continually struggling to find and fingerprint the latest strains of malicious programs.

You can hire your favorite hacker "by the hour" to perpetrate the attack on your behalf, operating as a cyberhitman to target whomever you like. This "as a service" model is the foremost reason why the volume of successful attacks has risen sharply over the past few years. It's not because there are more people with cybergrudges, it's simply that cybercrime is now an intrinsic part of the criminal landscape and is readily accessible to anyone who wants to use it in a criminal campaign.

Criminal Motivations and Capabilities

Understanding criminal motivations is key to understanding why you become a target and why you get attacked. It also helps identify whether the threat is likely to diminish by upping your defenses. What's interesting is that the motivation that drove the hackers of old—bragging rights—is consideration, since today's threat landscape is overrun with criminals.

Traditional white-collar crime, organized crime, terrorism, activism, revenge attacks, espionage, and opportunist hacking-for-profit are all considerations when we look at the categories of successful attacks over the past ten years. Furthermore, cyber is now a component and consideration of every single law enforcement investigation, simply because each and every crime has some sort of electronic fingerprint, be it from a mobile phone, CCTV footage, GPS logs, SmartWatch logs, or even a Bluetooth-connected pacemaker.

HACKING OF PACEMAKERS

Back in 2012, *Homeland*, a national security-related drama, featured a scene where the vice president of the United States was assassinated by terrorists who remotely accessed his pacemaker and gave him a massive electrical shock, triggering a fatal cardiac arrest. This might have seemed to some like an elaborate plot device to enhance the story and shock viewers, however, it's been proven in real life that this is a legitimate threat and something healthcare security teams are extremely concerned about.

Pacemakers have been around for a very long time and not posed this kind of threat, but what's changed? Simple, like many devices in our everyday lives, more and more health related implants are becoming remotely accessible, allowing doctors and healthcare workers not only to monitor their efficacy, but also to change the way they operate. When you get a pacemaker installed, sometimes it needs tuning to make sure that it's working best for your particular case. Previously, surgeons had to open you up and either change the device or physically modify its operational parameters, but nowadays, things are different. Devices are now being implanted into patients with Bluetooth communications stacks and software that allow them to be accessible from outside the patient's body and reprogrammed on the fly. This is the perfect outcome for the patient since the majority of tuning of the device can be done remotely (no more complicated surgeries and prolonged recovery times).

Security researchers at South Alabama University subsequently discovered that these devices were prone to electronic attack, with early models sporting some interesting oversights in the hardware and software stacks that leave the patient wide open to cyberattack. Read the research paper at `http://arxiv.org/ftp/arxiv/papers/1509/1509.00065.pdf`.

Some of the most devastating cyberattacks we've seen over the past few years demonstrate well how aligned the modern cybercriminal landscape has become with traditional crime:

- **Anthem**: This health insurance provider was hacked by an organized crime group in order to steal customer health records. Health records are extremely useful on the black market, fetching a much higher price than credit card records, since they can be used to create false identities, leading to much more significant profits and, unlike credit card information, your name, address and social security numbers cannot be changed.

- **OPM**: We looked previously at the attack on the US government's Office of Personnel Management, however, to classify it against standard criminal activity, it really falls into the category of espionage.

- **Ashley Madison**: This dating site was hacked by a group of activists who believe the organization was furthering immorality in society by encouraging people to cheat on their spouses. Activism in cyberspace is known as *hacktivism*, but it remains activism nonetheless. Ashley Madison is one of the first hacks that resulted in the deaths of at least two affected victims.

- **Sony Pictures**: The massive and sustained attack on Sony Pictures saw copyright material leaked onto the Internet, along with emails, celebrity contracts and a plethora of other potentially damaging material. This hack was attributed to North Korea by US law enforcement; however, it can't really be considered as espionage because it wasn't politically motivated. Rather, it was posited as revenge for the portrayal of North Korea's leader, Kim Jong-un, as a psychotic idiot in the movie skit *The Interview*.

- **Bureau of Meteorology**: The Australian government agency that provides national meteorological services was hacked in late 2015 around the same time as the international climate talks were being held in Paris. The identity of the perpetrator is unknown, but evidence so far seems to be pointing toward China, one of the primary protagonists in the conversations about cutting global omissions. Could this have been politically motivated to give them an edge in climate negotiations?

- **Iranian Nuclear Enrichment**: Cyberwarfare became the new media buzz-term when the Iranian Nuclear Enrichment program was set back a few years by a cyberattack on their centrifuges; devices that are crucial in developing weapons grade uranium. This attack, dubbed Stuxnet, was attributed to a joint US-Israeli attempt to slow down Iran's realization of their nuclear arms capability, so it must be attributed to espionage and cyberwarfare.

Some countries have become true havens of cybercrime, either because of lax local laws or a lack of enforcement of the laws, even if they exist. Just look at Nigeria, for example: the majority of phishing attacks seen in our mailboxes every single day originate from some of the poorest communities in Lagos, Nigeria. Lagos has become the African capital of cybercrime, with fraudulent activity a way of life for many of the country's poorest people. Criminals use social engineering techniques to convince their victims to send money for goods, services, and even love.

We've all seen those wonderfully colorful stories of billionaires needing to urgently move their fortunes away from the clutches of an evil empire and they desperately need *your* help… all you need to do to earn your 15% commission for helping them is make a small deposit into a foreign bank, just to activate the account, so the poor old billionaire victim can deposit their fortunes before fleeing the country. Victims pay them a smallish amount of money, maybe a few hundred dollars then, of course, they never hear from the criminals again.

Russia has become a global nexus of cybercrime, most of which is controlled by the Russian mafia, a.k.a. the Bratva. The majority of the world's ransomware attacks, privacy hacks, and banking scams originate from Bratva controlled hacking crews hidden behind the veil of an electronic iron curtain.

The tools hackers are using to scan systems, detect vulnerabilities and exploit weaknesses are diverse, plentiful, and highly functional. Furthermore, teams of extremely competent malware developers are deploying millions of code variants of new and devious exploits every day, making the job of the information security manager and her team continually harder and more complex. Tools, such as network sniffers, port scanners, vulnerability scanners, keystroke loggers, remote administration tools, and brute-force password crackers are just some of the well-known categories of tool openly available on the Internet for download and use.

The essence of the problem is this: threats are everywhere and cybercrime is just a new mode of operation for traditional crime; most crimes have some kind of digital footprint and your organization will be under continual attack 24 hours a day, 7 days a week, every week; you need to understand the threats your organization faces before you can adequately defend against them. The lack of visibility we have of what's really going on in our systems is the key: if you can see it, you can manage it. When they first deploy monitoring systems, most organizations are amazed at how often they are being probed, attacked, and even compromised.

Physical Threats

As an information security manager, your job extends to looking at all aspects of threats that affect your organization's IT systems and information, not just the technical attacks from hackers we've already briefly looked at. You need to consider threats from physical hazards such as the following:

- Earthquakes

- Floods

- Volcanoes

- Cyclones (hurricane)

- Tornados

- Heatwaves

- Forest fires, wildfires, and bushfires

- Landslides

- Cave-ins

- Collapsing sinkholes

- Crashes (planes, trains, and automobiles)
- Staff illness (pandemic flu, Ebola)
- Explosions
- Toxic chemical releases
- Nuclear power plant meltdowns
- Simple power cuts

The United States Federal Emergency Management Agency (FEMA) lists a variety of natural hazards in their useful document entitled *Are You Ready?*. This series of guidelines shows citizens and business owners how to deal with hurricanes, tornadoes, earthquakes, and floods, offering a plethora of useful advice and guidance. Most other countries have what's commonly referred to as *critical national infrastructure*. In most cases, you will be able to find government guidelines that have been extended to include the cyberdomain for protecting this critical infrastructure, so it's worth contacting your local government or federal government agency to see what's available to you in your own country.

■ **Note** You can access the *Are You Ready?* FEMA guidelines at `http://www.ready.gov/are-you-ready-guide`.

As an information security manager, you need to consider the environment you live and work, especially from a historical perspective. If there is a history of natural disasters hitting your region (maybe you live in a hurricane or tornado zone) then your threat analysis will feed into your overall business risk assessment. For example, if you live in a coastal region that regularly gets hit by a couple of tropical cyclones each year, then your data center, communications systems, working environments, transport systems, and even the location from which your IT administration and security staff work, all need to be assessed and hardened. If the risk is high of losing service, you need to invest money in physical mitigation, such as strengthening the building infrastructure and having a disaster resilience facility in a less risky location.

One of the key duties of the information security manager is to ensure that you put systems in place to alert you to these kinds of natural disaster so that you can put your emergency management plan into action should the threat manifest into an incident. For example, you should create an alert that warns of the spread of disease, such as pandemic influenza or the recent Ebola crisis. You could have an alert from the Centers of Disease Control (CDC) ping you with regular updates so that if a major outbreak of pandemic flu hit your workforce, you'd have time to get contingencies into place. How would you fare on a reduced workforce? What would happen if staff became afraid to come into the office or travel on public transport for fear of infection? You might consider planning a home-working option in the event of a crisis, even if the policy of your business is to normally work from the office. This way you might be able to continue operations where otherwise you'd not have enough staff to turn the lights on.

We will look at physical threats in more detail later when we look at protecting our people and our premises.

Vulnerabilities

In the previous chapter we looked at what vulnerabilities are and how they differ from threats. As a quick refresher, a threat is defined in ISO 27000 as "the potential cause of an unwanted incident, which may result in harm to a system or organization;" whereas a vulnerability is defined as "a weakness of an asset or control that can be exploited by one or more threats."

So far, we've looked at some of the threats our systems, our information and our people face, from the criminal underground, foreign governments and extremists, coupled with the physical threats that result from natural and man-made hazards. However, it's necessary to understand that these threats are of little consequence without a vulnerability that they will exploit should they manifest. If your systems are self-contained on a private network in a bunker hundreds of meters below the surface with no external connections to the Internet, then the threat of malware on a public website won't matter. It is therefore unlikely that a vulnerability in your system will be able to be successfully exploited. If your datacenter is located in the flight path of your local airport, then the vulnerability in your infrastructure could be the thickness of the concrete surrounding your building. What about the strength of the room on your datacenter? Would it withstand a light aircraft crashing into it? If there is a likelihood that an event like this might occur, the vulnerability is in the building infrastructure, so that is what you need to reinforce, otherwise, your mitigation might be to reduce the likelihood by relocating to a safer zone, away from the proximity of the airport.

But where are the vulnerabilities in our technical systems and, as an information security manager, how do you find where they in within the complexity of networks, operating systems and the application you manage?

Technical Vulnerabilities

There are many kinds of technical vulnerability you need to consider when performing a risk assessment for your business. Operating systems and applications have been developed from millions of lines of complex code and often have a variety of errors and oversights that are left in the system once compiled. These errors are not necessarily ones that affect operations therefore are not found until someone specifically tries to find ways to exploit your systems.

Even where development companies have the most rigorous of quality control systems in place, errors still slip through, some of which are so complex and hard to find that only the best and brightest security researchers on the planet will be able to locate.

When security researchers discover vulnerabilities, vendors are usually given a relatively short period of time to create a patch before the researchers notify the public about the problem. Often this is a few months, since the ethical security researcher will follow the process of responsible disclosure, to allow the vendor to check and validate the vulnerability, then develop the patch, which itself is tested to ensure that it does not introduce further problems. By way of example, when you receive Microsoft's monthly patch roundup containing application and operating security patches, Microsoft has likely been notified of the issue during the previous month. If the bug is severe enough, patches are sometimes released outside of the usual schedule, as a critical update, which needs to be installed as a matter of urgency. It is incumbent on the information security manager and the security team to receive these notifications, perform a risk assessment for their organization, and ensure that any vulnerable systems are patched as quickly as possible.

Most software vendors have their own security teams, who develop secure coding standards, enforce the use of security development processes and methodologies and perform analysis and code review. However, with limited time and resources, it's impossible to exhaustively test every potential failure mode for every single function in the software; otherwise, they'd never get their products shipped. This is why systems will almost certainly ship with a baseline of vulnerabilities when developers are not only building new code, but incorporating functions from external code-libraries that also may contain unknown weaknesses. A bug might be found in a shared cryptographic function that has been compiled into dozens if not hundreds of end user application, and in each case the vendor will need to wait for the cryptographic function to first be patched, and then recompile their own software and release a patch of their own.

COMMON VULNERABILITY SCORING SYSTEM (CVSS)

A system for scoring the severity of technical vulnerabilities has been created as open standard (free) for use across the security industry. This is known as the Common Vulnerability Scoring System (CVSS), which allows anyone who discovers a vulnerability to assess the complexity and severity of the bug, determine how hard it is to exploit and how damaging the weakness might be, looking at how much of a risk to confidentiality, integrity and availability it might be. NIST's National Vulnerability Database website has a great write-up on how CVSS v3 works and how to integrate its use with the NVD to calculate a contextual score that helps with your risk assessment. What this means is that you can use this as an accurate vulnerability rating in your organization as it takes into consideration other mitigating circumstances, such as whether you have firewalls or other security enforcing functions and how critical the affected system is to operations.

You can find out more about CVSS and its usage at `https://nvd.nist.gov/cvss.cfm`.

The CVSS calculator is at `https://nvd.nist.gov/cvss.cfm?calculator&version=2.`

Non-Technical Vulnerabilities

One very important aspect of being an information security manager is you need to be the guy who executives trust to make the best decisions for the business. Ask any senior Windows technician how to solve a security problem and they will build you an Active Directory with locked down group policies and throw in a couple of products from their favorite vendors that can audit and control the environment. If you ask a network engineer to solve the same problem, they will approach the solution in a similar way, just choosing different tech. In this case, they might specify a new firewall architecture, along with an Intrusion Protection system and a network access control system that locks down access, while auditing everything that passes through it.

While these are all viable solutions, if the question was related to fixing a vulnerability in a physical process, the security management guy might choose to solve the problem by employing a security guard or building a fence. As a security manager you need to properly understand how physical and process vulnerabilities affect your business and security and how they should be addressed within a holistic approach to your security architecture. In this section, we'll look at

- Physical vulnerabilities
- Process vulnerabilities
- People vulnerabilities

Physical Vulnerabilities

In the previous section in this chapter we looked at some of the physical threats our business systems and information might be affected by, such as fires, floods, and earthquakes. These are all dangerous and can affect our systems, but like any threat in the electronic world, they still need to exploit a vulnerability or weakness to have any kind of negative effect on our systems or information. The sorts of areas you need to consider, where non-technical vulnerabilities will affect your organization are

- Premises security
- Access control
- General staff awareness

You should study the floor plans and schematics of the buildings and premises your company resides in. Check to see what materials have been used in construction, as certain materials and standards will be stronger and more resistant to overheating, shock, shaking, and so forth. If you reside in Los Angeles, for example, making sure your IT systems are housed in modern buildings or datacenters developed using the Federal Emergency Management Agency (FEMA) building codes. If your business resides in an older building that has not been constructed using these standards, then that is what you should consider a vulnerability (to the threat of earthquake) where the risk is subsequently catastrophic loss of service to your business.

If you operate your business in an earthquake zone and you are in an older building that has the potential of being affected by a moderate earthquake, you can look to enhance your building's resistance to earthquakes through seismic retrofitting. For more information on this topic, check out FEMA's website at `http://www.fema.gov/building-codes`.

The following are other things to consider.

- **Perimeter**: Consider whether your perimeter needs a standoff distance to protect the building from intruders, potential rioters, or terrorists. In urban areas this is difficult to achieve, so it should be considered as a vulnerable part of your overall structure and delay with in your risk assessment

- **Loading bay**: You may have great security measures at the front and sides of your organization, but what about the loading bay? What vulnerabilities exist where deliveries are made? Is it guarded? Do you have good CCTV coverage? What about weekend deliveries?

- **Locale**: The neighborhood the building or datacenter resides in could also become a vulnerability (since it could be the reason threats are so prominent to your business). Criminal activity needs to be considered, as does the impact of having competitors nearby or oversight from foreign residents or embassies.

We'll look at the physical security needs of your business in a lot more detail later in the book, but for now this is enough to show you what kind of physical vulnerabilities can affect your business and what kind of things the security manager needs to be looking for when conducting a vulnerability assessment.

Process Vulnerabilities

The technical vulnerabilities in systems are just one perspective of where you'll find weaknesses that can affect a loss of confidentiality, integrity, or availability. Security managers need to be aware of the underlying processes that keep the business safe and ensure that there are minimal vulnerabilities in those that can also lead to a compromise. For example, a process may be dictate that the keys to the server racks in the datacenter are held by the security guard and an engineer needing access needs to seek written permission from the security manager, which needs presenting to the guards prior to keys being issued. However, if an attacker knows what the form looks like and has found a way to forge the security manager's signature, if this form is all the attacker needs to get the keys to the server room, then gaining malicious access will be easy.

Information security managers should regularly review processes, along with all relevant business stakeholders, looking at them from a variety of perspectives to see if vulnerabilities exist. Once you find a weakness, it doesn't mean it will be exploited, it just means that there is a likelihood that it could be. This is an essential factor in the risk assessment, where you determine the vulnerability, its likelihood, and the subsequent impact of a successful exploitation, to get that final value of risk. If the risk is high, you might consider treating it. In the case of this example, you might have the security guard call the security manager with a serial number associated with the form, seeking confirmation that you have indeed signed the form and it's associated with the access request that's being sought. A further ID check of the engineer, cross referenced with the request form and the reason for the visit could also be added. As you can see from this, we've not introduced any complex technology into the process, instead using the telephone and an ID number that can be checked on a register, which is trivial to set up.

The security manager needs to be careful not to over complicate the mitigation strategy, since simple physical security measures such as these can easily improve the security posture without investing money in a complex technical countermeasure. Also, experience shows that an unnecessarily complex or onerous process is often circumvented or ignored by the end user, resulting in a much less secure state than in the first place.

People Vulnerabilities

Finally, one of the biggest considerations the information security manager must make is that of how to deal with the vulnerabilities introduced into the organization by staff. People can introduce risk into the systems they manage, through complacency, carelessness, simply not understanding how to do something or why something should be done the way it's specified, or through malicious intent. We also use people as the developers of our systems, which is where many of these issues come from in the first place, and for any one of myriad reasons, bugs can be introduced into the systems you are developing (both from a software and a hardware point of view).

Often, though, the statement I hear from new security managers and other management teams within the business is that, "We trust our people, our people are loyal and wouldn't do that to us....". So why are people considered one of our biggest weaknesses?

People Can Be Compromised

It's true that we cannot know everything about our staff and colleagues. What goes on when they leave work is really none of your concern, but what if something they are involved in leads to them compromising their work environment or leaving them prone to blackmail or coercion? In some cases, depending on the sensitivity of the work undertaken by the member of staff, it's prudent to do some background checks and have regular interviews to make sure that nothing in their life puts them at risk.

We will look at people related security matters later in the book, but for now it's just worth seeing that vulnerabilities can exist in many different places, not just technology, so you need to be looking for weaknesses that can lead to loss in as holistic and pragmatic a way as possible.

CHAPTER 3

■ ■ ■

The Information Security Manager

Becoming an information security manager is an exciting and daunting prospect, especially given the task in hand of defending your employer's castle against the hordes of cybercriminals, hacktivists, and nation-state hackers, not to mention the ever present threat of a malicious (or even careless) insiders.

This chapter offers a whistle-stop tour of the information security profession, looking at the diverse range of job roles and career opportunities available, and then focusing in on the information security manager role and its responsibilities within the infosec career portfolio. Following that, we'll take a look at a useful framework that you can use to map skills and competencies against individuals (either yourself or your team members) so you can assess where you are on the ladder and what you need to do to climb up to the next rung or switch from one ladder to another. The skills framework that is most useful to base the discussion on was created by the Institute of Information Security Professionals (IISP) in the United Kingdom; however, the framework itself is based on the Skills Framework for the Information Age (SFIA), which is recognized internationally.

THE SKILLS FRAMEWORK FOR THE INFORMATION AGE (SFIA)

The SFIA Foundation introduced the Skills Framework for the Information Age in 2000. It has become one of the most widely used general skills frameworks available for the information technology sector. It's a useful resource that allows individuals and managers with organizational design and talent management responsibilities to map staff capabilities, including infosec skills, to a range of skills and competency levels.

Skills categories cover strategy and architecture, business change, solution development and implementation, service management, procurement and management support and the client interface, while competency levels range from one to seven. One is being the most junior level and seven equates to the most senior, with roles in the industry associated with CIO, account director, service director, and so forth. Employees who use skills with lower competencies tend to be the junior staff on the team, such as service desk operators, systems installation engineers, and content publishers. Businesses can use the SFIA framework to map to their own internal job roles and levels to allow managers to plot career development milestones for employees and identify internal talent.

You can learn more about SFIA on the SFIA Foundation's official website at http://www.sfia-online.org/en.

© Tony Campbell 2016
T. Campbell, *Practical Information Security Management*, DOI 10.1007/978-1-4842-1685-9_3

There are dozens of career opportunities within the infosec profession and it is certainly confusing as to where to start. Job roles range from the highly technical to business-focused (manager, risk, business continuity, strategy and advisory), as well as physical security roles, such as facilities designers. The interesting this is that all of these roles are in high demand and in short supply in pretty much every demographic around the world.

The information security countermeasures needed to cover every angle of electronic attack cover a vast array of people, processes and technology and to cover all the bases, the information security manager's role is the one that works across all towers of technical experts, risk managers, business continuity experts, facilitators, other managers, and even sales and marketing departments.

Our adversaries take as long as they need to plan an attack, methodically scanning each and every one of our systems for the chink in our armor that will let them break in. Invariably, the way the threat landscape is evolving so rapidly today, it may not be immediate or even tomorrow, but soon enough all the countermeasures you have put in place will seem worthless in defending the castle. This is the unfortunate reality and inevitability of working as a security professional and, while it's exciting, exhilarating, and also demoralizing, there is one constant you can always depend on: you'll never be bored.

Information Security Job Roles

Organizations of all types and sizes face internal and external factors and influences that make it uncertain whether and when they will achieve their objectives. The effect this uncertainty has on an organization's objectives is risk. (ISO 31000)

As you've already seen, information security is now a fully-fledged profession in itself, comprising a vast array of job roles that cover everything from the very technical to the highest levels of the boardroom, with developers, systems architects, risk managers, business continuity managers, testers, and operators all working toward the common goal of reducing information risk.

To anyone embarking on this journey, there are a couple of questions you need to answer before you can decide on which path to take. First, if you have a technical background, you might want to stay in technology and as such as you need to consider whether a security architecture career path might be for you. If you are a hacker and love tinkering with software code and reverse engineering, you might consider a career as a penetration tester. If your penchant is for management, or maybe teaching people about security and ensuring everyone is doing the right thing, you might be ready to take on the role of information security manager.

There are many job roles to choose from within the profession, such as the following:

- Information security manager
- Chief security officer
- Chief information security manager
- Information risk manager
- Operational security manager
- Digital forensics analyst
- eDiscovery expert
- Security architect
- Penetration tester
- Security requirements manager

- Security programmer

- Malware analyst

- Intrusion analyst

- Incident response manager

Believe it or not, this is not an exhaustive list and you'll find that different industries even have different names for exactly the same job role. This can be very confusing; especially to anyone new to this industry, but by the end of this chapter you should have a much better understanding of the landscape you are entering.

You'll also find that one organization's view of the skills required to tackle any given job role will differ to the next. For example, the manager of information security in one company might be called the *information security manager* (ISM). The very same role, with exactly the same skills requirements may be advertised as the *head of information security, chief security officer* (CSO), or *chief information security officer* (CISO). Confusing, isn't it? The reason for this disparity can be attributed to two simple factors:

- The maturity of the hiring organization: some organizations simply don't know what they want from a security manager. They know they need one (maybe a consultant told them so), but they have no idea how to go about scoping the role or deciding where the manager's role exists within the organizational structure.

- The level of seniority: the CSO and CISO roles are often board-level appointments, with the CSO being above the ICT function, holding responsibilities for information security, as well as physical security, process security and personnel security. CISOs, on the other hand, are sometimes appointed as a direct report to the chief information officer (CIO), where their responsibilities are limited to that of technical (cyber) security matters.

There is no right or wrong answer to how your organizational structure is created; however, the thing that's important is ensuring that someone is appointed with the authority to make security decisions and the responsibility for making it happen. In some organizations where information and technology is core to their central business function, the way the banking sector has become, then a CISO role may report directly to the CEO, with organization-wide authority for all aspects of security (people, process, and technology). Choosing the structure that's right for your own organization is a critical step in ensuring governance is strong, authority, and responsibility is duly delegated and managed effectively and all aspects of the security landscape are covered.

Another example that highlights just how confusing the industry can be is in the role of the *security architect*. In some cases, companies advertise for security architects who are a highly technical person that can design, build, and run technical components or functions, such as complex firewall implementations or security information and event management systems (SIEM). The very same job role, advertised by a consultancy firm, might require an enterprise security architect, where day-to-day activities include designing conceptual architectures, threat modeling, technical assurance, and strategic security advice for clients. Both jobs are advertised as a *security architect*, but the skills required by each company are entirely different from the other. You might ask why this is and whether anyone is doing anything to make things more consistent.

There are in fact many routes into the information security industry, some of which are easier to take than others. For example, to become the leader of a professional penetration testing team, (often abbreviated to *pen testing*), you'll need to work your way up from the bottom, in effect starting out as an apprentice. Junior pen testers are often hired because they are inquisitive; managers know the rest of the job can be trained, but this inherent aspect of an individual's personality is critical to success. I've even heard interview questions that ask what the candidate did on the weekend. If they reply by saying they took apart their new iPhone to see how it worked and managed to hook it up to their fridge, they'll get hired.

If you've worked as a network or systems administrator you're in a great place to start, especially if you spent time configuring Windows, Unix, and network systems. Taking the skills you've already learned, you'll already have an understanding of what it takes to build and secure a system; hence, you'll know where to look for vulnerabilities in those systems, vulnerabilities that could potentially be exploited in an attack. This is exactly what a penetration tester does. They figure out what the bad guys might do and demonstrate these threats to their customers.

What if you are into programming? There are plenty of coders that know next to nothing about security. This is why there are so many vulnerabilities being discovered in software applications all the time. By learning the techniques and weaknesses of modern programming languages, software frameworks and systems architectures, you can build stronger more robust code or even act in an assurance role where you review or design the security aspects of new systems before they are released. Today, this discipline of secure coding commands some of the highest pay in the programming sector and is certainly a worthwhile career if you are that way inclined.

Training, Experience, and Professionalism

Initially, it might occur to you that if you take a training course and pass the exam, the certification will be enough to highlight you as a security professional to prospective hiring companies. You might even be right and land your dream job after passing one of those exams. But are you really ready to stand up and be accountable to the board when the business suffers from an intrusion?

Ask yourself this, if you decide to read a book on brain surgery and fully understand what you've read, including what bits to prod and cut to remove a tumor, would you expect a patient to let you operate on them with nothing more than your knowledge? This should be somewhat of a rhetorical question, as the answer is almost certainly no. What makes the difference in the world of subject matter experts is experience. You'd expect that the surgeon would have passed through medical school, aced their degree, and then served under a mentor for many years before being allowed to even lift a scalpel. If you ally this to the context of information security, which is a highly complex field of study, would you expect someone to pay a lot of money for you to pen test their network if all you had was a book and quick e-learning certificate under your belt? Again, I'd hope not. Some of the best penetration testers have no formal qualifications at all, just decades of experience.

We need to collectively take this seriously and encourage professionalism right across the field of security, laying down a core body of knowledge that steers professionals through study and certification, but also uses the same techniques that the medical industry employ to mentor and encourage experience that will eventually lead to a security professional who can make the tough calls in the middle of a crisis.

Unfortunately, this isn't how the security industry works today, but I would encourage anyone in this industry, from the very junior to the very senior, to find a mentor that can help you develop and grow, while taking on your own apprentice that you can provide that same level of advice and guidance to. Choose carefully and this will be one of the most critical aspects of your development that will lead to your eventual success. Try and design your own career development program, that gives you experience across all the towers of the security industry, to allow you to get a fully rounded understanding of operational security, business security, architecture, physical security, and dealing with complex forensic investigations.

The final point by way of introducing this section is to consider where the best training ground is for new security guys, where we can target our hiring should we want to encourage new entrants to the industry to take up the mantle and set on their new career path. Technical jobs, such as Windows and Unix administration, can be a great place to start. Who are the ace engineers in your networking team or platform team? You know the ones, the guys who can script anything and tend to jump into the command line, build shell scripts and PowerShell scripts to solve the problems that the GUI guys don't know how to solve. These are the inquisitive types that really know how to tackle a problem that means they have the mindset needed to be in security. They don't have the fundamental knowledge of being a security professional, but that can be learned: it's the mindset that important. As the information security manager you need to understand this area of the industry, how to get new guys interested and skilled up to be your replacement, so you can move on to bigger and better things, but before you do you need to ensure that the legacy you leave behind is fit for the business in the future.

Career Planning with Professional and Academic Certifications

It's worth taking a quick look at professional and academic training establishments that provide information security courses and certifications to see what helps you plan your own career, and the progression and training of those you are responsible for.

The dilemma that you will find is choosing from what seems like dozens of certifications, university courses, and so-called expert short courses. Many of these offer no more than a certificate of attendance. It seems that the majority of managed security services providers these days offer their own special training and certification programs that complement the myriad other service offerings; usually alongside consultancy, security operations, architecture and incident response. As the guy with the training budget, the information security manager needs to know where to spend those all-important training dollars to get the most value for the business and make sure that you are developing yourselves and your team to manage the information risks the business is subject to.

First, there are a variety of self-appointed global authorities (I use the term *authority* in the loosest sense) that claim to be the best. Professional security certifications, such as Certified Information Systems Security Professional (CISSP) and Certified Information Security Manager (CISM), to name just a couple, are the two most widely accepted professional certifications. CISSP has gotten somewhat of a bad rap over the last few years, since the industry has noted (ISC)²'s slow progress in keeping up with rapid change in the information technology sector. It has been criticized for coming late to the party with technologies such as virtualization and cloud computing, for example, which are not entirely unfounded. However, irrespective of this criticism, and it's something that (ISC)² has now addressed, CISSP is still the most widely asked for (and known) certification when you survey the global information security job market.

Nevertheless, CISSP does pose a few problems of its own that are worth investigating. The certificate itself has created somewhat of a bottleneck for getting new people into the profession by limiting the candidate selection process to the elite CISSP certificate holders. CISSP is not really required by an organization for the role of firewall engineer, but the global understanding that security professionals are assessed by their having passed CISSP means that many job adverts for engineering roles request that the candidate have CISSP as a minimum. This leads to what looks like a shortage of candidates and creates a false barrier to entry for any network engineers who want to move into security-focused roles, even if they are firewall experts.

The re (ISC)² has set the requirement for CISSP as being to not only pass the exam, but also to have five solid years of information security work under your belt and have a professional reference and CV that backs that claim up. This is clearly not an entry level certificate and is exactly what is hampering wannabe security guys getting into the industry. If HR teams and hiring managers require CISSP for every security job and every security professional needs five years to get CISSP, you can see why this creates a problem. Many information security professionals already in the field, even ones who have CISSP (me included), consider the certification a mile wide and an inch deep. What I mean by that is that the relevance of the CISSP in hiring specialists, especially in very niche roles, is extremely limited.

All of this being said, (ISC)² has now recognized that this is a real issue and has made changes to address this in the industry and with the hiring/recruitment sector. They have uplifted the CISSP syllabus to include a variety of contemporary changes with regard to mobile computing, cloud computing and the technologies of virtualization (in networking, data centers, and all the as-a-service offerings). Alongside this, (ISC)² is also pushing the entry-level (one year in infosec) Systems Security Certified Practitioner (SSCP) certificate, aimed at junior security managers and engineers, which allows them to acquire a decent certification before they have enough experience to challenge the CISSP.

The lesson from this is that certifications are definitely worthwhile, but need to be considered as just one piece of the professionalism puzzle, rather than the be all and end all of career progression and job/skills alignment.

CERTIFICATE IN INFORMATION SECURITY MANAGEMENT PRINCIPLES

In the United Kingdom, the British Computer Society (BCS) provides a full curriculum of study for the security field. This has the backing of the UK government, with GCHQ using the Certificate in Information Security Management Principles (CISMP) certification as a baseline required to apply to be a government security professional. This is not the only way that an individual can get into being a government security advisor, however, it's certainly a straightforward way to prove your value to the security profession prior to taking on some of the GCHQ specific training. What's interesting is that this is so much more accessible than getting CISSP. CISMP does not have a five-year experience requirement, but it still manages to cover the same set of vertical domains that the (ISC)² syllabus covers. The primary difference with CISMP is the depth of knowledge in each domain required to pass the exam is shallower, simply because it's aimed at entry-level security professionals.

I think this is what makes this a great qualification, since it allows operations managers or technical managers to branch out into a career in security, taking the five-day CISMP course and getting enough of a grounding to understand organizational security, risk management, technical security and architecture, business continuity, and forensics, and take on a job role as a team leader under a more senior and capable information security manager. The five-year career development plan can then encourage the junior to challenge CISSP in the future, while in the meantime, they can still apply to become UK government security professionals through the CESG Certified Professional (CCP) scheme. What's also worth noting is that CISMP is not a UK-centric certification; therefore, its universal applicability means it's as valuable to a security professional in the United States as it is in Europe or Australia.

Learn about the CISMP at `http://certifications.bcs.org/category/15735`

Learn about CISSP at `https://www.isc2.org/cissp/default.aspx`

E-learning version of CISMP at `https://www.infosecskills.com/products/kits/certificate-information-security-management-principles-cismp`

Learn about the CCP scheme at `http://certifications.bcs.org/category/15865`

It pays to be aware of all the different aspects of the information security professional. As an information security manager, you need to know which controls are most important in each area and how they are implemented, and you need to be able to deal with the experts in each of these area so that you can scope their work, understand their reports and convey their complicated and often technical output to the executive board for assessment. The kinds of subject matter I'm talking about are covered in the majority of baseline qualifications, whether they are professional certifications or academic degree courses, as follows:

- Access Control
- Telecommunications and Network Security
- Information Security Governance and Risk Management
- Software Development Security
- Cryptography
- Security Architecture and Design
- Operations Security

- Business Continuity and Disaster Recovery Planning

- Legal, Regulations, Investigations, and Compliance

- Physical (Environmental) Security

These subjects need to be well understood if you are to become a security manager, however, if you have chosen a different route in your career trajectory, such as Penetration Testing, you need to also consider what else you need to skill up in. Pen testing is a true specialism rather than a generalist role, so professionals looking to move up the rungs of that particular career ladder can aspire to get CREST registered. CREST is the Council of Registered Ethical Security Testers, originally a UK organization but now operating globally, CREST provides a benchmark of certifications for the security testing industry and gives assurance to companies that the pen testers they hire know how to do the job properly. This is extremely important in this kind of role, since companies invest significant money in a pen test and, as such, expect the assurance that the pen testers know what they are doing.

CREST provides a syllabus that security training companies have used to develop hands-on courses in security testing. Furthermore, CREST also offers an examination service that allows testers to prove they have what it takes to do the job. A tester is added to the CREST registered list after 6,000 hours of experience (or three years) and become CREST certified after five years. This means that pen testers know their career paths and the way that their careers should pan out in the coming years.

Aspiring security architects can take CREST's CRTSA exam and become CREST registered after 6,000 hours of work experience in an architecture-related security role. Alternatively, they can take specialist architectural development training in areas such as industrial control systems security or national security and defense network security.

■ **Note** You can find more details about CREST here: http://www.crest-approved.org/. If you are based in Australia, CREST has a subsidiary organization that focuses primarily on the APAC region. More details on CREST Australia can be found at http://www.crestaustralia.org/.

The point of this discussion is that the world of infosec is changing every year, but the basics of global professionalism are beginning to stabilize. There is no better time to plan a career in security, ensuring you start with the right mix of work experience, certificates, and training and make sure that you strive to get as much experience across all the core competencies as you can.

What about the academic path? You might consider that if you jump into a university course and emerge at the other end of four years of study, you'll get a job as a security professional. In some cases this may help you, but it can be complicated. You will certainly gain the core body of knowledge you need to become a security professional while at university, however, the introduction, globally, of infosec courses into our further education portfolios has been even slower than the rationalization and proliferation of certificates in the professional training market. Universities were somewhat late to the party; however, nowadays, the majority of top tier establishments have one or more infosec courses in the portfolio. Most also have master's level and doctorate-level degrees that can be achieved. There are, however, two major drawbacks for anyone wanting to be an infosec professional:

- Unless you choose your course wisely, you will likely not emerge from university with professional experience, which is what most employers are looking for.

- Very few job adverts require further education, especially as a prerequisite for employment, so you may have wasted four years or more of career progression where you could have been exploring your passion for the subject matter in a practical way, while also getting paid.

So, the question is, is there really any value in going to university to study infosec at all? The simple answer is yes, but in reality it depends on your personal situation. I would recommend that anyone with the opportunity should take it since university will teach you to focus on the details of an investigation without the pressure of it being real. It also forces you (if you want to do well, that is) to adopt a disciplined approach to problem solving and research and develop a great approach to communication, both in the form of public speaking and written submissions to be reviewed.

■ **Tip** More and more universities are rolling out Work Integrated Learning programs, which can include partnerships with industry. These allow students to take a placement with a potential employer for a semester or a year with a potential employer, working in their chosen field of study/interest. If you have a choice, these will also provide more benefit that a flat study-only course.

These are many important aspects of being a security professional that should not be overlooked. I would personally hire an infosec degree student tomorrow as a junior in my team, understanding that I can get her to a professional level quickly, as long as she demonstrates the innate qualities of curiosity and tenacity that all security professional require. This could be a better option than someone who's had four years working in firewall management team who's not been exposed to risk management, business continuity planning or security architecture. Although the firewall guys are good techies, they usually don't have a grasp of (or even care about) these fundamental aspects of information security. Universities are now training students in all of these disciplines, so when they leave college, they are ready to put what they've learned into practice.

As the manager of the team, it's your job to make sure that your graduate staff gets all the experience that they need over the subsequent months and years to try all the areas they have learned about during their studies so they can determine where their passion lies, making sure they don't stagnate in a single role that stops their development as a professional. Managed properly, with regular training and mentoring, university graduates can become highly regarded and valuable infosec consultants within a short timeframe.

GETTING STARTED IN PEN TESTING

Should you aspire to be a top pen tester, like any other profession you'll need to start at the bottom and work your way up. This is exactly what apprenticeships of old would allow you to do, where carpenters and plumbers would hire a junior and mentor them in the trade until they were ready to go it on their own. This might have involved day-release to college but focused more on the work experience than the college course, but both are important to get the license to operate at the end of the apprenticeship.

Getting hired as an apprentice pen tester might involve you demonstrating that you have the right mindset to break into systems, rather than just having the willingness or interest in the subject matter.

A colleague once told me that he'd much rather hire an inquisitive novice with no coding or testing skills than someone who's experienced in coding, because the bad practices learned through years of enterprise coding are hard to undo. If the apprentice is genuinely inquisitive and loves to tinker with home-automation projects at the weekend, for example, they are more likely to have the right mindset for developing great pen testing tools of their own.

Trainee pen testers usually start with a narrow scope of work based on having specialist knowledge in one area of IT systems engineering, such as Oracle databases or using PowerShell scripting on

Microsoft Windows. The focus is on making these systems do things they are not designed to do, using a variety of tools and techniques to gain access. What's interesting is that this is exactly the same approach used by organized crime syndicates to recruit new members of their own highly paid and competent cybercrime units. Online forums assist them in their talent spotting efforts, with potential employees being targeted by the criminal recruitments teams to write malware for large sums of money. Ethics, as you might have guessed, are a matter of perspective, with one person's black hat being another person's hero. The underlying skills are almost always the same.

Having a technical background will pay dividends if you want to get started in information security, however, it's not essential for all job roles. Some job roles require a great deal of technical knowledge, right up to the expert level, however, to become a business risk consultant does not require you to have a detailed knowledge of networks and routers, instead you need to be attuned to the needs of the business and cognizant of the threats, vulnerabilities and consequences they are subject to. You can rely on technical teams to advise you as long as you know how to conduct the interviews and workshop the outcomes.

Careers and job roles have been discussed and debated within the industry for many years and are only now beginning to gain some traction as they become better understood. However, there is a need for industry bodies to make skills and job titles as ubiquitous and transferrable as possible so that industry and organizations understand them and national lock-in doesn't occur.

■ **Caution**   National or company lock-in refers to job roles that are specific to a single country, where the skills, competencies, and job role titles don't translate to an international equivalent. For example, most countries and businesses now understand what a security architect's role would be in the enterprise architecture team. However, if you're company decides not to recognize the role of security architect, insisting you are a technical architect, you may struggle in replying to a job advertisement that is looking for a security architect, simply because the role does not equate. Security architects should have skills more akin to a solutions architect or enterprise architect, so your company may be underrepresenting your ability to the market.

Using a skills framework, such as SFIA, means skills and competencies are well understood wherever they are accepted so, in effect, a job description and role in the United States that is defined using SFIA skills and competencies translates to exactly the same job role in the United Kingdom, Canada, Europe, or Australia.

Adoption of a global information security skills framework would be a panacea, however, as long as some nations are heading in that direction there is hope that one day it might happen. There will always be companies and countries that have a *not invented here* attitude, where they reject this simply because they didn't come up with it themselves. This kind of arrogance only serves to damage the global industry and makes it difficult for the rest of the security workforce to move around as freely and readily as it needed, so it's vitally important that, as individuals, we all strive to standardize our profession where possible.

Getting Started in Security Management

In an essay he wrote back in 1997, security pundit and cryptoexpert Bruce Schneier stated:

> *Present-day computer security is a house of cards; it may stand for now, but it can't last. Many insecure products have not yet been broken because they are still in their infancy. But when these products are widely used, they will become tempting targets for criminals. The press will publicize the attacks, undermining public confidence in these systems. Ultimately, products will win or lose in the marketplace depending on the strength of their security.*

Twenty years on and little has changed: security is just as difficult as it ever was, with the information security manager being the guy in the organization who keeps information and systems secure, while suffering the consequences when the business is hacked.

The job is actually very hard and isn't something that can be done alone—this is exactly why you need to understand all the detail we discussed earlier in this chapter, since hiring the right team is critical to your overall success. The recruitment process your organization uses needs to be tailored to hire security guys that have all the necessary skills, competencies, and industry experience to fulfill all the needs of your organization.

The Information Security Manager's Responsibilities

Your primary role is to identify, manage, and mitigate security risks on behalf of the business. This requires a special kind of person who has a solid understanding of risk management, impeccable communication skills, and the patience to explain complicated security concepts to a non-technical audience.

■ **Tip**   A risk, audit, or compliance manager is potentially responsible for managing risks, depending on the size and maturity of the organization, with business leadership (C-suite executives) dictating whether or not they are willing to accept the risk, and mitigate or manage risks.

Having a technical background will give you a head start in your role as information security manager role; however, it's not essential as long as you are willing to step up and learn about technical security. You will not be trying to become a technical expert, you have a team for that, but you should strive to at least understand enough of what your team is telling you to translate it into business speak while still offering them guidance and focus on how to do their jobs. Your job is a governance and management role, albeit with a significant slant on cybersecurity matters.

If you don't have the luxury of a large team (usually reserved for enterprises, banks, and government departments), then your role becomes significantly harder as you need to deliver against a wide variety of outcomes. A typical list of responsibilities attributed to the information security manager role might be as follows:

- Advising corporate leaders

- Monitoring and assessing security risks to the business

- Coordinating security matters across the enterprise

- Ensuring the business can recover from a security incident

- Authoring and publishing security policies
- Monitoring and reporting on efficacy of security measures
- Creation of a security culture that will use security to the benefit of the business
- Representing the business to the external security community

The information security manager needs the authority to undertake each these activities on behalf of the business and needs to have blockers cleared to ensure that the work can proceed unhindered.

Information is a significant component of most organizations' competitive strategy either by the direct collection, management, and interpretation of business information or the retention of information for day-to-day business processing. Some of the more obvious results of IS failures include reputational damage, placing the organization at a competitive disadvantage, and contractual noncompliance. These impacts should not be underestimated.

—Institute of Internal Auditors

You need to find the right balance between security, functionality, and cost, ensuring the business gets the best value from its investment in technology, processes, and your security team. Too much security leads you to losing support and this will hamper success. Too little security leaves the business exposed and, should you get hacked, data will be lost and you will take the heat.

You need to be cognizant of the needs of the business, knowledgeable enough to take the most pragmatic steps to securing what is most important for business operations and continuity, and to target an often limited set of resources at those areas that will deliver the best value and returns to the organization. You need to enable the business to perform and compete in today's marketplace, without impeding its progress through unnecessary or onerous controls and governance.

If a breach happens, you need to have the gumption to put yourself in the middle of the chaos and coordinate the incident through to conclusion. You'll work closely with all the relevant stakeholders, including the human resources department, executive management, technical teams, and public relations to determine culpability and the response. In some cases, if a breach is serious enough, maybe involving coercion, espionage (industrial or governmental), or criminal activities, you'll be calling in law enforcement and working closely with those investigation teams.

■ **Tip** It's a good idea for a security manager to build that network of contacts within local law enforcement and national computer emergency response teams, so if the worst happens, the process is understood and the right people can be made aware quickly. Time is often the most crucial determining factor in successful recovery from an incident.

You might ask how the information security manager knows how to do his/her job? Surely there must be a template to follow or some kind of standard? Well, there is. Most organizations will build a process framework, known as an information security management system (ISMS) that integrates corporate policy with legislation and compliance requirements, linking in external processes (such as risk management), procedures (how to do something) and records (items audited to demonstrate compliance).

The Information Security Management System

The ISMS specifies the requirements your business has for establishing, implementing, operating, monitoring, reviewing, maintaining, and improving information security. It provides you with a comprehensive approach to information security management, focusing on the management of risk. The principle underpinning the introduction of an ISMS is that an organization should design, implement, and maintain a consistent set of policies, processes, procedures, and systems, to manage information risks.

The most well-known framework for establishing an ISMS is based on international standard ISO/IEC 27001:2013 (as revised and updated in 2013).

ISO/IEC 27001 specifies a formal security management system intended to bring information security under management control as a process within your organization. This process should integrate with all of your other business processes, such as change management, asset management, organizational risk management, logistics, and supplier management, and so forth. Since ISO/IEC 27001 is a formal specification, it mandates specific requirements that are mandatory in order to become certified. However, many organizations will adopt the standard without trying to get certified, which is a perfectly good approach to improving security, as long as the lack of having a certification goal does not lead to avoiding doing some of the harder things the standard demands.

To help with the operationalizing of the ISO/IEC 27001 standard, another companion guideline document was released, known as ISO/IEC 27002:2013. This provides recommendations on implementing best practice for information security management for anyone responsible for initiating, implementing, and maintaining an ISMS, including the specification of security objectives and controls, and recommendations on how they could be implemented.

As I already said, you can get your company (or a single business function) certified against the ISO/IEC 27001 standard by an external accredited auditing body, but you don't have to get value from the standard. Finally, it's worth noting that ISO/IEC 27001 has been adopted by a number of governments around the world as the framework for delivering their own security requirements.

The rest of this book is dedicated to the implementation of the security controls that are inherently required for a standards-based ISMS. We don't specifically call out the cross references throughout the book, as it's aimed at anyone that needs to improve security, however, the structure of the book and the ensuing chapters align well with ISO 27001 as a governance framework.

CHAPTER 4

■ ■ ■

Organizational Security

This chapter examines the responsibilities given to the information security manager's role within an organization, taking a detailed look at what makes a security function effective, how organizational structures affect the success of the overall security program, as well as how certain aspects of security are aligned to business operations, while others are aligned to development, compliance and governance.

Security in Organizational Structures

We all know that the big boss is usually the chief executive officer (CEO) or the managing director. In businesses of significant size, the CEO typically reports to a board of directors, who are responsible for providing strategic direction to the business and ensuring that the CEO stays on-target and protects their investment.

Beneath the CEO, there are usually C-level executives who are appointed as custodians of business functions, such as finance, information technology, strategy, operations, sales, and marketing. In each case, these executive appointments come with titles, such as chief financial officer (CFO), chief information officer (CIO) and chief operating officer (COO).

Every member of the executive team has a subset of responsibilities discharged to them by the CEO, such as the CIO being responsible for the business's information and technology strategy, while the COO is responsible for day-to-day running of business operations.

The information security manager must work closely with whomever is responsible for business risk and become their ally. In many cases, the CEO will delegate information risk to the CIO, so the information security manager reports directly into that part of the organization.

In some organizations, where the level of security understanding is high and the executives understand the need for seniority in the security role to help with the execution of strategic security programs, the information security manager's job is elevated to a board-level position, acquiring titles such as chief information security officer (CISO) or chief security officer (CSO). The reality of today's business environment is that as security becomes increasingly more important in the boardroom, the most senior role moves up in the organizational hierarchy, making it more accountable and more effective.

Where Does Security Fit?

We looked at the role of the information security manager in the last chapter, highlighting how important it is to focus on the management of information risk on behalf of the business, especially with regard to critical business information and operational systems. Now we'll have a look at where that function sits in the organization.

Just to recap, being an information security manager requires you to have a solid understanding of information risk management, great communication skills and the patience to explain complicated and

© Tony Campbell 2016

T. Campbell, *Practical Information Security Management*, DOI 10.1007/978-1-4842-1685-9_4

abstract concepts to non-technical executives and board members. You'll have delegated authority from the CEO, possibly via another executive, such as the CIO, to undertake your security program on behalf of the business ensure that their tactical and strategic objectives are not hampered by security threats. You'll need the wherewithal to implement the most appropriate mix of physical, procedural and technical security controls available, making sure you don't focus too much on technology, especially if a simple process will suffice, such as hiring a security guard for $100,000 a year rather than a special, bespoke access control system that costs $500,000 per year.

In terms of fitting the security management function into your organization, it's best to focus on the creation of virtual teams that span the entire business to provide comprehensive support to the entire organization.

This allows senior management to delegate security responsibilities to team leaders, administrative staff, HR teams and facilities management groups, without requiring them to be part of the information security manager's immediate team. In Figure 4-1, you'll see that the information security manager sits at the top of the organization, reporting directly to the CEO, however, there are dotted lines into security guards, enterprise security architects, and even the induction training manager.

For example, the information security manager can discharge the responsibility for security induction and security awareness training to the education and learning department within the business, providing nothing more than an assurance function across the content and examinations. While each of staff members is controlled within the context of their own teams, they all have corporate responsibilities derived from the overarching information security policy.

What's most appealing about this matrix management approach, shown in Figure 4-1, is that you retain the experts in the fields they are in, while injecting security responsibilities into the heart of these functions, thus encouraging a cultural shift toward a more secure business.

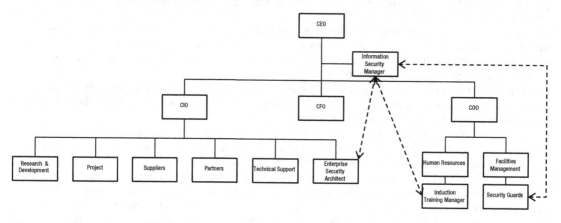

Figure 4-1. *Organizational hierarchies can contain a variety of security functions*

Intelligence subsequently flows back into the security team from these other business functions, allowing the information security manager to determine where policy, procedures, or controls may or may not be working. This bidirectional flow of information ensures that any revisions to policies or controls are based on evidence from the business.

This is an effective way to manage security throughout your entire business, especially if you work in an international organization with offices split across a wide geographical area. Regional security managers can report to the information security manager's corporate office, thus allowing regional information security managers an element of autonomy to manage local security matters in their own jurisdiction. This is a powerful way to delegate authority in an organization while still ensuring compliance at all levels, in all offices, wherever the locale.

To make sure that the delegation of security responsibilities is effective, you need to make sure that the requirements of the job are clearly communicated and all expectations are unambiguously set in their job description and job induction. This is achieved by documenting each responsibility in the role's *terms of reference*, describing each of the roles, responsibilities and reporting requirements of the job. These terms of reference become a contingent part of that person's overall job description and their employment contract should reference it so that it's official from everyone's perspective, including HR.

Where security responsibilities are a subset of a person's overall job function, these should be built into the line-manager's appraisal so that they are rewarded for performing their security duties well and understand what can happen if they don't manage risk on behalf of the business—that is, they may get breached, which can go on their permanent record.

Terms of reference should contain full, unambiguous job descriptions, fully defined scopes of work, explaining which processes, procedures, and work instructions must be followed by that member of staff to discharge their security responsibilities. This should also explain how they should deal with security breaches and what their responsibilities are should a security incident occur.

Aspects of confidentiality, integrity, and availability should be discussed in detail and reporting chains should be well-defined. Joining and leaving instructions should also be fully documented so that the process for new starters joining the organization just as clear as the process for staff leaving the organization.

It is difficult, especially in such a complicated world as information security, to be an expert in every aspect of the job and this is why you will more than likely employ a range of talent in your team to cover the technical security, physical security, and risk-related aspects of the job.

Nevertheless, it's difficult to ensure that you have all the coverage and expertise you need in your team, simply because you can't afford to have a team of thirty security guys as a core overhead in the organization as it will cost too much. If you use a team structure something like that shown in Figure 4-2 it will comprise most of the key functions that the information security manager needs to consider in day to day activities: security operations, architecture, risk management, and security testing.

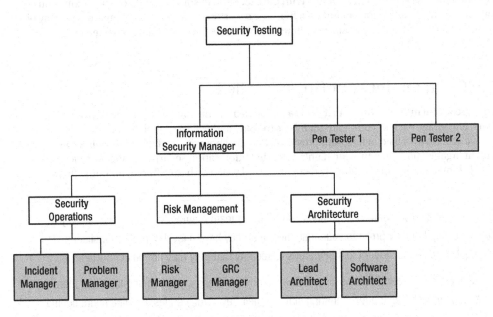

Figure 4-2. *Functional structure for the security team*

The core function of the security operations team is to manage the security of devices within the environment, as well as to monitor the external threat environment and react to early warnings of new threats to prepare the business to deal with these if they were to target the business. They will also react to system and security alarms and get involved in managing security incidents as they arise. Problem managers (a throwback to service management frameworks, such as ITIL) resolve ongoing issues that recur within the environment. Furthermore, you'll possibly see a team of analysts employed in the security operations team that watch consoles and ensure that all of the critical assurance systems used by the business are running and free of alarms.

The risk management team will conduct both technical and business-level risk assessments, run threat modeling workshops with architects and subject matter experts, and present a risk management plan back to the information security manager with recommendations of which risks can be mitigated, monitored, or insured against. This team will also liaise with external organizations, such as auditors and regulators to ensure smooth running of the business's compliance requirements.

The security architecture team works closely with the businesses change program and other project design teams to ensure that the business's overarching security objectives (translated into security requirements from security controls—remember the ISO/IEC 27002 control set) are met as technology and processes change. You will find that the team often contains security architecture specialists, such as software architects, infrastructure architects and even database security architects, as these are all extremely specialized and complicated areas of design and assurance.

Finally, the security testing team may be a component team within a larger testing organization, or dedicated as a smaller, more targeted team to the information security manager. This team will write test plans for the security architecture group, when new systems are transitioning into production, to ensure that the new systems or changes remain compliant with the overall business's security requirement set. When this testing team is not scoping test plans for projects, they may have the remit of conducting ad-hoc vulnerability tests on infrastructure, software, and websites, and if they have the required skills, they may also perform penetration testing of your systems. With the exception of some military organizations and multinationals, not many organizations maintain a full-time security penetration testing team, so it may be that this unit, in collaboration with the security architects, scopes the pen tests for external teams to come in and undertake the work.

License to Operate: Get Your Guys Certified

To build a truly successful information security management team, one that engenders trust from all of your customers, encourage each of your team members to study and get accredited in security related certifications. We've already talked at length in previous chapters about some of the most well-known and independent organizations that provide highly-regarded information security certifications for professionals. Most of these are internationally recognized and well worth the effort in attaining them.

■ **Note**   As we've already discussed, certifications don't prove a team member is experienced enough to do the job they are doing, but they prove to your customers that they have a level of professionalism and dedication to the job, forcing the student to study areas of security that they may not be comfortable in.

If you treat the requirement for certifications as you would a driver's license, you'll understand that there is nothing better than on the job training for preparing staff for their day-to-day duties, just like hours behind the wheel, just like the driving test, gaining a security certification proves that the team member should be prepared to make decisions on behalf of the business and understand the context of threats, vulnerabilities and risks as they are presented.

The International Information Systems Security Certification Consortium (also known as (ISC)²—pronounced "ISC squared") provides a series of information security qualifications recognized and well-regarded the world over. The most well-known of these is the Certified Information Systems Security Professional, or CISSP, which (ISC)² reports has over 75,000 certified members.

The International Council of E-Commerce Consultants (a.k.a. EC-Council) provides both foundation level and professional-level qualifications for penetration testers. If you have team members that want to get into the technical side of security testing, getting the Certified Ethical Hacker (CEH) qualification then going on to take the Licensed Penetration Tester (LPT) examination can add credibility to their resume. However, the most relevant penetration testing certifications, recognized globally, are those awarded by CREST and the OSCP or OSCE (Offensive Security Certified Professional and Expert). The OSCP, for example, relies on a 24-hour long practical exam, followed immediately by a further 24 hours to write up a high-quality report, proving that a tester who has passed this certification is both technically competent and capable of presenting findings back to a business audience.

Finally, since universities are now offering both undergraduate degrees and master's degrees in information security and specific subdisciplines, such as, computer forensics, it doesn't hurt to encourage your team, if it's what they want to do, to go back to school. Royal Holloway, for example, in the United Kingdom, pioneered an information security master's degree that incorporated a deep dive into cryptography, which led to them turning out a number of highly skilled infosec guys who were snapped up by the UK government. In the United States, the University of Washington also offers a variety of undergraduate and graduate courses and has also provided a number of modules of their courses as MOOCs via Coursera.

■ **Note**   MOOC is the acronym for Massive Open Online Course. MOOCs have become extremely popular with universities all around the world, with many now offering information security related courses that you can either audit (take for free) or pay a nominal fee to get a certificate. The two most popular of the MOOC providers are Coursera and Edx (https://www.coursera.org and https://www.edx.org).

These are just two examples of universities providing further education academic program in information security. Setting a degree course as a goal for team members is an excellent way to keep them fully engaged, recognizing that these kind of goals encourage continual professional development, not necessarily on the job training, but with the right management and mentoring, each one of your staff members can evolve into a highly successful security professional once their apprenticeship period is over.

Encourage a Culture of Security Awareness

What's different about information security in the business as opposed to other aspects of your organization's operation is that security becomes the responsibility of every single person. From the very top of your business, down to the very bottom, every single person has access to information that could be misused or abused if it got into the wrong hands.

Board members may well support what the information security management team is trying to accomplish, but sometimes can get ahead of themselves when it comes to getting the job done or their strategy executed. Top-level executives are often the first people to cut corners to get a result, simply because they believe they should be able to do so. Often it can be this attitude that leads to a gargantuan security breach and unfortunately it will be the information security team that takes the rap.

At the bottom end of the business, cleaners, facilities staff, and mailroom workers actually have more access to rooms and information than many of the mid- and senior-level staff; therefore, they need to be aware of the risk and attacks that could be mounted on them or their colleagues. Using social engineering techniques, an attacker will most likely pick on a target they believe vulnerable to suggestion, which oftentimes will be found in the lower paid ranks of the organization.

For this reason, you should always be seeking to encourage a culture of security throughout your entire business to ensure that all members of staff have security in their mind at all times. When they see something that looks or feels wrong or they encounter some behavior that is out of the ordinary or suspicious, instead of following the natural human trait of ignoring it, they should be encouraged, even rewarded, for questioning and reporting it. At all levels, the workforce needs to be reminded that it's OK to say no or ask a supervisor rather than risk a security breach.

The fastest and most effective way to change staff behaviors is to educate them through formal security awareness training. This will have to reach every single member of the organization, explaining to them how they should behave and deal with circumstances that could potentially cause a breach. Often, security awareness programs are designed and tailored for individual businesses rather than being off-the-shelf courses and in my experience this is the best way to run them. Since every business is different and the threats that staff are facing are also different, tailoring security awareness courses is actively encouraged and should be one of the key deliverables of the information security manager's team. Coupling this with some real-world testing and fire drills (where you set up an internal phishing campaign to really and properly test the workforce's response to an attack) is by far the most effective way of promoting and developing a security-aware culture.

I would suggest commissioning a specialist company that understands instructional design, since the initial investment will pay back dividends in the long run. The size and shape of the content of your security awareness training course will depend on the nature of your business and the kind of data you handle, as well as the market you operate in. For example, if you are a military contractor, you will have a significantly different risk profile than if you are protecting the secret recipe for a world-famous fizzy drink.

The most important factors when designing a security awareness program are ensuring that every member of staff knows what is expected of them and you can measure the success of the delivery of the course to management.

Security awareness training should not preach to staff about how they should do their job, instead it should teach them about the threats and risks they all face when then use technology. It should explain how viruses and malware operate and how attackers target their victims, explaining the dangers of removable media and surfing the web and what they should do to protect themselves when having to make use of these risky technologies. In context of your organization, breach and risk reporting lines should be well documented and explained in the course so that staff know what to do and when to do it.

If you decide to adopt a security awareness program, make sure that you build in metrics to test its efficacy by including an exam at the end that each member of staff is expected to pass. You can also consider reinforcing the messages of the security awareness training through the use of live drills and exercises where you use live pen tests to attempt to test the efficacy of your security awareness course and your security operation's team's ability to response and manage the incident.

■ **Caution** If you use pen tests to test your team's ability to detect and respond to incidents, try not to penalize them when a breach is discovered. This can be a real demotivator for your team, so instead use it as a learning experience, asking yourself why did this happen and what can you do to remediate it and stop it from happening again?

The question is also often asked as to how often you should recertify your staff in security awareness. It's very easy for people to forget what they learned during a course, especially if it completed more than six months ago, and there have been no security incidents to remind them of the response plan and their obligations. The majority of businesses that run mandatory security awareness programs recertify staff annually, meaning staff must take (and pass) the exam at least once a year, however, this is very much dependent on the company risk profile and on any external factors or influences that have impacted it over recent years. For example, political unrest in the country the company operates in or an environmental disaster caused by the company would require a level of security awareness throughout the workforce that other companies may see as unnecessary.

Finally, one reason that security awareness has become so important in today's information security landscape is that it has actually become one of the main controls an auditor looks for when assessing an organization's security maturity. It's a key control that you need to demonstrate compliance with, for example, to get certified as ISO/IEC 27001 compliant. Furthermore, training your staff in how to handle security incidents and protect themselves also protects the business from legal issues. Take, for example, an employee that copies data onto a memory stick and loses that device. If they have taken the security awareness course and passed the test, then there is no excuse for having done this—they have broken the rules. On the other hand, if they have never been told that they should not do this and never signed up to the policies they are bound by, a court might rule in their favor as the business is remiss for not instructing the employee on what is and is not allowed.

Security awareness programs save money and that should be all the information you need (for the business case) to pitch it to your CEO.

NIST SECURITY AWARENESS

NIST's Computer Security Division publishes Special Publication 800-50 *Building an Information Technology Security Awareness and Training Program* to help US government agencies and corporates integrate security awareness programs into their organizational ecosystems. This document is one of the best all-round explanations of how a security awareness program should be built, focusing on continually reinforcing the messages of the program throughout the entire career of staff.

The document lists four steps that are deemed critical to the success of awareness programs:

1. Design. Conduct a full assessment of the organization and develop a training strategy that is sent to the executive for approval.

2. Develop training and awareness material. Using a blend of existing and new material that is appropriate and in-context, create all the content required for the entire program. It's advisable to call in an expert contractor to help, since this is a specialized area of development.

3. Implement. Roll out the training and awareness material to the workforce, ensuring it's accompanied by a comprehensive communications plan that explains its purpose to all concerned.

4. Post implementation. Keep the content current and take feedback and continually hone and improve the delivery to ensure that staff remains engaged and the program remains fresh and relevant.

For more information on how to create your own security awareness program, you can consult NIST Special Publication 800-50 from the following link:

http://csrc.nist.gov/publications/nistpubs/800-50/NIST-SP800-50.pdf

Working with Specialist Groups

It's critical to your success to get involved in specialist groups that monitor and inform their members of what's important and what's changing in the world of information security. International organizations such as the Information Systems Security Association (ISSA) and the Information Systems Audit and Control Association (ISACA) are worth getting involved in, since they run regular education sessions and webinars relating to modern or emerging security issues affecting today's businesses.

In the United Kingdom, The British Computer Society (BCS) offers members a specialist group dedicated to information security, called the ISSG. The ISSG send alerts to members detailing new security issues, threats, and new technologies from vendors that are worth knowing about. There are many such bodies around the world, and it's well worth subscribing your information security team to these sorts of alerts, as well as other sources of such intelligence

The information security team should pass on specialist advice and guidance to anyone in the organization that needs to know about it. For example, if you receive an alert from Microsoft on a new critical security flaw in SQL server, you need to pass that on to the database team to assess prior to working up a mitigation strategy.

Every member of your information security team should aspire to keep up-to-date on industry trends, changes to organizational threats, new control measures, new methodologies for analysis of risk, changing legislative or compliance requirements, and the latest developments in technology. This should be actively encouraged by you, as the information security manager. This does not, however, mean that every team member should become an expert in every aspect of information security; that is impractical. Instead, each team member should have the necessary training and skills to be find the answers out and proffer the best advice back to the requestor so they can mitigate their concern or risk.

For example, if your security engineering team has recently attended a briefing on *cloud computing security*, they should brief the technical architects in your organization since they are the guys designing your cloud-based as-a-service offerings.

Encourage this kind of contact with special interest groups by building the requirements into each of their employment terms of reference, as well as individual development plans where they have time allocated for a certain amount of "self-education" time. If you are worried that this time will not be put to good use, monitor how successful it has been based on the number of courses, seminars, or trade shows they attend and set targets as key performance indicators for the whole team that you have to meet. Encourage them to provide feedback on every session they attend, in terms of cascading information to the business and running briefings, seminar, or brown bag sessions for peers.

Working with Standards and Regulations

Mandatory security requirements are often imposed upon your organization by external legislative bodies, where a legal requirement to adhere to some statute exists. These are known as *statutory requirements*, which flow down from the government, law enforcement, or legal system that you are bound by. Statutory requirements are typically jurisdictional and compliance often influences how your business organizes its security and incident response function. This is because incident response, and particularly reporting criminal matters to law enforcement, is tied to your country's own legislative requirements. For example, if someone undertakes an illegal action using your organization's IT systems, such as downloading pirated movies or illegal pornography, law enforcement must be notified.

You may be required to offer technical support to a forensic investigation into criminal activities on your systems as part of your statutory obligation to support law-enforcement in investigations. Privacy legislation may force you to notify a government agency and your customers if a data breach occurs, so again, this is a legal requirement that you need to be aware of and ensure that your systems are compliant, but also making sure that your staff are compliant.

Regulatory requirements are imposed upon your business by external organizations. However, unlike statutory requirements, regulatory requirements are imposed by trade bodies rather than legislative bodies, setting standards of how your business must operate in the sector you do business in. As the information security manager, you will need to be aware of the regulatory environment your business is operating in, ensuring you are compliant so that you can continue to trade in that way.

The global finance industry has extremely strict controls that are imposed on banks and finance organizations to help reduce international fraud and money laundering. In each country, there will be a local ombudsman looking after regulatory requirements, often calling out for organizations to meet specific security standards that allow them to trade. For example, any organization directly handling credit card information must maintain an active PCI-DSS (Payment Card Industry Data Security Standard) compliance certificate.

■ **Note** If you work in a business or industry that processes credit card payments and deals with storage of cardholder data, you will undoubtedly be required to adhere to the PCI-DSS. The PCI Security Standards Council is the global organization that maintains, evolves, and promotes this standard. More information about the standard and associated implementation guidelines is at https://www.pcisecuritystandards.org/pci_security/.

Advisory requirements exist, as the term suggests, to provide advice. They often arise from government agencies or utility companies advising businesses of what to do in the event of an emergency, such as natural disasters, fires, industrial accidents, or acts of terrorism. Advisory requirements are not mandated, instead existing to help organizations plan what to do in a crisis.

Most technology vendors issue *good-practice guides* for their customers that explain how you should configure their software or hardware to make it as secure as possible. These should be evaluated by your security team to determine if they are fit-for-purpose for the context of your business. Most governments have their own cybersecurity advisory units, publishing good advice that can be useful not only for government agencies, but also for commercial organizations. The following organizations publish cybersecurity advisories in each of their respective countries:

- **The National Institute of Standards and Technology (NIST):** This is a US government agency that publishes myriad standards and guidelines related to cybersecurity matters, many of which are referenced by other nations all over the world. In response to Presidential Executive Order (EO) 13636, NIST also created its own cybersecurity framework (akin to ISO/IEC 27001) that can help government agencies and businesses reduce cyber risks to critical infrastructure. NIST's cybersecurity framework can be found here: http://www.nist.gov/cyberframework/index.cfm

- **CESG:** Previously known as the Communications Electronic Security Group, this UK government branch of GCHQ is the United Kingdom's national technical authority for all aspects of cybersecurity. CESG provides a variety of advice and guidelines, good practice guides and executive briefing papers to UK government and industry, as well as providing a variety of product testing and assurance activities. CESG also runs the Certified CESG Practitioner scheme, previously known as the CESG Listed Advisor (CLAS) scheme, which certifies security professionals as having the requisite knowledge to provide consultancy and advice to UK government departments. You can learn more about CESG here: https://www.cesg.gov.uk/

- **Australian Signals Directorate (ASD)**: ASD is the Australian Defense Force branch of government that manages all aspects of communication security. It is very similar to CESG in the United Kingdom and published a series of documents, known as the Information Security Manual (ISM), that provide a security control set similar in construction to ISO/IEC 27002. In fact, the ISM can be used instead of ISO/IEC 27002 to deliver Australian government standard security, while using ISO/IEC 27001 as the process framework. ASD also provide an Evaluated Products List (EPL) which contains a list of products that have been tested and assured by ASD labs as being fit for purpose for Australian government use. You can find out more about ASD here: http://www.asd.gov.au/

Working with Risk Management

Risk management sits at the heart of everything the information security team does. As such, the information security manager should encourage the business to embed information risk management into every process it uses to deliver its products and services.

Every member of staff should be encouraged (and educated) to raise threats, vulnerabilities, and risks with the information security team when they are discovered or observed. This should instigate an assessment process where the threat, vulnerability, or risk is taken through the formal Risk Management process to assess its potential impact to the business, decide on remediation and mitigation strategies, and implement changes as required. Threats, vulnerabilities, and risks are recorded in a central register, known as a *risk register*, which will eventually become the focal point and core tool used to drive the whole risk management process.

Risk management process is iterative, as shown in Figure 4-3, comprising of the four key stages of identify, analyze, threat, and monitor. This continual cycle of reviewing the threats, vulnerabilities and risks on the risk register (more on this later) process is a continual cycle because new risks can emerge which require analysis and treatment.

Figure 4-3. *Risk management life cycle*

The following four sections look at each of the stages of risk management in enough detail to understand their impact on the business. The information security manager should begin to bake this into the organization's standard operating processes.

■ **Note** Risk management is a massive subject area and there is much documented on the efficacy of each of the different methods of risk assessment we can take for evaluating issues. Very often, there are conflicting viewpoints that further work to dismiss the risk management approaches used by some security professionals, while extoling the virtues of others. The reality is that risk is at the heart of everything we do as security professionals, however, the problem is that it's still somewhat of a grey area and determining what's best for your organization always needs to be in context of business imperatives. I'd encourage any budding security professional to research as much as possible on risk management standards, processes and general approaches, and then read *The Failure of Risk Management: Why It's Broken and How to Fix It*, by Douglas W. Hubbard, (Wiley, 2009). This book explains that there are many ways to make risk management work for you and your organization but the key is to not kid yourself that it's working just because you've followed a standard or a process—you need it to fit your business.

Risk Identification

The first stage of risk management is risk identification. You'll need to collate all threats, vulnerabilities, and risks that may be affecting the business. This information will need to be passed to the next stage of the risk management process for analysis, so you'll need to record each item in a format that can be analyzed and cross-referenced. As mentioned earlier, this record of risks is called the *risk register*, which becomes the focal point for the majority of risk-related activities.

A lot of information security managers, especially in smaller organizations, use spreadsheets or custom databases to record risk-related information. If possible, associate threats and vulnerabilities as pairs of linked items for each risk record as this allows you to best assess the risk in its truest context.

People who are new to the concept of risk identification can sometimes struggle to find all of the threats and vulnerabilities the business may be facing. There are a variety of ways you can speed this process up and ensure that you are getting as much insight from the businesses possible as to where potential issues may lie. The following list is not exhaustive, but gives you a good place to start.

- **Risk notification mailbox:** You can set up an email address that is open to the entire business that allows anyone to raise a concern. You will find that having eyes and ears operating in every corner of the business is extremely helpful and this will yield results above and beyond anything you will do formally (and it costs a lot less).

- **Threat workshops:** By facilitating workshops with teams within your organization you are actually engaging the subject matter experts who will best understand how they would exploit the systems they are responsible for. Asking a UNIX engineer how he would hack into the systems he administers (as long as he's a competent and accomplished sys admin) will yield amazing results that can help you determine where the risks lie. In the same manner, asking the facilities management team what the vulnerabilities in the building's alarm or CCTV system might be will help you see where your facility might be at risk from intruders.

- **Business impact analysis (BIA):** You can use a formal process known as *business impact analysis* to identify the impact of losing an information artifact based on certain threats. You might identify high-level threats, such as the lack of availability of a critical database, which provides a good place to start working through the risk assessment process. It's advisable to conduct a BIA in consultation with other business stakeholders rather than solely from the information security perspective, since there may be operational threats and vulnerabilities that are more important that technical security issues you may have come up with from a cybersecurity point of view. Some security managers find questionnaires the best way to engage the business, allowing you to correlate your findings across multiple teams, locations, and business units. NIST Special Publication 800-34 provides a useful BIA template you can use to get started: `http://csrc.nist.gov/publications/nistpubs/800-34-rev1/sp800-34-rev1_bia_template.docx`.

- **ISO/IEC 27002:2013**: ISO/IEC 27002:2013 contains a long list of security controls coupled with implementation guidance that you can use to assess how well your systems and security controls are current organized. You could start by auditing your business against this list of controls and use your findings (where you discover an omission or oversight) as a feed into your list of vulnerabilities. In essence, like many of the audit processes you will undoubtedly undertake as a security professional, you are performing a gap analysis that you can use to build a remediation plan.

- **Penetration testing**: Pen tests are undoubtedly one of the most valuable and comprehensive sources of threats, vulnerabilities, and risks. If you don't have the internal resources to conduct your own pen testing, start with a vulnerability scan of your systems, and then consider outsourcing the pen testing work to an external, certified company. If you happen to be in the United Kingdom or Australia, you can look for companies that are CREST approved, or something approved by your local government's national technical authority (such as the NSA or NIST). Pen testing will not only discover vulnerabilities but will also see if they can be exploited.

Risk Analysis

The analysis stage comes next. This is where you take all of the threats and vulnerabilities captured during the initial phase of the risk management process and establish whether or not they pose a real risk to your business. In effect, you are establishing the *level of risk* these threats and vulnerabilities pose. During this stage, you need to establish the impact and likelihood of each threat and vulnerability pair previously identified.

We already discussed the need to perform a BIA in the previous stage; however, you now need to consider the likelihood of the threat and vulnerability leading to a successful breach. Unfortunately, this is not so straightforward, but there are two primary methods you can use to do this, known as *qualitative assessment* and *quantitative assessment*.

Qualitative Assessments

Qualitative assessments are largely subjective. This technique uses no real empirical data and in some cases it's criticized as being all about guesswork and no science. However, this is not the case. You need to use a formula that can be relied upon to give you enough information to properly assess the risk. This will depend entirely on your organization, where you may find there is a method already being used to establishing likelihood in other areas of risk assessment (such as by your safety team, or even in the finance department). You can develop a probability scales that may have ratings such as these:

- Negligible, rare, unlikely, possible, probable

- Rare, unlikely, possible, likely, almost certain

- Low, medium, high

As you can see from the last of these examples, it doesn't have to be complicated, as long as there is some kind of delineation between each of the levels and you understand what it means when you claim a threat has the likelihood of HIGH of leading to a successful compromise.

Quantitative Analysis

Quantitative analysis is the "scientific" method for assessment that relies on having enough empirical data to determine a statistical probability of a threat occurring. For example, the probability of a volcano erupting in Southern Italy might be 75% for business operating near the foothills of Mount Etna. The probability of a power outage might be 5% during peak loading times, based on statistics you have obtained from the power company that supplies your data center. This is real data and takes the guesswork out of your analysis. However, the rule when using these kinds of statistics is to still be extremely careful how you apply them. It's easy to manipulate the numbers to lie for you and you need to ensure that you are making decisions based on impartiality rather than your own desire to buy some technology or relocate to another office, for example.

In Figure 4-4 I've shown a threat matrix that consists of impact ratings and likelihood ratings ranging from low to high. This is a typical threat matrix that you might see used in the majority of organizations, especially where the approach to risk management is based on a *qualitative* methodology.

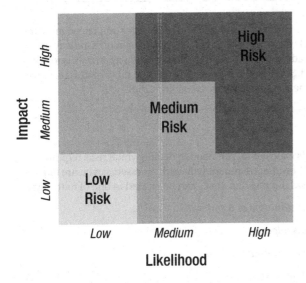

Figure 4-4. *Impact and Likelihood matrix*

From this kind of matrix, it's possible to estimate the risk attributed to any given threat and vulnerability combination. This is the information that the information security manager needs to get really good at presenting to the senior management board as it's this kind of presentation that will allow you to connect the esoteric world of information security to business imperatives and ask for money to rectify the problems.

■ **Note** For all intents and purposes, it is the attacker who determines the likelihood of something occurring, as well as the impact of that incident. The security manager can guesstimate the figures, but they are ultimately determined by a third-party and can be affected by a myriad of external factors.

This example is minimalist in the sense that it has an X and Y scale comprising just three graduations, however, some organizations use five or even ten divisions. You need to create the process that best suits your business—the more graduations you use, the harder it becomes to decide which one a particular threat goes in (is it a 4 or a 5?). Whatever you come up with (and you can always change it and improve it over time) you need to ensure that it's unambiguous in its description of each unit of scale.

In the example shown in Figure 4-4, locate the intersection of impact and likelihood (for any threat in your spreadsheet captures in the previous phase) to see what the risk level is. A few examples are shown in Table 4-1.

Table 4-1. *Sample Risk Ratings Based on Simple Impact Likelihood Matrix*

Threat	Vulnerability	Impact	Likelihood	Risk Rating
Malware	Unpatched System	Medium	Medium	Medium
Hackers	No webserver firewall	High	Medium	High
Journalist	HR document left in taxi	Medium	Low	Medium
Flood	Data center lost under water	High	Low	Medium

You can use as many levels as needed to define impact and likelihood and both scales don't need the same number of divisions. Some organizations have three levels of impact and six levels of likelihood. One way to help you, especially if you are in an industry that may already have standardized on a particular approach, is to see what international or national standards are adopted. Some business use ISO 31000 and ISO 27005 as these will work nicely with your information security management system if it's based on ISO 27001.

Risk Treatment

After establishing how much risk the organization is exposed to, you need to decide which risks require treatment—that is, how you will address them and how that treatment will work. In essence, you are looking at methods for lessening the probability of these risks manifesting. Risks can be treated in one of four ways:

- Avoid the risk, sometimes referred to as *eliminate* or *terminate*.

- Accept the risk, sometimes referred to as *tolerate*.

- Reduce the risk, sometimes referred to as *minimize* or *lessen*.

- Transfer the risk, also referred to as *risk sharing*.

Before we take a look at some specific examples of risk treatment plans, it's first important to classify the kinds of security controls you can use in treatment. These are all industry-accepted terms.

- *Physical controls* are real-world mitigations that reduce the risks to information. Examples of physical controls could be to introduce physical access control systems, such as secure cabinets and security guards, or physical intrusion detection systems, such as alarm systems and CCTV.

- *Procedural security controls* usually take the form of policies and procedures that define how staff behaves. Information security policy documentation and the subsequent processes, procedures, and work instructions used to enact the policies form the basis of your information security management system (ISMS). An example might be in the form of an HR process to conduct and employee clearance checks prior to hiring. Another example might be that your security guard walks around the perimeter of the building every hour to look for intruders or weaknesses in the perimeter than leave your business open to attack.

- *Technical security controls* are the traditional information security controls you'd expect to see in a corporate technology stack, such as firewalls, anti-malware products, SIEM (security information and event management) solutions, and vulnerability scanning systems.

Security controls usually provide risk reduction in one or more of four ways. The following are terms that you are likely to see used to describe a control's mode of assisting in risk reduction:

- *Preventative controls* directly protect the confidentiality, integrity, and availability of information by blocking the threat or removing the vulnerability. An example might be where a firewall blocks unauthorized ports or protocols from traversing your business's Internet connection.

- *Directive controls* are procedural controls. They tell your workforce what action needs to be taken to protect information, such as a procedure for locking the filing cabinet at the end of the working day.

- *Detective controls* detect and report unauthorized or undesired events. Detective security controls are often invoked after an undesirable event has occurred. An example might be the monitoring of audit logs or examining CCTV camera footage.

- *Corrective security controls* are used to respond to and fix security incidents. Corrective controls limit or reduce further damage from an attack. For example, antivirus products can be configured to quarantine and clean a system after it's been infected by a virus.

The choices made in risk treatment planning need to consider the cost of the planned mitigation, the business impact of installing or enacting the mitigation and the residual risk left over once the mitigation is in place. This relationship in terms of consideration items is shown in Figure 4-5.

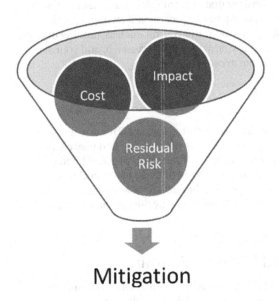

Figure 4-5. *Risk treatment assessment*

By way of example, a risk has been raised whereby the business is concerned that sensitive information on an open fileserver could be copied by a member of staff and passed on to a competitor, so reducing market share and losing IPR. As the security manager, you have been asked to look at ways to treat this risk through the risk management process instantiated in your team. The vulnerabilities are many: untrustworthy staff, open access to the file server, lack of control of information being copied off business systems, and so forth. In this case, when you run through the risk calculation, the impact is high, the likelihood is high, and so your risk is high. For this reason, you need to do something about it. However, when you look at the true impact of loss, it's deemed that the information, while important, would cost the business around $200,000 per year in lost revenues if it was no longer a secret. That's the true impact. The impact might still be considered high, according to our calculation (and the definition of high on your impact scale) but now you need to figure out what you can do to lower its rating to an acceptable level. You might consider throwing new technology at the system, such as a data loss prevention (DLP) system. This would cost $120,000 to install and you'd need a new guy in your security team to take on the load of running and configuring the new system.

However, is that the best solution? A DLP solution won't necessarily stop all forms of information egress, so when you re-look at the risk assessment, even after investing this money, the likelihood has dropped to medium, so the risk is still medium, and hence unacceptable to the business. Another option is to remove the data from the server's folder structure, install a new, high-security server, and change the access control system to prevent unauthorized access. This project costs $250,000 in capital costs of equipment, engineering and design work, as well as project management, testing, installation and data migration. This option is costlier than the value of the information, so is that the right answer for this business? Although lowers the risk, since it costs more than the value of the information and adversely affects the business, it's not tenable and should be rejected. It fully mitigates the risk, changing it to low, but it's too costly and its impact on the business is too disruptive. Finally, you decide to investigate the possibility of moving the files from that directory and adding them into a different, appropriately controlled directory only accessible by the directors. Changes costs $35,000 to go through planning and implementation, which is affordable, reducing the likelihood to low. This is acceptable by the business, and while a rudimentary example, it demonstrates the thought process you go through when assessing which mitigations make the most sense for the business.

The most important consideration when looking at risk treatment options is to be practical and realistic. Where a simple solution will reduce the risk significantly, consider that over complex and costlier option to see whether it's good enough. If not, look again. Maybe a combination of a process and technology will work best. Maybe you could look at a detective control rather than a preventative control, such as auditing that file store every day to see who's accessed it? The fact that you are looking at who has accessed it, and your staff knows you are doing so, may well be all that you need to prevent access.

Risk Monitoring

Lastly, once you have put your mitigations in place, you enter the risk monitoring stage. This is where you watch existing risks to make sure that they are not worsening. Your risks are not constant and may change under your feet as conditions outside of your control change. For example, the impact and likelihood of a risk can easily vary with time, such as your system's being infected by a virus. In terms of physical threats, if you work in a tropical location, then it may be that your risk is higher in the summer season when the threat of a tropical storm may be severe. At other times of the year, the risk is lessened by the very nature of the threat being lessened.

Business Continuity Management and Disaster Planning

The final aspect of managing risk at the organizational level that you need to consider when building your risk management capability is that of business continuity management and disaster planning.

These are both subjects that we'll cover in more detail later in this book, but for now, as part of your team's approach to risk management you need to make sure that you have interactions with the business unit that looks after business continuity planning and disaster resilience, since availability of information will undoubtedly be affected by issues identified through these two processes. Should the worst happen and your premises be flooded or drop into a sinkhole, you need to be in a position to recover to your continuity site in a way that still retains your information's confidentiality, integrity and availability. Information security is very closely linked with both of these processes and you'll find that in more mature businesses, these two processes are actually subprocesses of the information assurance function, covering security, policy, risk management, business continuity management, and disaster resilience, so information assurance is the high level function covering all aspects of security.

Working with Enterprise Architecture

Security architecture has become a core consideration within any business's enterprise architecture function and, quite honestly, if an enterprise architecture function does not include security architecture, it is categorically failing the business. In order to understand the role of security architecture within your organization, it is worthwhile starting with an explanation of what architecture really means. A general definition of architecture is that it typically represents how the components of a product, system, or service are organized and integrated together. An architect is the professional person who has the depth of knowledge and expertise to define how these products, systems and services are constructed, usually having deep understanding of legislation, guidelines and standards, as well as best practices related to integrating the components that architectures are constructed from (these components are the building blocks of systems that are usually best understood by subject matter experts).

Architects are found in the majority of industries, and while they may have different end results (bridges, IT systems, buildings and cruise ships, for example), the general approach to how they operate is primarily the same. Enterprise architecture has become a commonly found function in many enterprise businesses that CIOs and CTOs embed in their organizations to define systems, processes, and programs that interact to deliver business objectives, over both a tactical and strategic timeframe. Gartner's definition of enterprise architecture is as follows:

> *Enterprise architecture (EA) is the process of translating business vision and strategy into effective enterprise change by creating, communicating, and improving the key requirements, principles, and models that describe the enterprise's future state and enable its evolution.*

This definition shows that the scope of the enterprise architect's work includes the entire business, the workforce, all of the business's processes and, of course, the information and information technology the business uses in support of meeting its objectives.

To make the delivery of enterprise architecture consistent across the enterprise, a variety of frameworks and methodologies have been developed over the past four decades that assist architects in creating these building blocks, standards and guidelines. If we take a look back at where these frameworks came from, historically, the first of these was the Zachman Framework, published way back in the 80's. Zachman is considered the grandfather of enterprise architecture frameworks and is certainly worth taking a look at to understand where today's approach comes from. However, the most widely recognized and implemented architecture framework today, especially in the ICT industry is The Open Group Architecture Framework (TOGAF). TOGAF was developed back in 1995, coming from the US Department of Defense's Technical Architecture Framework for Information Management (TAFIM). Since then, we've seen many revisions, with each one improving the previous, making it increasingly more comprehensive and all-encompassing until today's most current revision of TOGAF version 9.1, released in 2011. At the heart of TOGAF is an iterative process known as the Architecture Development Method, referred to as the ADM. Each phase of the ADM defines what inputs are required from the previous phase, what steps should be performed during that phase and what outputs are passed into subsequent phases.

TOGAF also defines a construct known as the *content metamodel*, which is used to offer definitions of architecture building blocks, showing how these interrelate to each other. Now, this is where it gets interesting and for the astute among you, you may have noticed that there is no specific call out to security in anything you've seen so far. In November 2005, The Open Group published a white paper that discussed the role of security architecture in TOGAF. This paper is called the "Guide to Security Architecture in TOGAF ADM." The introduction it states: "Coverage of information security considerations in TOGAF ADM has, for several years, been acknowledged as a significant omission."

This acknowledgement was a breath of fresh air for security professionals all around the world who had been battling with their enterprise architecture teams about security matters since TOGAF was adopted. Generally speaking, since security was not a primary consideration of TOGAF, security was not getting a seat at the table in terms of strategic planning and as such security tenets and requirements were being overlooked in the early stages of architecture design. The paper went on to define a variety of security inputs and outputs for each ADM phase, something that entirely overlooked in older version of the framework. However, as this provided only at a high level and didn't discuss any of the detail related to implementation, it was still somewhat lacking in delivering fully into the security space.

TOGAF 9 included some of the content defined in the white paper, but it still wasn't covered in enough detail to really do the job properly, leading to architecture teams still ignoring the fact that security architecture was a specialized discipline, one that needed serious focus at every stage of the ADM if security was to be taken seriously by the business. This is why most technical security guys who move into architecture turn to a different framework, one that works as a complement to TOGAF but covers security thoroughly across the entire life cycle using an approach all of its own. This framework is the Sherwood Applied Business Security Architect, or more commonly referred to simply as SABSA, published by John Sherwood. As a framework for enterprise security architecture and service management, SABSA has a similar structure to the old Zachman framework, providing a methodology for developing risk-driven security architectures and security infrastructure solutions.

The main focus of SABSA is that its outputs must be derived from rigorous business risk analysis, since this concept lies at the heart of everything we do in security. The process analyses the business requirements from the outset, and creates a chain of traceability through the strategy and concept, design, implementation, and ongoing life cycle, to ensure that the business mandate is preserved. SABSA is a layered model like TOGAF, as shown in Figure 4-6. The top layer is the *contextual security architecture*, where the security requirements are derived for the business. Each subsequent layer goes deeper into the architecture, design, and implementation. What's excellent about this approach is that it also considers the *operational security architecture* throughout the entire framework, meaning that the operational considerations are built into the solution from the requirements phase and further elaborated and refined alongside the overall architecture. This, for most security architects, is the panacea.

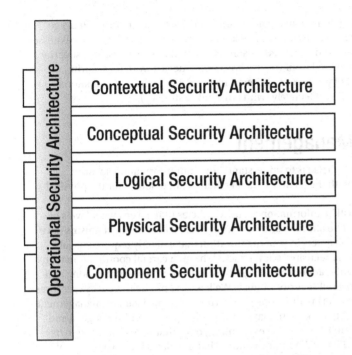

Figure 4-6. *The layers of the SABSA security architecture framework*

In October 2013, The Open Group published a whitepaper called, "TOGAF and SABSA Integration: How SABSA and TOGAF complement each other to create better architectures." This was authored by representatives of the TOGAF/SABSA Integration Working Group, providing groundbreaking collaboration between these two leading architecture frameworks. This whitepaper states: "TOGAF has treated security and risk either implicitly through stakeholder requirements or through a limited set of techniques in Chapter 21 (Security Architecture and the ADM). The Open Group Architecture Forum and Security Forum agree that the coverage of security and risk can be updated and improved."

■ **Tip**   If you want to learn more about SABSA, I recommend reading the official book, *Enterprise Security Architecture: A Business-Driven Approach*, by John Sherwood, Andrew Clark, and David Lynas (CMP Books, 2005).

The primary reason for explaining this enterprise and security architecture background to you, especially if you want to deliver a robust security management function to your enterprise, is to give you the context to confront the business if they are overlooking this critical function. You should now have the ammunition you need to advise them on how they would be best served by enterprise architecture if they added in a *security architecture* capability.

As an information security manager, your role is to provide assurance across the entire business, covering all of its projects, people, processes, and working practices to protect your information's confidentiality, integrity, and availability. In effect, this is the essence of the entire job.

If you don't have a robust approach to how you deliver enterprise security architectures, this can lead to projects not eliciting security requirements at the outset and subsequently systems transitioning into the live, production environment where the security considerations are minimal. Without a consistent security architecture approach, you'll discover security implementations that look like Band-Aids stuck into projects to paste over the security cracks and just about meet the poorly scoped requirements. Security testing will be scoped as minimal, amounting to nothing more than a quick vulnerability scan before the systems go live, and while it will look like you've passed the tests and it all looks good, there will be inherent weaknesses either in the direct components you have released or related weaknesses introduced because of a security integration degradation that will not be discovered until you are breached. The last word on security architecture is that this is a vital component of your organizational structure and without it operational security will be nigh on impossible to undertake effectively (with any kind of strategy).

Working with Facilities Management

The final piece of the organizational security puzzle is to understand how your information security management team works and collaborates with the facilities management team to look after the physical security of your premises.

At the top of your organization, there will be information security policies that govern what levels of protection certain kinds of information must be afforded and how strong the protection mechanisms have to be. However, there are very few information assets in your organization that will only require logical controls to protect them. This is why a physical security policy, enacted through careful coordination with the facilities management team will reap significant rewards for your overall security posture, as long as it is carefully coordinated and aligned to the overall security strategy. We'll look at physical security measures later in this book, but for now, it's worth considering the scope of security within the facilities management team and how you should interact with them to make sure that security principles cover both logical and physical manifestations. For example, you might have an access control policy that states you need to have two-factor authentication for access to CONFIDENTIAL information. That translates into two factors of authentication in your logical access, whereby users have a username and password combination coupled with a smartcard where both are required to access the database. If that database is in a datacenter and the data is stored on a physical server, then access to the physical server should also be subject to two-factor authentication. That might be implemented by datacenter technicians and managers being issues with smartcard that also require a pin number to be typed into a pin pad, so it's something the user has (the smartcard), and something the user knows (the pin).

As the information security manager, you will need to look at all aspects of facilities access control (including access to high-security rooms, such as datacenters), as well as alarm systems, monitoring and construction standards. You will undoubtedly get involved in discussions about security guards, guard dogs, fences and building perimeter protection, facilities locations (proximity to threats), CCTV systems, fire suppression systems and HVAC (heating, ventilation, air conditioning) systems, all of which need to be included in your overall information security risk assessment.

Conclusion

This concludes our look at organizational security and how the information security management function needs to work closely with all other aspects of the business to ensure that security requirements are properly built into projects and systems, while balancing an approach based on understanding the risks rather than having a knee-jerk reaction to vulnerabilities and threats. As you start to explore all of these different aspects of the job, you'll soon find that each area has a vast number of references, frameworks, standards, and methodologies that can be applied to make the job easier and to help you deliver information security more consistently. Let's now move on to look at how you start developing an information security implementation program.

CHAPTER 5

■ ■ ■

Information Security Implementation

This chapter looks at some of the implementation issues and impediments that the information security manager might encounter when trying to embed a security function in an organization, especially if security has not been taken seriously in the past or you are building a security capability from scratch.

Implementing a security capability should follow your standard project management methodology so that you can keep control of budget, deliverables, and outcomes, as well as establish stakeholders and outcomes that are tangible and measurable. At the end of this project, you'll have established organizational interfaces with all of the necessary business functions you'll need to co-operate with, as defined in Chapter 4.

CREATING A SECURITY STRATEGY

The concept of a *strategy* is often used to describe the way the business will grow or develop over a long period of time with a number of specific targets it wants to achieve: grow by 30%, establish a 55% market dominance, expand into Europe or Australia, and so forth. Strategic targets are often pitched as financial, marketing or technology related plans, so it should come as no surprise that security strategy refers to the laying down of high-level plans that show a considerable improvement in security posture over a defined timeframe.

Your security strategy must be realistic enough to influence the business to invest money consecutively over a defined number of financial periods (years, quarters, half-years). You can then use the money to achieve targets (or milestones) on a strategic plan, underpinned by tactical, short term plans.

Any good strategy will align itself with your implementation program but will project beyond its initial stages to a three-to-five year timeframe. Consider the implementation program as tactics that help progress you, step-by-step toward long-term strategic objectives.

For example, an organization could run three iterations of an information security implementation program over three years, successively building on the output of the previous stage to achieve the strategic objective. Each interim stage builds on the success of the previous one, but can also deliver strategic risk reduction in itself.

© Tony Campbell 2016
T. Campbell, *Practical Information Security Management*, DOI 10.1007/978-1-4842-1685-9_5

Acceptance of your strategy from the organization's board or C-suite is only possible if you include details related to the following:

- High-level objectives

- How the risk profile of the business improves with time

- Clearly communicating benefits as "value propositions"

- Trends in global and regional threats and vulnerabilities

- Aligning the security strategy with the business strategy

- Supporting the business's technical strategy

- Demonstrating a focus on cost savings

Lastly, your strategy should be *visionary*, demonstrating your organization's maturity and depth of understanding of information security practices and needs. It should be written in plain, non-technical language and must state the goals of the business as simply as possible; this document exists alongside marketing strategies, business plans and technical roadmaps, so it needs to be consumed by the same set of audiences that read the rest of the business's strategic literature.

Let's start by looking at how information security risk management integrates with your business risk management function, embedding security considerations and decision making into every aspect of business.

Integration with Risk Management

Risk management is at the heart of everything we do in information security. The information security manager must advocate a risk based approach for every security-related decision taken by the business, including even the simplest decisions, such as whether or not to buy a firewall for the perimeter defense or purchase some antivirus software for the desktop.

The Language of Risk

The most effective way to integrate your information security risk management capability with the rest of the organization is to educate everyone on the language of risk. Getting everyone speaking the same language means it becomes easier to communicate security decisions and requirements to the diverse variety of audiences that you will be required to engage with.

Start by making sure your own team (or your assurance team as well as any technical security teams in operations or architecture) understands information security risk management speak. Make sure that they also understand the full information risk management process, as covered in Chapter 4. If you need to send them on formal training, do so as soon as possible, since this will become the doctrine that underpins everything they do.

Build explanations of language and terminology into your security awareness training course, which we also covered in Chapter 4. Provide examples of where the terms are used and put some local business context around them so that your team can see the common usage in your own environment. Your ambition should be to walk up to and discuss a security incident, along with its risk to the business, and they'll understand how to prioritize it and raise it with the relevant teams. Exactly the same message could be conveyed to an engineer in your networking team, the chief financial officer (CFO), or the receptionist, and they will understand it.

If you use partners or outsourced service providers, you need to make sure that they are also on the same page in terms of their use of language. You need to make sure that when you talk to your infrastructure outsourcer or your development partner about a threat model or risk assessment, they understand what you mean and what to do with the information you provide them.

Use Existing Frameworks

When it comes to implementing a risk management framework, the last thing you want to do is reinvent the wheel. There may already be an accepted approach for business risk management that your financial department uses, especially in contract pricing or tender negotiations, since risk and contingency often plays a vital role in outsourcing deals, supplier pricing and business continuity planning. You should speak to the executive board about risk management and explain what you are trying to do from a security standpoint. If you tell the CFO that you are using his risk management methodology as your basis, you are more likely to get buy-in from the board than if you say you are introducing something entirely different that will need to be operationalized by the business.

■ **Caution** While I've suggested that you should adopt the frameworks and methodologies used by the business for risk management, you may find you need to adapt it to deal effectively with information security risk management. For example, if your business currently aligns itself with the ISO/IEC 31000 risk management standard, you can use this for information security risk management, but you should split out each assessment into three distinct areas: confidentiality, integrity, and availability. Most risk management frameworks ask for one specific business impact calculation as an input to the calculation, but in our case, you may need to do it three times, since some systems may not be so important from an availability point of view, but the information may be so sensitive that it has an extreme impact from a confidentiality perspective. This leads to two separate risk treatments, where your investment focuses mainly on solving the confidentiality problem, while only lightly touching the availability issue.

It's highly unlikely that your business doesn't have some kind of risk management approach already in common use today. However, if this is not the case, you should look to adopt one that is standards aligned and repeatable by all business units that may benefit from it. For example, you could introduce an overall alignment with ISO/IEC 31000, which has been adopted by the national government in various countries around the world, such as the United Kingdom and Australia. If your framework for delivering security outcomes is ISO/IEC 27001, this makes integration of the risk management approach really easy, as it works across all levels. From a lower level implementation perspective, you can look at ISO/IEC 27005 to help you build an information security risk management capability that sits at the heart of your own security service. Tying it all together, with frameworks, standards, and alternative methodologies, you will create a flow of information using a common language that integrates your information security management team with the rest of the organization's approach, as shown here in in Figure 5-1.

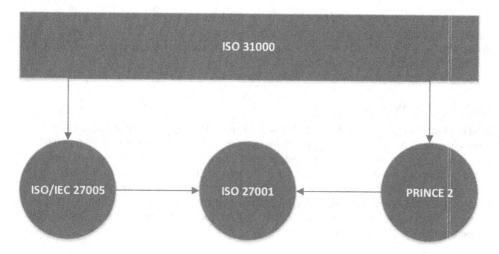

Figure 5-1. *Use frameworks and standards to build your security risk management capability*

■ **Note**   Most project management frameworks, such as PRINCE2 and PMBOK include risk management as one of the inputs to managing a successful project. You can speak to project managers about how they run risk registers for their projects and how those risks, once the project is finished, are transferred onto a corporate risk register for management by someone in the business. If this is done, you can make sure that any information security risks are managed using your infosec process, but the implementation of the treatment plan and any transference onto the corporate register can be handled through the existing project management processes.

Secure Development

Your systems development and software development teams will more than likely undertake any work as part of a project or through an ongoing change process that manages delivery of new or updated solutions into a production environment. Projects will typically be underpinned by a methodology for successful delivery, such as PRINCE2 or PMBOK, while service management delivery may rely on the underpinning processes of a framework, such as ITIL. Changes to the production environment may flow through a waterfall approach, or you may have switched to a modern agile approach, such as DevOps, which speeds up the delivery of incremental changes to production systems based on a streamlined governance and risk management approach.

The majority of formal methods for the management of projects and product release control (even within other frameworks, such as ITIL and DevOps) rely on the concept of managing deliverables that sit on the critical path. Projects can be divided into specific stages, as follows:

- Definition
- Planning
- Build
- Test
- Implementation

- Monitoring

- Adjusting

- Evaluation

Security needs to be a consideration from the very first stage, since during the definition stage, requirements are gathered. It's a worthwhile engagement model to work with the Project Management team to include the information security manager as a key stakeholder in all projects during this definition phase. That way, the information security manager takes responsibility for supplying policies, security governance frameworks, corporate non-functional security requirements (relating to confidentiality, integrity, and availability) and internal standards (technical or non-technical) to the project manager to impose on the development team.

There will also be a myriad of functional security requirements (technical ones) that need to be imposed on the development team. If you have a security architecture function established in your business, this project definition stage would be the engagement point where the developers are required to discuss technical security issues with the architecture team. In more mature organizations, you'll more than likely find well defined secure build standards for all common systems and architectures, which form the foundations of new or changed business solutions.

Security Architecture Awareness

When a new project is initiated, make sure that the project management and engineering teams are aware of your role and the importance of security architecture in designing their solutions. Start by workshopping security outcomes with engineering teams as to why products and systems need to be designed with security in mind from the get go. Many software engineers have not been exposed to secure coding practices and may well be skeptical at the beginning of your discussions. You'll need to provide examples of how attacks occur and how weaknesses built into systems at the design stage end up costing ten times more than issues discovered in production systems. You can also look to implement programming tools (integrated development environments) that assess the security of code as it is written and prevent developer behaviors that create insecure code. This helps the developer learn better coding while on the job and drives a better business outcome.

■ **Tip** If you can bring a penetration tester or a code reviewer into this initial session it can really help bolster the strength of your discussion. An external face is also a useful psychological trick to get the developers to listen since they may have more respect for this "external expert" that they do of other competing internal staff.

Always provide reasons for specific coding practices being proposed. For example, if you are telling developers to switch off unused facilities or not advertise product versions from the system, then explain why that is bad and demonstrate how it can be used to assist an attacker. This kind of practical discussion not only convinces the developer to follow your guidance, it engenders trust and makes them more likely to come back to you when they have questions.

ARCHITECTURE IN CONTEXT

Security architecture, just like security strategy, is a relatively new concept used to map an organization's security controls to the enterprise. An *architecture* is defined as "the complex or carefully designed structure of something," which is how requirements are met by the organization. Akin to technical architecture, security architecture often adopts a framework approach for implementing controls and objectives to be delivered to the enterprise in a consistent and cogent fashion. This obviates the problem of bespoke solutions, where one department approaches a problem differently to another, sometimes referred to as Shadow IT. Furthermore, having a strong project governance function, with the need for a clear and approved business case for any new systems, will also prevent the propagation of parallel, differently architected systems that are built to achieve the same outcomes across the business. A security architect makes sure that new projects follow enterprise-adopted design patterns for security solutions, helping to mitigate risks and enforcing accepted and pre-tested security controls.

A *security architecture* defines a set of security "principles" that communicate the controls needed to implement a solution. These principles reflect the requirements of the organization's policies, standards, guidelines, design patterns, legal requirements, or compliance obligations.

A common approach to security architecture is to define a security domain so that common controls can be developed to protect that domain, such as all network devices using a common approach to securing services, with a common set of requirements placed on the operational teams to only permit certain protocols and administrators must only use privileged accounts under direct supervision from a colleague. These security principles will be applied across all the systems and solutions within the business, both in a logical and physical perspective, taking into account people, processes, and technology.

Most systems can also contain cryptographic solutions to protect data or use public key infrastructure functionality to secure data and communications. If there are implementations of cryptographic systems in the product specification, ensure that the developers know how to configure and use them. Again, if in doubt, explain the purpose of the technology and demonstrate its operational implementation. You could even assist in configuring it, suggesting the most appropriate key lengths, expiry dates, cryptographic cypher-suites, and so forth. It is often the security manager's job to clearly articulate to the developers how the business may need to comply with certain standards, legislation and practices, which will be independently audited and potentially incur significant penalties for noncompliance.

■ **Tip**   Give one-on-one briefings to developers to break any "pack" mentality that might be adopted in a more open workshop. You can use this time to ask them to put on the attacker's hat and consider how they'd break the systems they are building. By doing this, you achieve two outcomes: first, you find where the control points in this new project need to be, but second, and more importantly, you begin the process of shifting the developer's mindset away from functional coding to be one of defensive coding.

Security Requirements

Throughout the life cycle of any project, security requirements must be managed and delivered by the subsequent systems or products. There are various sources for security requirements you can call upon, such as:

- Risk assessments
- Governance frameworks
- Legal and regulatory frameworks
- End user requirements

- Best practices

- Internal standards and guidelines

We've already looked at the risk management process in Chapter 4, so we don't need to revisit that here. Needless to say, however, that taking the output from a risk assessment will help you decide on the types of controls required to protect the information your project will be interfacing with.

The rest of your security requirements can be obtained from legal and regulatory sources, best practice guidelines (such as ISO/IEC 27001), end user requirements such as privacy concerns, as well as any internal standards or guidelines that have already been developed.

■ **Tip**   The Payment Card Industry Data Security Standard (PCI-DSS) is a proprietary information security standard for organizations that handle cardholder information for the major debit, credit, prepaid, e-purse, and ATM and POS cards. It was created to increase controls around cardholder data to reduce credit card fraud via its exposure. If you process credit cards or debit cards in your systems, you have to comply with the standards and potentially be independently assessed.

You will need to be able to trace requirements through the entire development life cycle, showing at each stage where those requirements have been met. This level of traceability can inform two additional kinds of project acceptance checking: functional testing, where you make sure that what's implemented meets what was specified; as well as negative testing, which ensures that your system deals with invalid input or unexpected user behavior in a way that remains secure.

For example, if a user were to type a long alphanumeric string into a username field on a web form, the system should recognize this as incorrect input and raise an exception. The purpose of this sort of testing is to detect situations where the system could be manipulated into an exception state by the user, potentially bypassing your security controls.

Organizational Interfaces

The areas we just covered (risk and architecture) are two of the most important aspects of implementing your security program across the organization. However, there are a variety of other interfaces you'll need to consider, along with their associated process flows, modes of communication and security decision points, and these need to be considered as you start to hone the role of the information security team within your business. The following list of business functions will need to be included in your roll-out plan to ensure that they know what the security team does, and when to call them.

- **Human resources**: The HR team hires people, deals with personal information, and sometimes (depending on the type of business you are) handles government clearances and national police checks. For this reason, it's important that you work closely with the HR team to understand the sensitivity of the information they manage, and ensure that any policies, standards, or processes you build work alongside and complement HR processes.

- **Security operations**: You might already have a security team that manages incidents; however, their role is focused on very operational tasks. Since your new information security function is providing a level of strategic assurance, you need to join up your world with their world to turn policy and guidelines into specific operational activities.

- **Physical security**: You will more than likely have a facilities management capability that looks after your building, remote sites and offices, and IT infrastructure. Make sure that you work with them to ensure that security is covered adequately from both a physical and logical perspective, and look to build mutually beneficial capabilities, such as critical infrastructure surveillance, to increase the overall benefit to the business.

Post Implementation

The business outcome for implementing your information security program is to deliver improvements in your business's security posture that can be considered *value for money,* and to reduce the risk to business operations. You cannot do this without the cooperation from the rest of the business, so establishing these critical business relationships and interfaces is essential in getting to a workable outcome.

Whoever in your organization is charged with business planning should be able to help you understand how the business expects to meet its strategic goals. This team will also provide you with details of up and coming acquisitions and mergers, overseas branch offices, or changes in the organizational structure that may affect your security program's success. Imagine, for example, an overseas branch office that introduces a range of new threats that have not been on your extant list of organizational threats. For example, you might suddenly have to consider your business operations in a region of political instability, or in a tornado zone. Both of these pose very different threats to the business that you may not have had to deal with before, and may affect projects from a whole variety of different perspectives. On a similar note, if your company is highly successful and sets about acquiring a third-party company, this acquisition may drive an increase in infrastructure loading and access control issues that you may not have considered before. As such, you'll need to assess your security architectures, security requirements, physical security requirements, HR and clearance issues, and a myriad of other concerns, in order to be confident that your information systems will be as secure post-acquisition as they are today.

Conclusion

Standards, frameworks, and other kinds of security guidance are all useful resources that can help you build a better, more robust security management capability, allowing you to meet legislative or industry obligations while keeping your business and information secure. However, you need to weigh what's really important to your business and build a security management system that is relevant, proportionate and taking into account your organization's risk appetite and approach to business continuity. To illustrate, take a look through the ISO/IEC 27002 control set, which offers best practice guidance on implementing an ISO/IEC 27001 compliant information security management system. If you are a large, information-centric organization or government department, then this may well be the right thing to do and the investment in compliance will be worthwhile. However, a smaller organization of 50 employees, who mostly work from home and use cloud-based systems such as Salesforce and Office365, would find the alignment with ISO/IEC 27002 far too onerous for their organization and entirely inappropriate. Standards and frameworks are useful, just make sure that you also include common sense when deciding what to implement.

CHAPTER 6

■ ■ ■

Standards, Frameworks, Guidelines, and Legislation

Something I often hear is that the security industry has failed. Pundits love to write articles that suggest our ability to secure information, data and systems, cannot be governed by management frameworks alone and it's the focus on these frameworks that means we are not focusing on threat management and incident response. Nevertheless, I wholeheartedly disagree with this sentiment, especially since the purveyors of this rhetoric are the same salesmen who have a wonder-product that solves all of your security problems.

In the real world, no one should take a standard and implement it for the sake of it. You need to consider the context of your organization along with the things that make sense to you within the legal, compliance and risk landscape you operate in. Security standards, therefore, have to be used properly. If your reason for implementing a standard is simply to prove compliance, this approach will serve to get a tick in the auditor's checklist, but still leave you exposed, since your focus will be to do just enough to get certified. Take, for example, the International Standard ISO/IEC 27001, second edition published in 2013. Right at the front of this standard, it states:

> It is important that the information security management system is part of an integrated with the organization's processes and overall management structure and that information security is considered in the design of processes, information systems, and controls. It is expected that an information security management system implementation will be scaled in accordance with the needs of the organization.

It's incredibly important to take all of these standards, best practice guidelines, and frameworks and make them your own. When people say the system is burdensome or over-complicated for their organization, then they do not understand the essence of what a standard provide. Standards must be integrated within your business's quality management system (QMS) to ensure that it is maintained and accessible, which may mean you have to consider aligning your document structure to the requirements of ISO 9001.

Further to the issue of implementing the standard based on requirements, a worrisome trend in the legal sector is to use the lack of standards as an attestation to lack of security, even to the point where the attorney general in California has stated that any organization that doesn't have the 20 controls listed in the Center for Internet Security's Critical Security Controls document (https://www.cisecurity.org/critical-controls.cfm), would not be considered as having reasonable levels of information security. A sweeping statement such as that doesn't consider the infinite nuances that must be analyzed, assessed and administered within every single organization, from the very small to the very large, where small business trying to implement this list of prescriptive controls might not even be earning enough revenue to justify it—and based on a risk assessment, half of those controls make no sense. But when the state's top legal man makes these sorts of statement, business leaders will stand up and take notice and may rush headlong into

© Tony Campbell 2016
T. Campbell, *Practical Information Security Management*, DOI 10.1007/978-1-4842-1685-9_6

building a security solution that is overcomplicated, overpriced, and overly oppressive, thus damaging the bottom line while adding no value. Unsurprisingly, an increasing number of public officials are seeking a one-size-fits all solution to the so-called "security problem," when in fact anyone working in security knows it is not as simple as that. Security is an intangible yet intrinsic attribute of everything we see and do in all aspects of existence, so trying to suggest that it can be achieved by adoption of a standard or framework, without understanding context, will never succeed.

Regulation ends up trumping education, since it's easier to create an artifact that demonstrates compliance than to accept the fact that we're never 100% secure, and measuring what's reasonable has more to do with the threat assessment that most people think—because this changes continually. What I mean by this is easy to illustrate with a physical security example. Do you feel your house is secure enough from burglars? If you answer yes because you have a burglar alarm (commonly used as a deterrent, especially when it's not monitored by a security company), then for today's threats (opportunist burglaries) it's probably adequate. However, what if you get a great big bonus from work and buy a fancy sports car? It's kept in your garage where your old Ford used to be kept, but now the value of your car is greater, it's more of a target. You might consider adding a new security service to your home, where your alarm now covers the garage and is monitored by a local security firm. For now, you may be safe, since no one really knows (in the local criminal fraternity) that you have such a prize parked in your garage. Now, your son happens to mention to some friends at school that you have a new car. The word spreads that you have a Porsche, right through the school community, where word ends up in the ear of the child of a local car thief—at this stage, your threat level has increased, since you are now on the radar of that specialist car thief.

The difference now is that you are not likely to be targeted by opportunist burglars or novice car thieves, you now face an all-new and greater threat from an advanced criminal gang, who has the resources, means, and motive to "boost" your prized wagon. The one saving grace is that car thieves at this level often work to order; however, if an order comes in you are on the list. The reality is, if you properly understand the crime rates in your local and national locale, as soon as you have something of value, you should be able to do a risk assessment relating to that item and build adequate security in the context of your own circumstances. If you live on a busy road where neighbors are often home and there is a neighborhood watch in operation, there is less vulnerability than if you live on an isolated farm and are out at work all day. The controls you put in place, therefore, will be entirely different, depending on circumstances. So the circle of security continues to turn, where threat and vulnerability drive risk and impact, and investment in controls is designed to reduce that risk.

■ **Note** Cyberinsurance is a relatively modern phenomenon. As well as deploying additional security controls, information security risks can be transferred via an insurance product, much in the same way you take mitigate the risks of a crash or car damage by taking out car insurance. Be aware that some risks are treatable using insurance, but others—such as risks to reputational damage or loss of life—cannot. Furthermore, the terms and conditions for most cyberinsurance products caveat that specific basic levels of security controls are in place. Using the car analogy, this is the same as the insurance company demanding that your car is garaged, alarmed, and has an immobilizer fitted, but you'll get further premium discounts if, for example, a tracking device is installed.

Why Do We Need Standards?

Standards are documents that have been published by a recognized body, such as the International Standards Organization (ISO), to help communicate a common understanding of the specifications and processes needed to assure the delivery of reliable products and services. For this reason, standards have been created to address the majority of considerations we have in delivering products or services to customers, be that from a government department providing a service to citizens through to pharmaceutical manufacturers developing new medicine for cancer patients.

Standards typically detail the protocols and requirements of a particular deliverable, such as in our case, an information security management system, so that its incorporation into any given organization is consistent.

From an information security manager's perspective, security standards provide the fundamental reference models for development of security capabilities, by establishing consistent ways of delivering security controls that are understood and adopted by the entire organization. Standards also help us deliver systems that can be independently verified as fit for purpose, allowing companies to seek additional assurance that they are doing things in a way that is adequate to satisfy legislative and commercial requirements.

There are a variety of benefits you can realize from standards as a security manager, which are worth considering:

- Standards can be used to demonstrate to customers that you are serious about security

- Standards can allow you to better coordinate organizational changes across all stakeholders, as the implementation of a standard will often impose compliance across the entire workforce

- Standards can also be imposed as a requirement on subcontractors and suppliers to help strengthen the security of your upstream and downstream supply chain

- Product and services that are certified as compliant with security standards can gain a competitive advantage since customers will invariably feel confident in its supply

- Standards can help make your internal security controls and processes compliant with partners, customers and the government, making doing business easier across diverse markets

This chapter covers a variety of standards that are relevant around the world as well as a number of guidelines and best practices that are considered relevant to information security. But the most critical considerations as a security manager are picking the standards, guidelines, and best practices that help you do business better and protect your information from the risks that you carry as an organization, without overspending or needlessly spending money on controls that are not relevant to your industry, services, or customers. So, standards are great references, and in some cases are required to do business in certain industries, but should be carefully considered by the security manager and the business prior to committing to seek certification, as they can also add a significant and continual overhead to the running of an organization which can invariably affect the bottom line of profitability.

Legislation

Most countries have a legal system that has evolved over hundreds of years, based on experiences that have tested law enforcement and the judiciary on how to deal with criminals. Legal systems are built to best suit the needs of both governments and citizens so that order can be maintained and a fair and consistent outcome of individual cases can be guaranteed. I know it's not always possible to guarantee but this is the underlying essence of what it does.

In the majority of cases, laws are constitutional since first being passed as a historical bill or act to protect landowners, businesses, or citizens. In jurisdictions such as the United Kingdom, the origins of the legal system date back to as long ago as mediaeval times, and this is demonstrated in some of the archaic regulations that are still upheld today. Newer countries, such as the United States and Australia, still have a similar approach to law; however, the legacy regulations seen in the United Kingdom and Europe are not present. However, most legal systems are tested through precedent setting in court, so a judge can decide on the outcome of a trial making the punishment a contemporary equivalent, even if the regulation demands payment in something archaic such as gold or chickens.

In the modern world, where trade often spans international borders (especially online), there is a distinct blurring of jurisdictions, therefore security in the context of business demands the information security manager understands these legal obligations in all the jurisdictions the business operates. It's critical that a security manager understands which laws must be adhered to in whatever business context the business is focused on. Today, for example, the European Union publishes directives to member countries, proffering guidance on how certain security controls should be adopted in member states, where the member state is expected to police the law and report on the outcome.

■ **Caution**   Misinterpretation of European Union directives is not uncommon. It's often seen that one country's enforcement of an EU directive is entirely different to another's, making it difficult to enforce the law across borders, even under a common legal framework.

In the United States, an equivalent legislative body exists at a country level, setting Federal Laws. These are disseminated and integrated into the body of state law and enforced at that level by the state police. When issues cross from one state to another, and jurisdictions are crossed, then it becomes a federal matter and it is passed to the FBI to prosecute.

This means that the legal system of one state can vary to the next, but it's the common set of countrywide laws, enforced at the federal level, that provides consistency. From a business point of view, compliance with the legislative systems of your trading partners may prove troublesome where they are outside of your legal control. If a corrupt government demands payments from companies earning more than a certain amount of money, through what appears to be a tax on the rich, this may simply be the cost of doing business in that country. However, if the company discovers fraud within the management in that remote jurisdiction, and you are based in California, you need to consider how you report that fraud and how you work with local police to prosecute the offender. If the country's laws don't deem the person's activities as fraudulent, then it will be impossible to prosecute from California.

■ **Tip**   As a security manager, your advice to the board should always be based on risk assessments. In this case, regarding cross-border risks to doing business, if there is too much risk going into a particular country, then you should balance the risk of doing business there against the overall need for entering that region. If there are huge benefits in terms of say, manufacturing in a foreign location, one way of dealing with the risk would be to establish a manufacturing subsidiary in that location, thus not exposing the rest of the business and its information to that level of risk.

Due to this complexity and the individual nuances of each country's interpretation of law, as the security manager, you should seek qualified legal advice before expanding into new territories. Most businesses will have an internal legal team who can deal with these kinds of issues, so be sure to work closely with them. By understanding the regulations, guidelines and laws of all the territories you operate in, as an information security manager, you'll be able to provide advice and guidance to the rest of the business that will help protect them from financial, reputational and, in some cases even physical, harm. From a security perspective, find out about intellectual property rights and the legal protection thereof, as well as any special requirements for records management that might be different to what you already do. Furthermore, look into what's needed for data protection and privacy protection and find out if there are mandatory breach notification rules you need to abide by. Check out the laws pertaining to computer misuse and lawful interception, since undertaking certain kinds of security testing, even by qualified and authorized testers, can put testing staff at risk of being arrested and tried as felons. Lastly, look at the local rules relating to cryptographic technologies and associated key material, since some jurisdictions treat cryptographic material as armaments and must be handled as such.

EXPORT CONTROLS AND THE WASSENAAR ARRANGEMENT

Encryption systems are essential when building information security capabilities, used to provide a variety of authentication, confidentiality, and integrity related functions. Within a single geopolitical region or country, governments will usually control how cryptographic technologies are used and by whom. The reason for this is often pitched in terms of national security, where encryption can be used by the government to uphold secrecy, but also used against the government to prevent law-enforcement or intelligence services eavesdropping on criminal communications. Most governments control the export of such cryptographic technologies from their country to other nations, treating the strongest, proprietary encryption algorithms with the same level of protection as they would armaments, such as guns, munitions, and ballistic missiles.

Because of this, suppliers are required to closely align their activities with governments, hence working under strict controls related to where they can and cannot supply to. To make dealing across international borders easier and more consistent, the Wassenaar Arrangement was created in 1996 to control export, to ensure that cryptographic technologies didn't fall into the wrong hands. The "arrangement" protects all countries that have signed up to its terms from purveying strong, military-grade cryptographic material to rogue governments or nations, since this technology could, eventually, be used against the selling nation. By way of example, a terrorist organization might use a strong cryptographic algorithm to encrypt its plans to attack a US government target. You can see a full list of all the nations who participate in the Wassenaar Agreement by looking on the website at http://www.wassenaar.org/participating-states/.

If you believe that a country's laws don't apply to you because you are not physically doing business there, you may want to think again. Not understanding a law or being aware about some kind of regulation is not a valid excuse for not abiding by it. If you break the law in a country you are participating in, you will be prosecuted, so always speak to your legal team and advise them of your findings. In most cases, the decision to proceed or not is not the security manager's to make, however, you should position yourself as someone who is trusted enough by the executive team to be consulted in these kinds of matter.

Privacy

Privacy is of massive international concern and has been in the headlines a lot over the past five or so years. Many of the big security breaches we've heard about in the news have negatively affected individuals' privacy, where businesses' systems have been hacked and information obtained by the attacker relating to customers' private personal data.

There is often a perceived tension between what's best from a security point of view and what's best from a privacy perspective. On one hand, to maintain national security and safety, law-enforcement and intelligence services should have as much access to data as possible, however, we each have the right to protect our personal (private) information from prying eyes, seemingly without exception. Privacy laws have been introduced in many countries, enforced through the application of fines and awards for damages for serious breaches. The essence of this legislation is that individuals have a right to privacy and companies making use of private information must adhere to a set of technical and procedural guidelines to ensure that they uphold those requirements. Nevertheless, privacy laws differ from country to country, and it's worthwhile knowing what the law is within all the jurisdictions you trade in. For example, companies trading in the United Kingdom fall under the EU Data Protection Act (DPA)—or at least they did until Britain decided to exit from the European Union. Things are not as clear now, which creates a legal precedent for the protection of all types of personal information. Contrast this to the United States, where sector-based statutes, enforced at the federal level, provide governance, but are specific to the kinds of data in that sector, such as the HIPAA (Health Insurance Portability and Accountability Act) guidelines for the healthcare and health insurance sector.

The European Union's data protection legislation suggests that citizens have the right to request access to any personal information held that relates to them. This applies to private companies and government departments alike and includes the ability to find out who has access to that personal information. Individuals also have the right to request changes to personal information if they find it misrepresents them or is somewhat inaccurate.

■ **Note**   To find out more about global privacy regulations and how laws are implemented in different countries, Forrester's Global Heat Map is a great reference. You can view that on their website at `http:// heatmap.forrestertools.com`.

US-EU Safe Harbor and Privacy Shield

In October 2015, the 15-year-old international Safe Harbor Privacy Principles scheme came under fire when a lawsuit filed by Austrian activist, Maximillian Schrems, attacked Facebook's handling of his personal information under EU privacy laws. The outcome of the hearing saw the court invalidate the Safe Harbor agreement, which underpinned how many US companies managed customers' personal information when it originated from systems running in the European Union. Under the old scheme, companies in the United States would be able to self-audit and certify that they were compliant with the EU regulations and data protection standards, thus allowing them to pass customer data to the United States, unhindered and effectively unaudited.

Maximillian Schrems argued that even if American companies were taking adequate measures to ensure that data was protected, the US government did not and thus European citizens' data was at risk due to US government surveillance. The courts ruled that the transferring of personal information where the only control is that of Safe Harbor self-certification is illegal, which affected more than 5,000 companies that were self-certified under that old agreement.

■ **Note**   The court ruling of Maximillian Schrems v. Data Protection Commissioner can be found at `http:// curia.europa.eu/jcms/upload/docs/application/pdf/2015-10/cp150117en.pdf`. It's well worth a read.

On July 12, 2016 US Secretary of Commerce, Penny Pritzker, along with EU Commissioner Věra Jourová, approved the EU-US Privacy Shield Framework as the replacement for Safe Harbor. You can find out more about Privacy Shield at `https://www.privacyshield.gov/welcome`.

Employer and Employee Rights

Employer and employee rights are dictated by each country your business operates in. The legal systems and precedents can vary considerably depending on the local privacy laws, so it's worth consulting a local employment lawyer prior to hiring staff in an unfamiliar jurisdiction.

Rights will also vary from one industry to another, such as where staff in the transport industry or mining sector may be prohibited from partaking in alcohol or drug taking, which may be enforced through random drug testing. If an employee maintains a safety-related role, for example, where they are responsible for ensuring customers cannot be hurt through company negligence, then the company should publish a policy detailing the requirements of the role (and what's expected of all supporting staff) so that it's completely clear what's expected, and well understood as to what the company will do to sure this remains so.

As an information security manager, you should make sure that you discuss employee rights and employer rights with your local Human Resources team, making sure that anything related to confidentiality, privacy and safety is fully explained in your information security policies and that all requirements related to employer or employee rights are upheld through business processes and technology systems and you have tested your compliance across the entire enterprise. Since there are potentially massive fines if you are found to be non-compliant, it's easy to justify expenditure on auditing this aspect of the business and remediating any findings of non-compliance.

Computer Fraud and Abuse Laws

Most countries now have some kind of legislation that prohibits hacking and the abuse of information technology. Let's take a look at some examples from America, the United Kingdom, and Australia to see how this legislation is enacted and what it means from an information security perspective.

■ **Tip**   If you are the information security manager or person responsible for security within your organization, you should always be aware of the information security requirements your local laws contain. Being unaware is not an excuse, so do your research. If you need to, educate your executives so that they understand why you are putting certain processes, procedures, or technologies in place.

We'll start by looking at the laws relating to computer misuse and fraud in the United States of America.

US Computer Fraud and Abuse Act

Congress enacted the Computer Fraud and Abuse Act (CFAA) in 1986. The primary objective of this act was to remove any ambiguity from previous legislation.

The CFAA includes provision for dealing with categories of misuse not previously catered for in US law, such as prohibiting the distribution of malware and committing hacking offenses, such as unauthorized access to computer systems or denial-of-service attacks. Interestingly, and ahead of its time, the authors included a clause that criminalized the trafficking of authentication related items, such as passwords, so the modern trend for selling these on the black market is catered for by the CFAA. Section (a) of the act focuses on anyone who accesses a computer system without appropriate authorization, such as in the following quotation:

> *Whoever having knowingly accessed a computer without authorization or exceeding authorized access, and by means of such conduct having obtained information that has been determined by the United States Government pursuant to an Executive order or statute to require protection against unauthorized disclosure for reasons of national defense or foreign relations, or any restricted data, as defined in paragraph y. of section 11 of the Atomic Energy Act of 1954, with reason to believe that such information so obtained could be used to the injury of the United States, or to the advantage of any foreign nation willfully communicates, delivers, transmits, or causes to be communicated, delivered, or transmitted, or attempts to communicate, deliver, transmit or cause to be communicated, delivered, or transmitted the same to any person not entitled to receive it, or willfully retains the same and fails to deliver it to the officer or employee of the United States entitled to receive it. (1986)*

Section (b) goes on to look at those who attempt to use computer systems to commit an offence under any of the sections listed in (a), while section (c) details the punishment for any breaches of sections (a) or (b).

Section (d) states the following: "The United States Secret Service shall, in addition to any other agency having such authority, have the authority to investigate offenses under this section," then goes on to delegate authority and responsibility to the Federal Bureau of Investigation for any cases that might involve espionage, foreign counterintelligence, or information protected against unauthorized disclosure for reasons of national defense or foreign relations. The rest of the CFAA can be found at https://www.law.cornell.edu/uscode/text/18/1030.

■ **Tip**   You can address the issue of users saying they didn't know the law by implementing log on banners that explain their obligations as users and the laws they are held accountable to. As a security manager, this is the kind of thing that you can actively do to help mitigate the issue of users claiming they didn't know the rules. Most operating systems (Unix and Windows) have this capability.

UK Computer Misuse Act

The UK's Computer Misuse Act was introduced in 1990. It included the introduction of three new offenses that criminals could be prosecuted for undertaking:

- Unauthorized access to a computer.

- Unauthorized access with the intent to facilitate further offences.

- Unauthorized modification of computer material.

Over the years, like most legislation in most countries, there have been a variety of amendments to the original act to include clearer guidelines for punishing offenders and details relating to serious offences to complement the Serious Crime Act of 2007.

In the United Kingdom, the misuse of computers can include any the following activities:

- Hacking (unauthorized access) of computer systems

- Unauthorized interception of communications

- Interference with computer systems that could lead to a denial of service

- Computer related fraud and forgery

- Infringement of copyrights

- Downloading and sharing of illegal material such as pornography or bootleg films

- Trafficking in stolen informational goods, such as credit card numbers, bank details, email addresses, passwords, digital signatures, and encryption keys

An interesting website to read through is at http://www.computerevidence.co.uk/Cases/CMA.htm. It contains the details of a selection of interesting computer misuses cases that have gone to trial in the United Kingdom and links to a variety of external websites that contain the details of the cases, along with the outcomes.

Australia's Cybercrime Act

In Australia, the primary provisions on computer crime are found in Part VIA of the Crimes Act 1914. Like many countries, these provisions data back to the late 1980s and had not been substantially updated by the turn of the century. The one exception is that search and seizure provisions were added in 1994, but like the rest of the act, remained stagnant after that. To try and deal with the outdated aspects of commonwealth law, Australian state governments introduced their own legislation to try and better define what constitutes computer-based crime within their own local jurisdictions. However, after much debate, in 2001, the Australian federal government introduced its new Cybercrime Act, in an attempt to update and modernize the law in this area. Following that, the governments of New South Wales, Victoria, the Australian Capital Territory and South Australia updated their own laws to align with the provisions details under the Commonwealth Criminal Code. The Cybercrime Act, 2001, can be accessed at https://www.legislation.gov.au/Details/C2004A00937.

Records Retention

Some documents are deemed constitutional by law for a given company operating within a given country. Documents, such as minutes from a company board meeting, audited financial records and contracts of employment are all considered legally admissible documents that have to be tightly controlled. These documents are retained over a predefined timeframe (maybe, five years for financial data) and made available for inspection should an audit be undertaken. These kinds of documents are known as *records*, which often pertain to an audited history of company operation.

Timeframes for retention vary depending on the types of records being kept. This is usually dictated by the legislation and compliance rules within the country you are operating in, however, multinationals that deal in various jurisdictions will need to be compliant in each of the areas they operate in, ensuring those records are available for the required number of years. For example, if you destroy your financial records after five years in one country but find they are needed for an investigation in another country after seven years, your company could be subject to a heavy fine or even imprisonment of executive directors. In some cases, legislation also dictates that some data has to be destroyed after a set period of time, such as the personal records of staff members after they have left employment.

To start with, the security manager should collaborate with the business to create a records retention policy and schedule that details the requirements within the legal jurisdiction you operate in. Policies explain which requirements need to be met, while the schedule can be used to explain what documents need to be stored and over what timeframe they need to be made available to auditors. The policy should also consider data protection and data classification aspects of the records and ensure that certain documents that must be destroyed have evidence recorded that attests to this destruction. This proof may be called upon later in court so this information is a vital record. For some guidance on how to manage these kinds of records, the International Standards Organization has created a standard called ISO 15489-2.

Read more at http://www.iso.org/iso/catalogue_detail?csnumber=62542.

Intellectual Property and Copyright

Intellectual Property Rights (IPR) is a messy area of law that again, varies from one country to the next. IPR laws protect the rights of individuals and companies in relation to creative works, such as documents, literary works, plans, prototypes, formulae, patents, trademarks (such as a logos or unique patterns) and designs.

■ **Note**   Within the European Union, a design is defined as "the appearance of the whole or part of a product resulting from the features of, in particular, the lines, contours, colors, shape, texture, or materials of the product or ornamentation." A design patent will be used to protect the overall visual appearance of the design and can refer to both two-dimensional elements, such as drawings or a particular fabric weave, or three-dimensional features, such as the multidimensional shape of the final product.

Copyright protects a fairly wide range of artifacts, applying to any form of written work. In recent years, copyright law has been extended to include software protection, where computer programs are described in the same manner as literary works. The duration for which copyright applies differs from one country to another, so it's worth knowing the copyrights laws not only of the country your company works in, but if you have employees working overseas, check the copyright laws in the country they are resident in. You should also be aware that protecting copyright is only possible in countries where copyright laws are respected and treaty agreements to uphold copyright law have been established. For example, copyrighted material produced in the United States will automatically be protected in the United Kingdom and vice versa. Furthermore, while the People's Republic of China has agreed with, and aligned itself to, the major international conventions on protection of rights to intellectual property, it's fair to say there are many infringements. It's often US copyright holders that report their work being plagiarized or even recreated in full in foreign countries without the owner's permission.

Now that your head is properly spinning with regulations and legislation from around the world, let's take a look at some of the information security standards and frameworks that have been designed to help you structure your approach to building an effective security management system.

The ISO/IEC 27000 Series of Standards

The range of standards within the ISO/IEC 27000 series cover a variety of security management recommendations and best practices that can be adopted to help you build a fully comprehensive information security management system (ISMS). Many people misuse the term ISMS, suggesting it's a single document or set of documents that details all of your security. This is kind of true, but misses the fact that, just like any other process model, such as ITIL (service management) or TOGAF (enterprise architecture), it can be applied to any or all processes and will be built and developed in context across the organization as it matures.

Similarly, there are aspects of the security framework that can be and should be customized to make sure that it's appropriate for your needs. Without this level of customization, the resulting set of processes, procedures, and work instructions will become such a burden and overhead to your business that it will be deemed a failure and to onlookers will seemingly add no value.

Any experienced ISO/IEC 27001 implementer will explain that much of the preparation required in getting the ISMS ready is in finding out how the organization works, interviewing stakeholders, and undertaking a risk assessment. This highlights what the risk tolerances of the executive are, allowing the ISMS to be tailored, contextualized, and streamlined for the size, shape, and complexity of the business.

For example, if you don't do software development, you won't need a detailed assurance plan for the *systems development life cycle* control area. On the other hand, if you are building an ISMS for a multinational enterprise with many third-party contractors involved in massive project delivery, having a unified information security process that drives security requirements into all these projects and solutions makes a lot of sense.

When you embark on an ISMS project, the result should be based on your using common sense, practicality and logic to ensure what's delivered is the best fit for your business. Let's start by looking at ISO/IEC 27001, which we've already mentioned briefly, then we'll take a look at ISO/IEC 27002 before finishing up with ISO/IEC 27035, the standard for information security incident management. At the end of this section I've also included a table of the other ISO/IEC 27000 standards in this series that are currently published but not covered here in any detail.

ISO/IEC 27001

As I mentioned earlier, ISO/IEC 27001 is a specification for an ISMS. Being a standard, it is filled with words such as *shall*, denoting the requirements that must be met to be deemed compliant. Like other standards, you can be audited against the requirements it specifies and use the results of the audit to achieve official compliance and certification, which may be used to help you tender for business in certain markets and attest to your security capabilities in relation to customers, suppliers, and partners.

The ISMS includes your business's organizational structure, its security-related policies and procedures, and requires you have clearly defined roles and responsibilities for all aspects of security management, and the entire security management system defines an embedded management approach to information security, covering:

- People

- Process

- Technology

The ISMS should be built in consultation with the executive management of your company and sized accordingly to ensure that it is fit for purpose for the particular nuances of your business. Furthermore, the ISMS is not something that is put in place and never changes—since it is a management system, it is a living entity within the business and requires continual assurance to make sure that it delivers what the business needs. If your organization decides to branch out into new markets, changes structure, or takes on a new subcontractor, the ISMS needs to be revaluated in the context of the people, processes, and technology requirements for this change.

Each chapter within the ISO/IEC 27001 standard contains guidance on how you build compliance in a particular area of your business. The table of contents is as follows:

- Introduction

- Scope

- Normative references

- Terms and definitions

- Context of the organization

- Leadership

- Planning

- Support

- Operation

- Performance evaluation

- Improvement

- Annex A: Reference control objectives and controls

If you are just starting out on the road to implementing ISO/IEC 27001, jump right into the annex and take a look at the specific control areas you need to focus on. Also, take a look at ISO/IEC 27002 and cross reference these control areas with the specific chapters in that code of practice, as this will give you an indication of just how much work may or may not need to be done. However, when it is time to start designing and implementing your ISMS, you'll be consolidating what are often ad hoc processes into a more mature management system, building a robust security management process model that provides repeatable and dependable results.

■ **Tip** Get copies of all the standards you will be implementing and ensure that they are available for all of the security team to use and reference. Make sure that all your standards are available in a document library and if revisions come out, always get the latest issue and update your ISMS to align with revisions and updates.

It's worth speaking to your management and senior executive leadership team before you embark on an ISMS implementation project since it will invariably affect the whole of your organization and will cost money (time, investment, and resources) across many disparate business units. The standard clearly states that management "shall demonstrate leadership and commitment with respect to the information security management system," which can be achieved through the publishing of compliant information security policies that promote good security practices for the whole organization.

▓ **Caution** An ISMS can be a costly exercise. This is why management support is so important. Don't start working on socializing the idea with middle management until you have top-level management buy in. You will invariably offside a lot of people who see you building empires, so ensure that the edict comes from above so that there is no dispute when you start making changes.

Getting Certified

If you decide you want to get your ISMS certified against the ISO/IEC 27001 standard, you will need to contract the services of an external organization, often known as a *certification body* or a *registration body*. All certification bodies have gone through the required accreditation process to be allowed to issue certificates. They will have gone through the full assessment process with your national accreditation body, proving they have the skills and competencies (knowledge and experience) needed to meet the international requirements for certifying against any given standard.

▓ **Tip** Certification bodies are not normally allowed to provide consultancy services in the same domain as their certification. This is seen as a conflict of interest. Make sure that you use a fully accredited certification body if you want to gain certification against ISO/IEC 27001, as this will ensure that your certification is legitimate and valid for the three-year period they are allowed to assess you for.

If you achieve certification through an accredited certification body, you will be subject to maintenance audits (sometimes referred to as *surveillance audits*) where the certification body comes and check that you remain compliant with all of the requirements of the standard.

ISO/IEC 27002

ISO/IEC 27002 is not a standard, instead it is pitched as a "code of practice," which really means it is simply a collection of guidelines that you can follow to meet the requirements of ISO/IEC 27001. Organizations can use ISO/IEC 27002 to help them prepare for an ISO/IEC 27001 implementation, however, compliance with ISO/IEC 27002 will never be tested, instead the specification of ISO/IEC 27001 will be what's used to deem you compliant or not. Some people refer to ISO/IEC 27002 as a control set. This is a good way to look at it, since it provides a series of individual controls that can be used to meet the higher level requirements of ISO/IEC 27001. As such, this means you can decide to not follow ISO/IEC 27002 at all, swapping it out for a completely proprietary control set—either one you have built yourself or one that is provided by your government, for example—and as long as the individual controls can be mapped to the requirements of the ISO/IEC 27001, you can still claim compliance and pass your audit. The contents of this code of practice are as follows:

- Introduction
- Scope

- Normative references
- Terms and definitions
- Structure of this standard
- Information security policies
- Organization of information security
- Human resource security
- Asset management
- Access control
- Cryptography
- Physical and environmental security
- Operations security
- Communications security
- System acquisition, development and maintenance
- Supplier relationships
- Information security incident management
- Information security aspects of business continuity management
- Compliance

PLAN DO CHECK ACT

The 2005 version of ISO27001 recommended that the Plan Do Check Act (PDCA) model should be used in implementing your ISMS. However, the latest issue (2013) has removed this mandate and offers no specific method to undertaking continual improvement, other than saying that it's required. A variety of other standards and frameworks also recommend PDCA as the approach that should be used to ensure continual improvement, such as in the Information Technology Infrastructure Library (ITIL) process model for IT Service Management. ITIL recommends that PDCA lies at the heart of the Continual Service Improvement (CSI) process. But where does this concept of PDCA come from? It dates back to the 1950s when it was introduced by W. Edwards Deming, where he stated that business processes are continuous feedback loops, allowing managers to identify and improve those aspects of the end-to-end model that need fixing. This update, to be successful, should be first planned then implemented, then its efficacy assured through a measured review, using any aspects where it's not met the goals as an aide to help decide what action to take next. And so on. It sounds sensible, right? There was some surprise from purists when PDCA was removed from the 2013 version of ISO/IEC 27001, however, instead of trying to be too prescriptive, the intent was to allow flexibility of how improvement are introduced into the security management system, since there are often external drivers that require updates that don't follow such as rigid formula.

ISO/IEC 27035

An information security event is: single or a series of unwanted or unexpected information security events that have a significant probability of compromising business operations and threatening information security. (ISO/IEC 27035: 2011)

ISO/IEC 27035 is entitled, *Information technology—Security techniques—Information security incident management*. The introduction to this standard clearly states that "it is inevitable that new instances of previously unidentified threats will occur," and "insufficient preparation by an organization to deal with such incidents will make any response less effective, and increase the degree of potential adverse business impact." This standard is designed as a reference that will help organizations and especially security operations teams:

- Detect, alert, and accurately assess security incidents

- Manage the response to security incidents so that the process is consistent and repeatable

- Assess the potential business impact of vulnerabilities that have not been exploited and inform the business as to how best to deal with them

- Report on the efficacy of the information security incident management process and ensure that the business learns from all previous incidents and vulnerabilities

As we saw in Chapter 2, threats originate from either internal or external actors and carry out unwanted activities or have intent to carry out something that will have an adverse effect on the business. Threat actors are looking for ways to exploit vulnerabilities or weaknesses in your systems in order to affect the confidentiality, integrity or availability of your information (either systems or services), leading to some kind of harm. Figure 6-1 is taken from the ISO/IEC 27035 standard and shows the relationship between all the different objects that comprise the information security incident chain. Objects that are shaded are pre-existing and are materially affected by the unshaded ones, leading to an incident.

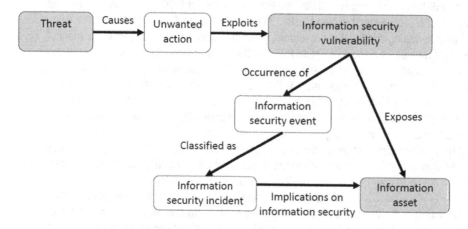

Figure 6-1. *Relationship of objects in an information security incident (ISO/IEC 27035:2011)*

The main focus of the rest of the standard is to ensure that you build a standard, repeatable process for managing incidents that allows you to improve information security management in general, helping build a consistent approach to reducing adverse business impacts (based on a risk-management approach), which leads to feedback from each incident informing the security team how to strengthen the organization to become more resilient to information security incidents in the future. The following are the five phases of information security incident management:

- Plan and prepare
- Detect and report
- Assess and decide what to do
- Response
- Lessons learned (continual service improvement by any other name)

Annex A contains a useful set of cross-references to ISO/IEC 27002 (albeit the older standard from 2005), but I'd suggest that the best part of this document is Annex B, where they provide real examples of information security incidents, along with their underlying causes. Annex C provides guidelines on how incidents and security events could be categorized, however, you may already have a process for doing this for other kinds of incidents if you already perform standard service-related incident management, so this should only really be used if this is all new to you—quite often customer contracts will define the kinds of SLAs defined within this section of the standard, so reverse engineering that contract and applying your findings to the clauses in the standard to ensure that they are all covered is a great way of making sure you cover all the ground you need to. Finally, Annex D is probably the most useful part of the entire standard since it provides a selection of example information security event, incident and vulnerability reports and forms that you can easily incorporate into your ISMS for future use.

List of Published ISO/IEC 27000 Standards

Table 6-1 contains a complete list of all the ISO/IEC 27000 series of standards currently published. There are others in preparation, covering topics such as intrusion prevention, storage security, network security, and digital evidence, so it's worthwhile making contact with a standards organization and subscribing to their bulletins so you know when these new standards are published.

Table 6-1. *ISO/IEC 27000 Series of Standards*

Name	Description
ISO/IEC 27000	Information security management systems — Overview and vocabulary
ISO/IEC 27001	Information technology — Security Techniques — Information security management systems — Requirements
ISO/IEC 27002	Code of practice for information security management
ISO/IEC 27003	Information security management system implementation guidance
ISO/IEC 27004	Information security management — Measurement
ISO/IEC 27005	Information security risk management
ISO/IEC 27006	Requirements for bodies providing audit and certification of information security management systems
ISO/IEC 27007	Guidelines for information security management systems auditing (focused on the management system)
ISO/IEC 27008	Guidance for auditors on ISMS controls (focused on the information security controls)
ISO/IEC 27010	Information security management for inter-sector and inter-organizational communications

(continued)

Table 6-1. (*continued*)

Name	Description
ISO/IEC 27011	Information security management guidelines for telecommunications organizations
ISO/IEC 27013	Guideline on the integrated implementation of ISO/IEC 27001 and ISO/IEC 20000-1 (for service management)
ISO/IEC 27014	Information security governance
ISO/IEC 27015	Information security management guidelines for financial services
ISO/IEC 27017	Code of practice for information security controls based on ISO/IEC 27002 for cloud services
ISO/IEC 27018	Code of practice for protection of personally identifiable information (PII) in public clouds acting as PII processors
ISO/IEC 27031	Code of practice for protection of personally identifiable information (PII) in public clouds acting as PII processors
ISO/IEC 27032	Guideline for cybersecurity
ISO/IEC 27033	Five-part standard dealing with network security issues, such as reference networking scenarios and secure communications
ISO/IEC 27034	Application security
ISO/IEC 27035	Information security incident management
ISO/IEC 27036	Information security for supplier relationships — Part 3: Guidelines for information and communication technology supply chain security
ISO/IEC 27037	Guidelines for identification, collection, acquisition and preservation of digital evidence

Business Continuity

Business continuity management (BCM) is the discipline of contingency planning, where practitioners will help prepare organizations for large scale incidents, such as natural disasters and terrorist attacks, where the normal disaster recovery options available to businesses are no longer relevant.

As the need for business continuity has grown over the past decade, standards were required to help align the requirements of BCM with organizational processes and systems and provide a benchmark for certifying systems and organizations as being prepared for these kinds of incidents. Australia, Singapore, and the United Kingdom all created their own standards alongside the standards created in the United States. In the United Kingdom, British Standard 25999 was introduced to standardize the approach to continuity management systems, from which organizations could elect obtain a certification against that standard. However, it became apparent that an international standard was needed rather than all of these individual country-centric standards, so an international team of business continuity experts was assembled which led to the publishing of ISO 22301 in 2012.

ISO 22301:2012 is by far the best business continuity management standard and has been created to allow the business continuity managers to create a plan that is appropriate to the size and complexity of the organization, so it's fit for purpose whether you work in a small business or a large multinational.

Furthermore, organizations can seek certification against ISO 22301 which allows them to demonstrate their resilience to these catastrophic events to regulators and customers, showing they have invested in the level of resilience required for servicing their customers. In the context of national critical infrastructure, for example, this is an essential step in confirming you can continue delivering services to your customers even under extreme circumstances, so is an effective was to ensure that you garner public and regulatory support for investments in continuity systems.

From an information security perspective, it pays dividends for security managers to be aware of the overall business continuity plan for the organization, making sure that in the event of a catastrophic incident, the security controls you manage within the organization are not undermined within the context of the continuity system. Working closely with the business continuity team allows you to clearly explain the risks to the people who are designing the systems so that critical information risks that may be dealt with through technical controls in normal operation are handled properly when the continuity event happens. Some risks may be accepted during this special circumstance, however, others that are controlled with technology may have to revert to procedural controls for the period of time you operate in the context of the continuity event. For example, you might have a special gateway component that protects your internal network from the threats of the Internet, however, and your staff use corporately supplied computer systems to access and process information. But in the context of the continuity event, your employees are all now working from home, using their personal computers to continue their work. Considering these issues in advance will help you devise the plans, processes, and systems that will continue to provide the right level of security during this kind of exception to normal running.

Information security managers should familiarize themselves with the details of ISO 22301 and help their organizations understand all of its nuances and requirements. Successful business continuity management is a continual and ongoing effort, like the rest of the information security process, so you need to make sure you have trained and experienced people working on your BCM plans and a fully endorsed directive from the organizations top executives, along with appropriate budgets and time to develop the systems and processes that underpin success.

Risk Management Standards

There are a variety of standards that can be used to help you build a risk management process for your business. However, before jumping in and announcing to everyone that you will be adopting one standard or another, you should first assess whether you are already using a process somewhere else within your organization.

I've consulted many organizations that are starting on their information security management journey but don't even know that they have a risk management team. Many businesses already use ISO 31000 as the basis for how risk is identified and managed. It might not necessarily say it's based on the standard, however, if the process model looks anything like Figure 6-2, then at some point this standard was referenced to build your system.

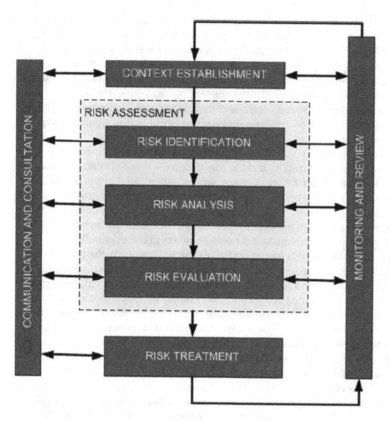

Figure 6-2. *The ISO 31000 risk management process (figure taken from ISO/IEC 27005)*

ISO 31000 and ISO/IEC 27005 are both standards that can be used in information security risk management. ISO/IEC 31010 can also be useful because it covers a variety of risk management techniques, going the next level down in terms of a referenceable process model. You'll find that systems that purport to be based on ISO 31000 are really implementations of ISO/IEC 31010, so try reading both before you decide on anything specific for your business.

ISO/IEC 27005 focuses on the specifics of management information security risks. So, ISO 31000 provides a great foundation for managing risks right across your organization, however, there are nuances of managing information risks, since each risk may have multiple ratings from different perspectives (depending on whether the impact being modeled affects confidentiality, integrity and/or availability), so this all needs to be considered in your process. The other main difference is the continually assessing iterative process that information security risk management follows, as shown in Figure 6-3.

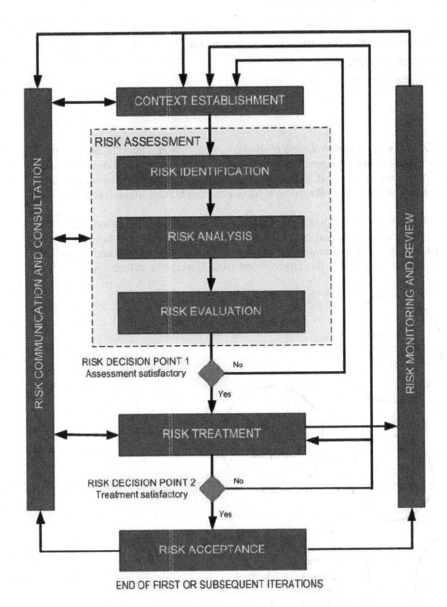

Figure 6-3. *The ISO/IEC 27005 information security risk management process (ISO/IEC 27005)*

As with all standards, the Annexes are full of useful information. At the back of ISO/IEC 27005 you'll find Annex B which lists examples of assets and shows how they should be identified in terms of the business impact of loss, while Annex C provides an example list of typical threats. This is a great reference for new security managers who need inspiration when it comes to threat assessments (and it makes a good reference for anyone planning to write a spy novel). Lastly, Annex E is of particular value to those of you wanting to operationalize risk management as it shows examples of how real risk assessment approaches could work. Work through all of these and at the end you should feel comfortable enough with this process to actually perform a real risk assessment.

■ **Tip**   ISO Guide 73:2009 is yet another useful standard to add to your collection. It offers a compendium of terms that describe, categorize, and manage risk.

COBIT

Control Objectives for IT (COBIT) was created by the international business systems auditing organization, ISACA, who claim to be the world-leading, independent, not-for-profit members' organization who promote best practices for information systems. In the past, ISACA was an acronym for Information Systems Audit and Control Association, but like many organizations who achieve notoriety of their adopted acronym, they are now simply, ISACA.

With the release of COBIT version 5, ISACA has neatly packaged a multitude of different tools, resources, and guidelines that will help you govern, audit and assure the delivery of business information systems, from the perspectives of risk management, information security, regulatory and compliance and the overall governance of enterprise IT. COBIT 5 is based on five fundamental principles (shown in Figure 6-4).

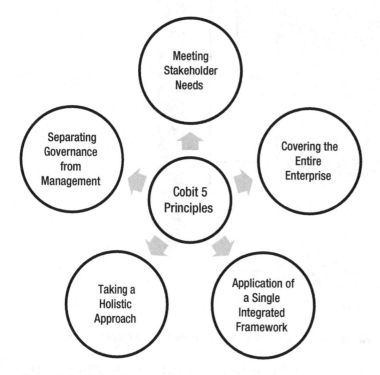

Figure 6-4. COBIT 5's five key principles

The five underlying principles work together to ensure that the whole of the enterprise gains the benefits from striking a balance between "the realization of benefits and the optimization of risk and use of resources." Within the framework, you'll find all of the processes you'll need to incorporate into your management system to drive the creation of business value by using optimized information technology. COBIT is one of those systems that organizations can align with to help govern all aspects of the IT value chain, and since this includes information security, it's a fairly good reference model to use to audit your security maturity against, since it looks at not only the security controls in isolation, but pits them against the organization's tolerance to risk and how the whole of the enterprise architecture delivers outcomes for the business.

COBIT can also be integrated with capability maturity models, with a tight coupling to Carnegie Mellon's CMMI, which unsurprisingly, is now administered by a subsidiary of ISACA called the CMMI Institute.

CAPABILITY MATURITY MODELS

The concept of capability maturity models is not new. They've been around in the software development world since the late 1980s, but the modern notion of the so-named Capability Maturity Model comes from the US Department of Defense, where they used a scale of 1 to 5 to classify the maturity of software development contractors. The scale starts at 1, with the least mature, denoting an organization with no formally defined processes and development follows an informal, ad hoc methodology. At the other end of the scale, an award of 5 denotes a process model that is formally defined across the enterprise and the processes have formal measurements and feedback incorporated into them so that the organization can continually assess and optimize them in line with changing business needs. A further enhancement of CMM was delivered by a Carnegie Mellon's Software Engineering Institute (SEI) and an expert panel from government and industry. This new model was intended to be more robust and enterprise capable, making it useful for all processes, not just those associated with software development. This new model was called CMMI, where the "I" stands for integration. CMMI is no longer a software focused maturity model and its principles are inherent a variety of maturity assessment methods used for all sorts of enterprise operations.

Since COBIT is an enterprise-wide governance model for instilling best practices across the entire business, then it goes without saying that a combination of COBIT and CMMI make for an extremely comprehensive framework for corporate governance. And the nice thing is, even if you decide to use the ISO standards as the basis for how you deliver security management and security operations, you can assess the maturity of your processes using CMMI and audit it using COBIT. Sometimes have a separate view from an audit perspective allows you to see flaws and omissions in your process model that one standard or framework might not.

From a security perspective, COBIT assumes that you cannot deliver enterprise-grade security with point solutions (single purpose technology or controls in just one part of your network). Information security is treated like a process, as it should be, and, as such, becomes inherent in everything the organization does. COBIT can be used to achieve this.

■ **Tip** The COBIT 5 framework can be ordered from ISACA's website at `http://www.isaca.org`.

Payment Card Industry Data Security Standard

The Payment Card Industry Security Standards Council (PCI-SSC) was set up in 2004 and tasked with building a standard for the payment card industry that would combine the policies and best practices of each of the five main players in payment card services: MasterCard, Visa, American Express, Discover, and JCB. The result was the Payment Card Industry Data Security Standard (PCI-DSS), which itself has been through a number of iterations to its most recent revision, version 3.6, published in April 2016. The essence of the PCI-DSS framework is the specification of 12 top-level compliance requirements separated into six groups, which are called *control objectives* (no surprises there). The following are the twelve requirements.

- Install and maintain a firewall configuration to protect cardholder data.

- Do not use vendor-supplied defaults for system passwords and other security parameters.

- Protect stored cardholder data.

- Encrypt transmission of cardholder data across open, public networks.

- Use and regularly update anti-virus software on all systems commonly affected by malware.

- Develop and maintain secure systems and applications.

- Restrict access to cardholder data by business need-to-know.

- Assign a unique ID to each person with computer access.

- Restrict physical access to cardholder data.

- Track and monitor all access to network resources and cardholder data

- Regularly test security systems and processes.

- Maintain a policy that addresses information security.

As you can see, this list of requirements is fairly comprehensive, albeit at an extremely high level, but if each of these control areas is properly design and managed, then customer card data should be safe.

These days, compliance with the standard is mandated to all companies that process, store, or transmit cardholder data. However, formal certification is not enforced for everyone, since Visa also runs another scheme known as the Technology Innovation Program (TIP) that can be used instead. The other aspect of compliance to understand is that smaller merchants and service providers do not need to be checked by an external audit, instead going through self-assessment to maintain compliance; however, if cardholder data is stolen, the issuing service provider has the right to investigate and if the self-assessment is found to be lacking, they will still be liable for the losses and potentially fined.

▓ **Caution**   Organizations that let their compliance lapse will suffer heavy fines and penalties should they incur a security breach and cardholder data is compromised.

Health Insurance Portability and Accountability Act

The Health Insurance Portability and Accountability Act (HIPAA) was enacted by the US Congress in 1996 to help protect health insurance coverage for healthcare workers, imposing a set of national standards pertaining to electronic healthcare information and patient data related to how providers, health insurance plans and employers use that data.

HIPAA law applies to all businesses that have access to health information; however, the law does not require businesses or individuals to be certified. Since HIPPA is a Federal government act, unlike PCI-DSS it isn't something you can get certification against, instead it's a collection of regulations that lay out the rules for proper handling of personal health information.

It's also worth understanding that HIPAA requirements vary depending on the role and the type (sensitivity) of the data being handled.

■ **Tip**   You can read the full text of the act at `https://aspe.hhs.gov/report/health-insurance-portability-and-accountability-act-1996` and if you want more information, you can contact the US Department of Health and Human Services at `http://www.hhs.gov/hipaa/for-professionals/index.html`.

Conclusion

There are myriad standards, frameworks, legislation, guidelines, and best practice references that can inform information security managers about how security controls should be implemented. A fair proportion of this guidance is country specific, especially where data protection and privacy rules apply, further supported by a plethora of industry-specific guidance that can help information security managers advise their executive managers on the best controls to implement to keep the business safe and secure.

As a security manager it pays dividends to align yourself with your organization's legal team so that you garner an understanding of the context of your business and take this back to the security governance team to ensure that these legislative requirements are represented as technical and procedural security controls and embedded into the organization's culture.

The best advice I can offer a new security manager at this stage is to read as many standards and guidelines as possible, familiarize yourself with the ISO standards and PCI-DSS standards (as both are comprehensive and all encompassing) and performance of more of these standards in your own organization to see how you fair. This will give you an indication of how mature your current information security posture is and you can then use this to inform your management on where you believe you need to get to. Don't overemphasize the need to become compliant with any given standard, unless it is absolutely necessary for you to remain in business (such as PCI-DSS), but use the best bits of each standard to help you define security controls and processes that are right for your specific needs.

CHAPTER 7

■ ■ ■

Protection of Information

In this chapter we'll look at some of the most well-known protection mechanisms that you can use to stop attackers from accessing your business's most important information assets. We'll discuss approaches you can take to valuing your data, including how to incorporate a classification scheme into your business in stages, so that the cost can be absorbed over a longer period of time. We'll also look at some of the most commonly used defenses for building barriers around your data, keeping out those who are not authorized. We'll finish off by looking at some of the more contemporary approaches used in information protection, such as digital rights management.

Information Classification

Performing a risk assessment is one of the fundamental tasks you'll perform when considering which protection mechanisms should be used to defend your information. We looked at risk assessments in Chapter 4, so you should be fairly familiar with how to undertake one of these by now; however, one thing that wasn't covered back then was how you go about attributing a value to the information you are protecting.

This value you place on information is extremely useful when deciding how much you are willing to invest in protecting it. This value can be used to skew the results of your risk assessment so that more sensitive information is given more appropriate and stringent security controls, which costs more but is limited only to those highly valuable assets (the information you are protection) as well as highly desirable targets (the information attackers will place value in). This ensures that your hard fought budget is spent on only protecting what's most important to the business rather than protecting everything with the same level of rigor.

In fact, all information has a value, whether it's in the public domain (such as product descriptions on your website), or the secret recipe for your world-famous black fizzy beverage. Therefore, you'll need a way to attribute an appropriate value to each category of data. One of the most popular ways to value data is based on its sensitivity; that is, the amount of secrecy required when handling or accessing it. An information classification scheme is often used by organizations to identify the sensitivity of individual information assets, where information can be labeled as CONFIDENTIAL, UNCLASSIFIED, or TOP SECRET (to use just three examples.) The reality is that any number of categories can be used as long as the definition of each category is clear and unambiguous. You users need to be able to implement it and make classification decisions themselves without having to refer to the security team each and every time they create a new document.

Any good information classification scheme identifies the minimum and maximum level of sensitivity that is used in your business and you need to accompany the description of the categories with succinct guidelines as to how information assets are labeled and handled.

By way of example, we'll look at the kinds of classification levels used by government departments across the world as these can be adopted and imported into similar schemes that work for commercial organizations, small and large. For the rest of this chapter, we'll use the following levels of classification:

- UNCLASSIFIED

- RESTRICTED

© Tony Campbell 2016
T. Campbell, *Practical Information Security Management*, DOI 10.1007/978-1-4842-1685-9_7

- CONFIDENTIAL

- SECRET

- TOP SECRET

■ **Caution**   Over-classifying information is as damaging as under-classifying it. If the majority of information becomes classified at any single level, that level becomes the lowest common denominator. This has the negative effect of diluting the value of that level of classification.

If you decide that an information classification scheme is needed in your business (and let's face it, why wouldn't you?), you need to ensure that complacency doesn't creep into the workforce, where it's misused or underused. The very worst case is where you build systems that are capable of protecting information up at the higher classifications of SECRET or TOP SECRET but employees don't quite understand its use and end up over-classifying all their data or under-classifying data that really should be protected better, simply because the instructions for using the scheme are not clear.

Use of the higher levels of protective marking (such as SECRET and TOP SECRET) should be strictly limited. Figure 7-1 shows a typical classification scheme that might be seen in governments around the world (or something very similar to this). National schemes such as this would be maintained by a central government resource that looks after information security, such as Government Communications Headquarters (GCHQ) in the United Kingdom or the National Security Agency (NSA) in the United States.

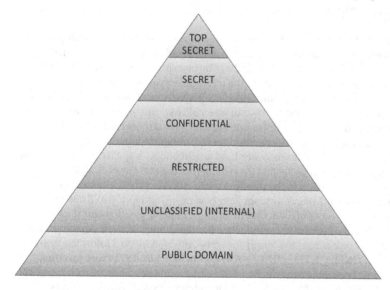

Figure 7-1. *The information classification pyramid*

I've purposely represented the information classification scheme shown in Figure 7-1 as a pyramid. Each layer represents the volume of data within the organization that should be classified in this way. At the very top of the pyramid, TOP SECRET represents an extremely small percentage of the information the business produces. This is commonly reserved for government departments that manage national security matters, where the consequences of losing control of information at this level could have national or international repercussions, or lead to extensive loss of life. It's less common for private organizations to use TOP SECRET as a classification for their own data, but really it's just a label and as long as its meaning is understood then it doesn't matter what it is.

At the bottom of the pyramid, you'll see the PUBLIC DOMAIN classification. This is subtly different from UNCLASSIFIED (INTERNAL) since it's information that is truly without value. Internal information, while UNCLASSIFIED, may still contain details of employee projects, communications with managers, and personal employee details that while not really sensitive, still need an element of protection from the outside world. This is the information that flows around our business networks every day, but we still protect it to a certain extent using our perimeter defenses, such as our firewalls, email filters, web content filters, and data loss prevention solutions.

■ **Tip** As a rule, use the minimum number of classification levels you can get away with. When you start trying to devise a classification scheme for your business, start with just two levels: PUBLIC DOMAIN and UNCLASSIFIED (INTERNAL). Then ask yourself (and your stakeholders), what would happen if this, for example, payroll information was leaked to the outside world? If it's decided that you need a second level of protection, then you might decide to make that CONFIDENTIAL. Next ask yourself, what about our corporate strategy, or these secret plans for our new automobile or software solution? If you see the damage caused by leaking those to be high (and higher than the payroll information) you need another level. You might call this SECRET, or HIGHLY CONFIDENTIAL, or you might decide at that stage to drop CONFIDENTIAL to SENSITIVE and reuse CONFIDENTIAL for the highest classification.

An important term we now need to introduce is *originator*. When any new item of information is created, the person creating it is known as the *originator*. This person must assess the impact and consequence of unauthorized access or misuse of that document and as such they will use the classification scheme to label it. The classification indicates that information has been properly identified and from then on it will be handled appropriately. However, if someone else comes into contact with that information asset, have they the right to reclassify it? This comes down to how you establish the rules around originator control. Some organizations will say that any information classified above a certain level, such as SECRET, automatically gets attributed with an addition label that designates it as originator controlled: such as ORCON. So, a document might have the label of SECRET ORCON. The reality of this is that only the author (or the group that issued the report) has the ability to change it—so making it effectively read only for anyone else. Again, as with many of these additional labeling functions, it's more likely used in defense and national security organizations rather than public businesses, but it's still an important concept, especially when you start to consider information integrity rather than just looking at confidentiality. If an intelligence report is to be trusted, then the consumer needs to know that it's as the originator intended and has not been altered, so a security mechanism may be required to attest to its authenticity.

The classification you select for an information asset may result in additional security requirements and controls being required for protecting it, with the controls being based on a security risk assessment, and expressed as requirements that must be met by people, processes, and technology. For example, if you sell a black fizzy drink and you want to protect the recipe, you might mark all the documents that contain that recipe with SECRET. However, if you need to send one of these documents to another manager, you will need to make sure that your email system has the following security features built into its implementation:

- Encryption

- Limited distribution

- Limited administrator access

- Limited staff access (maybe with higher levels of clearance than the general population workforce).

Based on this list, *encryption* can be used to prevent unauthorized access to the data. The *limited distribution* security control could be implemented by some software that check a directory (such as Microsoft's Active Directory) to see if the recipient is allowed to see that level of classification of email prior to leaving your email client. *Limited administrator access* could be configured to help reduce the ability network and server administrators have of accessing your email using their special (elevated) privileges. Finally, *limited staff access* could be implemented to make sure that only people with the appropriate level of clearance (employee checks) can see the emails and read the attachments, such as when they are in a shared mailbox or public folder. By following these principles, you can apply the same kind of protection mechanisms in the filesystem, on web servers, or any other information storage and collaboration platform, thus providing a simple set of security requirements that your technical guys have to try and meet when they design or upgrade systems.

As you might have guessed, the controls that will be woven into your enterprise to achieve all these outcomes can be onerous and costly, which is why you need to be very careful not to over classify. If you only have one document in your entire business that needs this level of protection (that secret recipe), then you might decide it's better to keep copies on two secured, encrypted hard drives, with one at a remote location, both stored in physically secure, fireproof safes, protected from the elements. That way, the document is well protected using physical security measures rather than complicated and costly network controls, while still making it accessible to managers that need it, albeit from the CEO's office.

Implementation of appropriate security controls to match the classification scheme should be based on your business's risk appetite (which you would have established early on during your security implementation project). Furthermore, some businesses will have the classification imposed upon them by external factors, such as becoming a defense contractor, for example, so you might need to demonstrate compliance with the government's classification schemes, and demonstrate compliance with their specific set of security controls.

■ **Tip** Protective markings can change with time. A highly sensitive document today may become less sensitive tomorrow; therefore, you should integrate some process or mechanism to allow the downgrade or complete removal of protective markings should that be possible. The *originator* should decide how temporal change affects the classification of an asset. An *originator* might extend the duration of a security classification, change it, or even reclassify portions of it. Furthermore, you also need to be aware of archived copies of data, as well as data that needs to be disposed of since the changing protective makings over time will also apply to information in these different states of its life cycle.

Business Impact Levels

Some organizations use the concept of business impact levels (BILs) to assist in the information classification effort. These BILs providing a clear method for assessing and quantifying the impact of loss of confidentiality, integrity, and/or availability of a business asset, unlike normal information classification which often focuses only on confidentiality.

A BIL calculation will still be somewhat subjective, just like any normal risk assessment, normalized onto a scale ranging from, for example, one to five. A rating (BIL) of 1 might relate to *low/medium*, whereas a *catastrophic* loss of confidential, integrity, or availability would be attributed a rating of 5.

You should assess each security tenet of confidentiality, integrity, and availability independently, and then use the highest rating as the asset's overall impact level. This means the subsequent classification rating you attribute to the data will be appropriate and will cater for all of the BIL ratings whether it's from a confidentiality, integrity, or availability perspective. This means that any security controls you impose on the systems, people, and networks where the information is stored, transmitted, and processed, will be commensurate with its BIL and will adequately protect it at that level of classification.

Most of the time, BIL ratings will have an equivalent level of classification. The following set of examples explains how BILs can map to classifications:

- Public domain information on a website that is low confidentiality but cannot me modified by an attacker due to the risk to the company's reputation (so both availability and integrity are considered high). So, the protective marking is UNCLASSIFIED, but the systems and information is treated as CONFIDENTIAL in terms of protection mechanisms, since its availability and integrity BIL is 3.

- Health records that are normally treated as CONFIDENTIAL, with a BIL of 3, need to be accurate to a level of BIL 4 prior to and during surgery. Therefore, this information is treated as SECRET for a short period of time prior to being transferred into the standard system that manages medical records.

- A military logistics system that manages individual orders of supplies has information records that are deemed RESTRICTED (BIL of 2) from a confidentiality perspective. However, the whole database (of aggregated orders) could be used to inform an enemy of troop deployments, therefore the entire dataset is attributed a BIL of 5, meaning that the protection mechanisms are as they would be for TOP SECRET, even though the individual records are much less value on their own.

FURTHER READING ON BUSINESS IMPACT LEVELS

You can find a variety of useful guidelines and standards for implementing BILs from the following government resources around the world:

- NIST's Framework for Improving Critical Infrastructure Cybersecurity can be found at http://www.nist.gov/cyberframework/upload/cybersecurity-framework-021214.pdf.

- The New Zealand government uses BILs as described at https://protectivesecurity.govt.nz/home/protective-security-governance-requirements/business-impact-levels/.

- The Australian government's Protective Security Policy Framework incorporates BILs as described at https://www.protectivesecurity.gov.au/governance/security-risk-management/Pages/Businessimpactlevelsguidelines.aspx.

- The UK government's classification scheme also uses BILs, as per the descriptions at https://www.gov.uk/government/uploads/system/uploads/attachment_data/file/251480/Government-Security-Classifications-April-2014.pdf.

There are many other good references on the Internet that can help you decide whether to include BILs in your classification scheme. You don't need to be a big organization to make these applicable to the way you operate, but you do need to make sure you educate your users on how they are used and how the levels translate into protective marking decisions.

Implementing Information Classification

Engagement with business stakeholders at the beginning of the program is essential to socialize the new rules and carefully manage the expectations of all business stakeholders affected by the change. When the time comes to implement an information security classification scheme, you need to make sure it's well planned and tightly controlled throughout the project. One of the most important things to consider is your education plan as even the best classification schemes won't achieve anything more than confusion amongst the workforce if the users don't understand it. Costs can also get out of control and teams that misunderstand the objectives of your project can end up working against you rather than with you, resulting in an exponentially harder task of getting the crew on your side using this newly conceived security "overhead" in their daily activities.

Even if you decide to adopt a national standard for classification, such as the one used by your government, implementation still needs careful planning and handling. You'll probably find that many of your staff already uses classification schemes in fiefdoms of the business, such as in the human resources department or amongst the staff in the finance team. They understand that the information they manage on a day to day basis has a security consideration and if the business hasn't told them how to handle it before, a diligent manager may well have made something up. You might find that the human resources team already marks personnel records as PERSONNEL IN CONFIDENCE or COMPANY CONFIDENTIAL. As long as you make sure your new classification scheme caters for all of these disparate schemes and normalizes the approach, ensuring the new classification levels are meaningful in the context of the old one, it should work just fine. Nevertheless, you may find resistance if the finance department always labels subcontractor contracts as CONFIDENTIAL, but your new scheme dictates these documents should be labeled as RESTRICTED FINANCE. The finance team may initially be resistant to that change as it seemingly lessens the security of their information as well as forces them to relabel their old documents.

You need to unambiguously explain the new protective marking of RESTRICTED FINANCIAL actually affords better levels of security to their contract information than the previous parochial CONFINDENTIAL marking. Your new scheme brings with it technical and procedural controls that align security controls and protection mechanisms with true security requirements, risk assessments, and business impact levels.

■ **Tip**   The project could likely classify 80% of all existing business document types during the delivery phase, thus the classification guidelines can then be applied to the less common or unusual documents and information that remains at the end.

Figure 7-2 shows a conceptual overview of a high-level plan for rolling out a classification scheme to your business. The important aspect of this is to build the education material after your initial pilot since it's likely that the initial pilot project will show you where your scheme may need modification. The education material needs to be as easy to consume as possible, backed up with workshops and one-on-one discussion with heavy users—that is, those users who will be creating and consuming a high volume of classified or other data.

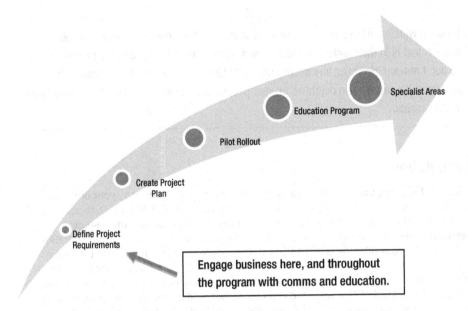

Figure 7-2. Sequencing the implementation of a classification scheme

Pick a friendly business unit as your pilot project, but make it one that isn't too close to home as it needs to be representative of the business and the challenges you'll find elsewhere. For example, if you have a great relationship with the human resources team, that would be a good place to start. Try not to implement your pilot classification in the IT department since this won't be representative of the true business impact of its adoption—IT people can overcomplicate some aspects of business change while not providing the input you need on its impact of underlying business processes, especially with much of their day to day documentation comprising systems procedures and standards of a technical nature.

Information Classification or Systems Classification?

When you plan the introduction of a classification system, one of the first roadblocks you'll hit is questioning how you will reclassify all the data on your file servers, email systems, and document management systems, especially when these collections of data are so jumbled up.

Will you need to individually open every single file and attribute it with a new classification? The simple answer is, yes, but only over a protracted timeframe. Many information security managers start by focusing on classifying systems rather than data, designating certain servers or document repositories as particular classification levels. This means that the finance department's server will be classified as CONFIDENTIAL and as such, all information assets on it are treated as CONFIDENTIAL whether they are or not. This way, at least the ones that are reaching that high watermark of protection requirements will be treated properly. Over time, as new documents are created using the classification scheme, you'll find that the dataset becomes cleaner and cleaner and if you have a retention policy that moves information into long term storage over a certain age, then you'll be clearing out the old, badly classified data over the next few months or at worst, years.

■ **Tip**   One was of dealing with legacy information classification is to let the workforce know that post a certain date, all information that is in their folders will be archives, unless they have specifically moved it into a special folder that you don't remove. However, any information in that special folder must be classified as per the new corporate guidelines. It's certainly an overhead on your people, but ensures that they follow the process or their legacy data will disappear.

Tactical Implementation

In the short term, start by classifying the lowest common baseline of information used by your business. If the majority is UNCLASSIFIED, then deem all of your systems and networks UNCLASSIFIED, then only look at increasing security where information needs to be more protected than in your baseline systems.

Once this baseline has been universally accepted by the workforce, the next stage of implementation will be a lot easier. Decide who your pilot users will be and start profiling their information. For the sake of argument, we'll use the human resources (HR) department for this rest of this section to explain how we'd implement this program of work. Since HR often holds *personal* information your employees, under most countries' privacy law, this kind of data will need extra protection and hence HR is responsible for its security. Let's say there are two classifications needed, over and above UNCLASSIFIED. Information related to pay and benefits, where they store bank account details, employee names, and addresses and clearance information, requires the protective marking of CONFIDENTIAL. This applies wherever data is accessed and used anywhere in the organization. For your pilot program, you'll not have any control of the information when it passes out of the HR department, but for this proof of concept it is fine. Furthermore, the HR department also maintains the executive payroll information, considered highly sensitive by the business and something that external attackers (journalists, shareholders, and competitors) might want to acquire. You've already determined that CONFIDENTIAL applies to the majority of personnel records, so you need a way to further protect this special payroll information. You decide to implement a special handling caveat to identify this information as "limited distribution." It can only be accessed and distributed within the HR payroll staff and you need technical controls to make sure that this is the case. The payroll staff is trusted by the business, with special clearances that further attest to their trustworthiness. Therefore, you decide to use the protective marking, CONFIDENTIAL PAYROLL, designating any information or systems with this classification must be protected to the level of CONFIDENTIAL, but only accessible to payroll staff.

BOXOUT ABOUT CODEWORDS AND CAVEATS

Some governments use special modifiers on their protective marking schemes to further define handling requirements or special distribution groups. These are often referred to as *code words* or *caveats*. Code words can be assigned to groups of similar information, related to a single topic, such as PAYROLL or OPERATION TOOTHBRUSH. Anyone involved in Operation Toothbrush would be allowed to see data with that code word associated with it, and the people, processes and technology within the organization that are not "read into" that code word, would not be allowed to see it. By "read in" I mean the business would indoctrinate the staff member into the purpose of the code words and as such tell them the rules of engagement. Once someone is read in, the attributes of the systems they use would permit them to see the documents associated with that code word.

Caveats are also handling designators, but operate on a slightly different demographic. Instead of being compartmentalized on the basis of something like an operation, it's limited by an attribute relate to the person, such as their nationality or seniority. You might see a government document labeled SECRET

NOFORN. As such, only people who have the clearance to read SECRET information would be allowed to see it; however, they also need to be US citizens (NOFORN means no one with another citizenship). It's possible for someone to be cleared to SECRET without citizenship, so this caveat would stop them from seeing this information. Similarly, if a piece of information is deemed CONFIDENTIAL, it may be visible to the HR team and the finance team, but if it needs to be limited to the executive then you might give it a caveat of EXEC ONLY. That way, the CEO's CONFIDENTIAL communications to his executive team would be labeled as CONFIDENTIAL EXEC ONLY.

When you implement a protective marking scheme, you need to decide how these documents will be labeled so you can explain that to the workforce. For example, you might decide that all documents need to be labeled in the header and footer and the protective marking needs to be written in capital letters and colored red. Emails need to designate the classification of the message body by putting the classification in the email subject line, such as the following:

```
Subject: CONFIDENTIAL EXEC ONLY Corporate Update on New Executive Hire
```

Once you start using these protective markings, you'll find that you may need technology to help you enforce it and apply it consistently. Furthermore, the metadata that is used to describe each kind of information must also be secured and its integrity assured. There are many companies that provide data labeling technology, where, for example, add-ins for Microsoft Office and email clients are used to add pre-defined labels (metadata) to all new information resources.

■ **Note**   One good example of the kinds of software you can use to label information is Boldon James' Classifier suite. Classifier can be used to build a policy-based classification solution that allows users to easily label documents, emails, photographs, notes, files, and folders. These labels can then be intercepted and read by special handling software to make sure that the information is only accessible by those members of staff that should see them. This is just one example of classification software and there are many others out there that do a similar job (see `http://www.boldonjames.com`).

The final point about running your pilot program is to make sure that you have well-defined objectives and scope since it's possible that projects like this can simply run on and on without your learning from them. Sometimes pilot projects end up as production systems, so you need to make sure that the implementation of technology, processes, and workflows with the target users are trialed for a period of time, and then removed again from their daily activities. This will do two things. Allow you first to hone the service for wider roll out and fix any issues you discover during the pilot, as well as providing an internal advocate of the solution, since removing it should make them concerned that they are once again less secure and less in control than they were when they introduced your system. Now it's time to move into strategic implementation.

Strategic Implementation

Your classification solution will undoubtedly be formulated from a combination of user training, processes, and technology that controls and enforces the rules around the labeling. Your security controls at each level of protective marking will be commensurate with the levels of protection (and therefore risk reduction) you are trying to achieve for anything marked with that label. It may be that, for example, you decide to implement specific controls at CONFIDENTIAL to ensure that only people who have been cleared to read that information can get it. To that end, you'll need ways of assuring this. You might have something inside your email system that reads the label of a communication and matches it against the directory service that profiles each of your users. That way, if someone isn't cleared, the email system prevents CONFIDENTIAL messages being sent to them. You might also decide that you unencrypted network means anyone monitoring traffic could read these CONDIFENTIAL communications. So, you decide to introduce end to end encryption to protect each message. These two controls will work together to enforce the underlying rules you have defined for CONFIDENTIAL information, based on your technical assessment of where the existing systems are weak.

Once your pilot implementation has finished, and you have learned from your mistakes through honing the program to meet the needs of the whole organization, it's time to roll it into your production environment. Information, networks and systems will then be evaluated against your newly published classification guidelines explaining why certain classifications have been selected for each individual information type and system asset. You will then design a security architecture that delivers the process and technology aspects of your controls appropriate to the underpinning classification, usually created from a security threat model (see Chapter 14).

Identification, Authentication, and Authorization

Three terms you will hear a lot about in information security are identification, authentication, and authorization. These three words are tightly coupled together to create an access control capability that identifies who the user is and grants them access only to information they are allowed to see. Identification and authentication work together to attest to a user being who they say they are, usually relying on a username and a password combination. Together these two functions constitute the standard "login" process users use to get onto their computers. Authorization is the next level of access control, where you access to specific resources will depend on a number of attributes, such as who you are, what levels of privileges you have and what groups you belong to.

From this description, you can see that this IAA process will work harmoniously with your classification scheme since you can start to see how you'd align group memberships and user attributes with access control decisions. If you are in the group called CONFIDENTIAL PAYROLL, then you get access to that data. If you're not in the group, you don't, even if you have access to the systems and the network.

Access Control Models

In computer systems, authorization is the term used when the system designates access rights to resources, such as users accessing certain folders or network file servers. Authorization means that the system will provide this access based on a predefined access policy, where the policy states that only HR employees are allowed to access the personnel records.

These access policies are implemented as access control rules, based on technical blueprints or standards defined within your organization, usually leveraging a number of different, yet integrated, technologies, such as your Active Directory, network access systems such as your VPN or Citrix remote desktop solution, along with authentication systems such as passwords and tokens or biometric authentication services.

There are a variety of different types of access control models in use today, however, for the sake of this book and its applicability to the relatively new information security manager, there are three most commonly used models that need discussion:

- **Discretionary access control (DAC):** This is where access to resources, such as files and network shares, is determined by the owner of the resource. You will find this is most commonly found in the systems we use at home and in the typical business office, such as the standard Access Control Lists (ACLs) used in Microsoft Windows.

- **Role-based access control (RBAC):** This model of access control relies on users being members of special groups that map to the access that role is allowed. The *attributes* of the group are used to define the *rights* of the role. This means that a user can be a member of many groups, therefore they have the responsibilities of multiple roles, which define the level of access they have to individual resources.

- **Mandatory access control (MAC):** With MAC, users are granted access to resources based on the classification of the asset and the clearance level of the user. This is mainly seen in a military or national security context, with very few systems technically capable of implementing this model.

The majority of access control models use a function known as a *reference monitor*. This controls access of a subject to an object, as shown in Figure 7-3.

Figure 7-3. *The reference monitor mediates access control decisions between subjects and objects*

Subjects are typically users or computer processes that request access to objects. Objects are files, directories, and/or system resources, such as memory and printers. An entity can be both a subject and an object, depending on whether it's being accessed, or it's the entity accessing the object. Access requests define the type of operation that attempting to be performed, such as whether it's a *read, write, update,* or *delete* request. Therefore, the reference monitor is the operating system's process that mediates all access requests related to object access, either permitting or denying the request to the subject.

The majority of modern operating systems use an *Access Control Matrix* to help conceptualize the reference monitor's operation and provide a simple explanation of the policy behind how access decisions are made. This concept has been built into both Microsoft Windows systems and Unix/Linux based systems (including Apple Mac OS X). The matrix shown in Table 7-1 shows how the rights a subject has to an object translate into an access control matrix.

Table 7-1. *Example Permissions Matrix*

	OS	Alice's Files	Bob's Files	Accounts DB
System	Read, Write, Execute	Read, Write, Execute	Read, Write, Execute	Read, Write, Execute
Alice	---	Read, Write, Execute	---	---
Bob	---	Read	Read, Write, Execute	---
App	---	---	---	Read, Write, Execute

In the example shown in Table 7-1, Alice has permission to access any objects she creates herself, with the comprehensive set of rights: *read, write,* and *execute.*

Her colleague, Bob, has a business requirement to read Alice's files; hence he is given the *read* permission. Bob also has *read, write,* and *execute* on his own files, but this is not reciprocated with Alice. Alice is given no access to Bob's files.

As you can also see from this example, two of the subjects are not real people. One of them is the *system* account while the other is an application, called an *app*. The system and the app accounts both have read, write, and execute rights to the accounts database, while neither of the two staff members have this level of access. In reality, this serves to limit access to the accounts database to only using the authorized interface, which uses the app account and to the system account, which could be compromised directly or indirectly and used to bypass the app and directly access the accounts DB.

System accounts are typically targeted by attackers for such purposes.

■ **Note**   Rights are also referred to as *permissions*. You will see these terms used interchangeably within the context of access control and file systems in operating systems.

In Microsoft Windows systems, access control is handled using *Access Control Lists* (ACLs). *Access Control Entries* (ACE), are then added to ACLs to establish the complete lists of accounts that can do something with the object.

An ACE is a structure that specifies a single set of permissions linked to a user or group in relation to a file or folder (or registry key, printer, etc.).

Linux and Unix systems have the concept of an *owner* and an *owning group*. For any given object, administrators specify the permissions that subjects have when accessing the objects. In the basic Unix model, permissions are *read, write*, and *execute*. Most Unix implementations support an extended version of this model, so in reality the entries look more complex, but the principles remain the same.

Microsoft's ACL model was introduced in Windows NT then subsequently enhanced in Vista and Windows Server 2003. Windows permissions are a lot more fine-grained than basic Unix permissions, which means that you can get quite creative but there is also room for mistakes. In Windows, for example, you can also specify a *deny* attribute, which prohibits a user or group from accessing a file or folder object. Windows also has a permission called *full control*, which allows subjects to do anything at all with the object. This is equivalent to *ownership* in Unix, with the exception that multiple users or processes can have this attribute.

The final piece of this permissions and access puzzle we'll look at here is called *role-based access control* (RBAC). This is a model that is frequently used by applications and middleware. The problem with ACLs relates to manageability—things get complex really fast, especially when you start limiting certain users or groups of users from access certain applications. The concept RBAC introduces to your access control model is that access in now based on the role the user assumes in the organization, where access to a resource is based on acting in the context of that role rather than the user's personal identity. As an example, an employee works as an accountant in the finance department. As a result she has access to financial records. If she leaves and a new starter takes over her role, that employee needs access to all of the same information. As such, the role of accountant is what dictates his access, not his personal identity.

RBAC is extremely powerful if implemented properly, but it does involve the organization understanding what it means in regards to how they operate and having tighter control over role changes, new hires, and exiting employees.

Implementing such a model can also be tricky. In Windows infrastructures, for example, it involves creation of active directory groups for every single role in the organization, and then users are placed in those groups to give them the permissions to do their job.

It's also possible that users can have more than one role. For example, a service desk user might also be an office first aider, so she will have two roles to perform. As a result, she is a member of the Service_Desk group and First_Aiders group.

NIST'S ROLE BASED ACCESS CONTROL MODEL

If you are new to the concept of RBAC you might think it seems relatively simple. However, as you start looking at implementing it, you see just how complex it quickly becomes, as well as how powerful it can be. NIST publishes one of the most comprehensive reference documents on RBAC, which covers a variety of implementation levels, each with increasing functionality, as shown in the following figure of The NIST Model for RBAC (Sandhu, Ferrailo, and Kuhn).

Level 1   Flat RBAC

- Users acquire permissions through roles
- Supports many-to-many user-role assignments
- Supports many-to-many permission-role assignments
- Supports user-role assignment reviews
- Users can use permissions of multiple roles simultaneously

Level 2   Heirarchical RBAC

- Flat RBAC+
- Must support role heirarchy (partial order)
- Level 2a requires support for arbitrary hierarchies
- Level 2b denotes support for limited hierarchies

Level 3   Constrained RBAC

- Hierarchical RBAC+
- Must be able to enforce separation of duties (SoD)
- Level 3a requires support for arbitrary hierarchies
- Level 3b denotes support for limited hierarchies

Level 4   Symmetric RBAC

- Constrained RBAC+
- Must support permission-role review with performance effectively comparable to user-role review
- Level 4a requires support for arbitrary hierarchies
- Level 4b denotes support for limited hierarchies

The most basic kind of implementation of an RBAC model would go something like this:

- A group of roles is defined and individual user accounts are created

- Users are assigned to the roles (remember, users can be assigned to one or more roles)

- Permissions, as they relate to roles, are defined and mapped onto all objects the role needs access to

- Permissions are then allocated to roles

- When the user logs in, she assumes the roles and permissions associated with her job

Roles structures don't need to be flat (as per figure). They can also be hierarchical or nested. Roles related to managers or executives can be allocated the same permissions as team members as well as additional roles of their own. Constraints can be added that restrict access, such as:

- **Static Separation of Duty** (SSD): manages conflicts of interest. This enforces constraints on roles. The classic example is a *Payments Clerk* not being allowed to perform the same duties as an *Accounts Receivable Clerk*.

- **Dynamic Separation of Duty** (DSD): places constraints on roles. DSD allows users to have two or more roles, but only in separate sessions. This prohibits users from having all of the permissions within the same session.

Cardinality is also discussed in NIST's standard. This allows you to define a finite number of roles a user can have in any given group of roles. A good example is defining that no user can be assigned more than three out of the four roles in purchasing equipment over a certain value.

System Privileges

As a function of both classification and ID&A, we've looked at the concept of an *originator.* This is the person or process responsible for creation of an object. In most models, originators have full control over an object, while third-party subjects are constrained to lesser levels of permission, such as having the READ ONLY attribute.

In technical parlance this is referred to as *object ownership,* as a component of the overall access control and authorization model. However, there is an additional consideration related to technical access to systems, known as *privilege* models that you need to know about.

Operating systems segregate access between users using *access control lists,* but they also limit access hierarchically, where certain users have more *privileges* to perform functions within the operating system. The most powerful accounts in a Unix system are known as *super users* and have what's known as *root access* to the operating system's most powerful functions. It's the *super user* (abbreviated to SU) that does things like change access permissions, shutdown and reboot systems, run scripts, compile executable code and install new software. User accounts can be created with lesser privileges to limit the power (and hence damage) they can do should their accounts be compromised, malware be installed in their session or they decide to do something malicious.

Security best practice is to use only the most privileged accounts to set the system up, before giving other users (both administrative users and standard users) specially defined accounts that have only the privileges needed to perform their duties. This restricts the damage a user can do if he tries experimenting with privileges they don't understand.

Microsoft's Windows (since Windows NT) uses *privileges* associated with users or the *system* account.

■ **Note** Privileges differ from access rights as they control the user's ability to manipulate system resources and perform special tasks, whereas access rights control access, when assigned to objects using ACLs restrict access to controlled resources (files, folders, and registry keys—in Windows, for example). As the information security manager, it's really important that you understand the difference between permissions and privileges as this is often confused even amongst the administration staff.

The administration accounts installed on both Windows and Unix systems by default are extremely powerful. Granting access to these accounts should be tightly controlled. It is common for privileged administrative accounts to have longer and more complex passwords.

It is also considered good practice that every user should operate using only the privileges necessary to complete the job; hence, any given subject should only have the privileges necessary to complete the given task. This is known as the *principle of least privilege.*

Just because an administrator can create/delete user accounts, they shouldn't automatically be allowed to create/delete user documents and other files. The principle of least privilege is a guideline for designing systems whereby you make sure that users have just the right level of privilege to do their job. Excess privileges will lead to having users or administrators who have more power than they need, which can lead to both accidental and malicious misuse of their levels of access. This is also a key issue in expanding the attack footprint (the number of systems that an attacker can access), since more accounts with administrative privileges or more privileges within existing accounts will give an attacker increased chances of success in gaining access to sensitive files.

Consider a disgruntled user, for example, who logs in using an administrator account rather than a user account (yes, this really does happen, especially in smaller businesses). If that user decides to delete some key corporate files, alter or steal the company's customer database, or take ownership of HR's personnel files, then that will be trivial as a domain administrator. If the user has basic user rights and no more, then they are limited on the damage they can cause. Of course, there is the question of who you should trust. How many administration staff do you physically have? While it's a good idea to segregate the duties of your privileged account holders as much as possible so that no one person can completely undermine your security controls, you will always be constrained by the number of people you have.

■ **Note**   One of the most widely publicized threats businesses face today is the so-called *insider attack*. The more privileges a user has, the more likely they will be able to undermine your security. Trust in staff needs to be earned and especially trust in administrators should be underpinned with continual monitoring and checking that they are trustworthy. Use background checks to reduce risk and conduct regular reviews with your administrative staff, including psychometric evaluations and financial audits, to ensure that they are not open to coercion, bribery, or corruption.

Clearly there are other means by which an insider might compromise your systems or information, such as through the poor implementation of controls, or a lack of proper patching, but for this chapter, we're considering insider threats from the point of view of permissions and privileges.

In some cases, organizations have been known to force privileged users to take mandatory holidays. During this period, someone else takes over their role and sees how the other administrator has been operating. This provides a valuable second pair of eyes on these most critical business functions to look for both malicious insiders and even complacency in following process.

Separation of Duties

We have already discussed rotating another member of staff into a privileged role so that they can check that the incumbent user is following the rules and not inadvertently (or maliciously) causing the business harm. There is a similar security principle known as *separation of duties* that can also be applied to further reduce the risk of any one member of staff having too much control or power within your organization.

Separation of duties is easiest explained using an example: imagine a team of administrators with different privileges all mapped to their individual accounts. When they log in, they get are attributed with the privileges by the operation system and they can then go about their business. One administrator can do some tasks, but not together, while his colleague can do different tasks but not the same tasks that the first administrator can. This has the effect of separating their duties from each other. However, the real power in separation of duties comes from making sure that where critical business functions occur, where the impact of compromise is high, no single user wields all the authority. For example, if you want to stop rogue administrators from creating new accounts within your active directory, build a workflow whereby the administrator cannot directly create accounts, instead they are provisioned though a trusted third-party application where it also requires the sign-off of a responsible manager prior to account creation. Another example, often cited in security texts, that explains the principle quite well is that of the accounts payable department in your company. No single user can authorize a payment to a third party, just in case they are feeling fraudulent on a particular day. Instead it requires at least two validated signatures within the finance team before it can be submitted to the bank. This way it significantly reduces the risk of corruption and would require multiple members of financial team to be colluding for an attack to be successful (a lot less likely).

▪ **Note**   To fully implement separation of duties across an organization adds a high level of administrative burden, especially to do it properly. This is by no means an easy task and can cause delays in critical systems recovery, especially during an incident or outage. It can work in military and government departments but for small or medium businesses, it should be considered with caution.

Separation of duties works on many levels, psychologically as well as technically. The fact that staff is being watched by the security team will make it harder for them to cover their tracks since they don't have access to your security information and event monitoring solution.

In the information security management world, it's considered best practice to separate the duties of system administrators from users, having both sets of people are monitored by a separate auditing team. Each group can be split up into subgroups, such as administrators for user accounts, administrators for servers, backup administrators, and network administrators. The user group might have power users who need more complex privileges, while office staff only uses email and office automation tools so they could be further limited in what they can do. The auditing team could be split into analysts and investigators, where the analysts monitor what's going on, while the investigators have more power to dig into the data and interrogate systems and people.

▪ **Tip**   Separation of duties is also sometimes referred to as *segregation of duties*.

Delegation of Privileges

Another principle in security management that often gets overlooked, unless organizations are progressive in their understanding of the risks related to their system administrators. Taking just Windows systems as an example, however this applies to all operating systems, administrators often have god-like rights over the operations of the computer system, allowing them to do practically anything they like, including reading information that users might have considered personal or private, or even classified.

The reality is that if you are a local or domain administrator on a Windows system or have the root account on a Unix system, there is little you cannot do. These accounts come as default when you install the operating system or the domain and as a result need to have the power to install software, configure system policy, take backups, and restore information, as well as access the file system, even when access control lists say they cannot. There is a function in Windows, for example, that allows administrators to override the basic access control set up by users, where they can *take ownership* of files and folders created by another user. This could be disastrous if, for example, those users have SECRET information that the administrator (read, Edward Snowden) should not access.

■ **Caution**   If you only have a small IT team it's harder to minimize the privileges you need for each of the administration roles. Taking the worst case scenario, you only have one IT guy, then she will need to be able to do everything the domain administration account would allow her to do—and there are no real limits. If this is the case, then you'll have to rely on auditing what she does, alerting when certain highly privileged functions are used, such as taking ownership of files or running a manual system backup. You can also use regular management interviews with her and background police checks to make sure that she's not become vulnerable to something that could see her leverage her position of power for her own malicious use.

How do we manage this? When we design the systems, start first by looking at who will be administering it and what duties they will be required to perform. If you have a large team of service desk technicians, second line and third line support and, potentially, a highly-skilled fourth line engineering team who do the design work, then you can immediately see that the service desk guys, who largely spend their time resetting passwords and unlocking accounts, don't need to ever have these domain administration rights. Start by creating them standard user account, and incrementally assign the rights they need to do their job, rather than starting with all your support staff having domain administration rights.

■ **Caution**   Clearly, If a user departs your organization on bad terms, and no one can access the business critical files/folders they created, then having an administrative level account who can take ownership of those files and then make them available for other users and management as appropriate, is a critical part of systems recovery and business continuity. So always have at least one account that you can use as a failsafe, even if all of your others are locked down.

EDWARD SNOWDEN

Edward Snowden was employed by the National Security Agency (NSA) as a computer systems consultant, with administrator-level privileges to the NSA's internal network. For whatever reason, and there is much speculation as to whether his story told publicly is the truth or was he simply an unknowing victim of espionage, he used the privileges he had to copy a massive number of highly sensitive, national security documents from their network and released it to the media, claiming it was in the public interest to see what the US government was up to. Snowden had the highest level of clearance and, as such, was trusted by the NSA to run their systems. He proved through this deception and leaking of TOP SECRET information that he was not trustworthy, irrespective of whether his motivations were altruistic or criminal.

Would delegation of administration have stopped this? Potentially it might have helped. If he had of had less rights to NSA systems, then he may not have been able to get the documents off their network. This would have slowed him down considerably as he would have needed to copy the documents off the screen, print them (which may be have been flagged) or somehow photograph them using a smartphone, which again may have been noticed. If he was designing systems, he didn't need production passwords. If he was administering production systems, he didn't need domain administrator rights for all his work—he could have been better controlled.

Finally, if all of this was entirely impossible to stop as he needed those rights for his work, then every time an administrator uses a "privilege function" should raise an alert to the security operations team, who should seek a change request or some kind of rationale why the work was being done. As it turned out, none of these controls were in place. Edward Snowden became disenfranchised with the US government for one reason or another and misused his position of trust to leak millions of documents. As a result, he seriously undermined the United States' national security capability and reputation and could well have jeopardized military and intelligence operations, putting countless lives at risk. Using delegation of administration coupled with comprehensive auditing and alerting, this could have been prevented.

CHAPTER 8

■ ■ ■

Protection of People

Often the most vulnerable aspect of your enterprise is not your technology systems, instead it's the weaknesses introduced by staff that are often the hardest to find yet the most harmful. Your staff might be simply unaware of what their security obligations are, or they might be complacent about security controls or internal procedures because they don't see their worth. This lack of awareness or complacency can leave staff susceptible to social engineering, which clever fraudsters will leverage to further their own ends. Furthermore, there is one more group of internal workforce threat actors you'll need to consider, although this is the group that most management types don't want to acknowledge the existence of: corrupt employees. These are the guys who hold a grudge against your company, or have some kind of personal vulnerability that can leave them open to attack. This kind of threat is categorized as the "insider threat." That's what the essence of this chapter focuses on: how the security manager can integrate mitigation strategies into the information security management systems to counteract some of these insider threats, while building a workforce culture that is aware of the threats and knows their obligations.

This chapter and the next both focus on the non-technical aspects of information security, where you will consider how you build trust in your employees, educate them and explain what the threats and vulnerabilities are that affect them directly when handling of corporate information.

Human Vulnerabilities

We've all seen how enterprises protect their network perimeters and information systems, using technology such as firewalls, content checkers, intrusion prevention systems, proxy servers and event management systems to detect, alert, and respond to attacks. Your end user computing platforms (workstations, laptops, and tablets) are protected with anti-malware software suites that are configured to audit and alert the security team when a threat or anomalous behavior is detected. Complimentary technical controls, such as application whitelisting will prevent users from running malware (either accidentally or maliciously) on your most vulnerable systems, while a sound approach to patching systems and applications will ensure that new vulnerabilities are not exploitable. You'll more than likely have a good backup solution that allows you to recover systems that have been corrupted, while your corporate access control systems will ensure that users can only get to the information they need, while delegating only the appropriate rights for administrators to prevent them from being your biggest threat. However, even with all of this technology and process-related security, there is one thing that is certain: your people will be the attackers' primary target. Humans really are the weakest link in every single reported incident, with publicized breaches having some common component of user mistake, malicious intent, or cavalier approach to corporate processes and procedures.

Unfortunately, every technical system, no matter how well you have designed its core security capabilities, is prone to exploitation if the people using it or managing it make mistakes. As an information security manager, you need to consider the workforce you are trying to secure as just another business asset that needs to be considered when you are building your protection mechanisms. People, like computer systems, have their own innate weaknesses (vulnerabilities) and are subject to threats and attacks just like anything else. However, there are a couple of added complications, unlike IT systems, people can make mistakes and pretend to be on your side, even when they are not.

© Tony Campbell 2016
T. Campbell, *Practical Information Security Management*, DOI 10.1007/978-1-4842-1685-9_8

Information security managers need to target the risk assessment lens on the user and administrator communities within the business, since the likelihood that information will go astray, even with the very best technology, is high. If your executives are careless enough to leave documents on the train, follow the links in dodgy phishing emails, or blindly follow the instructions from the spoofed CFO email address, then information will be compromised, systems will be infected and money will be lost. Information security managers need to be considering special controls within the information security management system to help build a culture of security within the business. We've previously discussed security awareness training in Chapter 4, where we looked at some of the ways it's possible to engender a level of awareness of the threats the workforce faces every day. However, security awareness training is just one of the controls you'll need to develop, since this won't address attacks from malicious insiders who don't care about your rules or best practice.

WHALING: BUSINESS EMAIL COMPROMISES

In early 2016, the FBI reported that *business email compromise* was one of the most rapidly escalating global scams, costing billions of dollars all over the world. Hardly surprising, given the low-risk, high-reward nature of this kind of crime. This kind of attack has been dubbed whaling by the security community to align with the other two kinds of email attack: phishing and spear-phishing. Just in case you don't know, phishing is where tens of thousands of email are sent in an attempt to lure a few careless users to click a link to download some malware or open a malicious attachment. Spear-phishing takes this one step further in its effectiveness, since instead of casting the net wide and hoping to get a few bites, the attacker targets specific individuals with more targeted messaging, such as using real names and information gleaned from social networks or other open source repositories to make the phishing attempt more believable. Whaling takes the concept of spear-phishing one step further as the attacker is after the "big fish" which will yield the biggest bounty for landing it. In most organizations, those big fish are the CEO, CFO and anyone with financial responsibility who has the ability to authorize payments of large invoices.

The FBI's statistics of over US$2.3 billion being purloined since October 2013 through to February 2016 were collected from around 17,000 individual businesses that had been successfully targeted by attackers. This sample ranges from businesses reported approximately 80 countries, but since many cybercrimes go unreported, the issue is probably a lot worse.

Whaling Attacks

Whaling Attacks are normally conducted against the most senior people in an organization. The concept of business email compromise has become a primary method of attack for whaling purposes, where the attacker uses specific, legitimate data collected on their target to craft a social engineering attack that is entirely believable. The attacker will spend a lot of time before the attack conducting research into the target company's employees, creating profiles of the employees who are responsible for the company's financial management. The attacker will learn the context of their roles, learn the kind of special language used in the business, and even run tests against the targets in other companies to see if they work.

Next, the attacker requests a wire transfer using a very specific dollar amount, usually related to products or services the company consumes from partners or suppliers. For all intents and purposes, this looks entirely legitimate and feasible to the unsuspecting target. The victim then receives an email from someone else in the business, such as the CEO requesting they pay their supplier for an order of hardware or provision of a service. Since this is so normal, the victim won't suspect anything until they review their inventory and realize they've been duped. By this stage their money has been transferred offshore and is being laundered through layers of organized criminal fences meaning recovery will be neigh on impossible.

Protection Mechanisms

There are a few ways businesses can protect themselves from this kind of attack. Starting with staff education, the nature of this attack should be regularly communicated to all potentially vulnerable staff to be on the lookout and question anything that's out of the ordinary. Security awareness training (as discussed time and time again in this book) is the best control you can put use develop a security culture in your business.

As the information security manager, it's your job to be advising the finance department and CFO on how they can bolster the processes they use for payment of bills. Look at the workflows used to pay creditors and make sure that there are secondary authentication and verification checks built into them. For example, a simple phone call to the company on the email to verify their bank details would be a good start. You could also implement a system for registering payees on your financial system so that only fully authenticated accounts can be paid.

Social Engineering

The term *social engineering* is used to describe the actions undertaken by a hacker who uses the same sort of tricks a confidence trickster (conman) might use to discover information about their target. Quite often, the social engineer will assume a pretext, which is a false identity that they will use to blag their way into your organization.

Simply by asking the right questions, maybe pretending to be one of your company's senior managers, or potentially someone in great need (such as someone with a medical emergency or someone late for an important meeting), the social engineer will convince the end user to give up some vital information that can help him gain access to your systems.

It's largely irrelevant what information social engineers are targeting, since it's the general vulnerability of staff that is the weakness and it could be anything in your business that the attacker considers worthwhile. In the same way that we recommend patching vulnerabilities where fixes are available, there are things you can do immediately that should help protect your people against the threat of social engineering.

You might be wondering why criminals would choose such a bold method to attack your business, especially when it's much easier and stealthier to attack from afar over the Internet. The answer is simple: social engineering, to those who are good at it, is so much easier to use to attack a target than a complex technical attack, especially since human nature is to instinctively trust strangers, especially those in need. For example, a social engineer might fool someone into giving over their password by saying they were from the "internal security team" or your bank's security team, since those are people you should innately trust. This is much easier than having to run special software to try and hacking their password (unless, of course, their password is weak).

When we look at teaching people to be aware of social engineering and it's underpinning methodology, we need to explain to people exactly how they are vulnerable, ensuring the workforce knows who they should be trusting and what they should and should not expect third-parties to be asking for—if they know that your helpdesk will never ask for a password over the telephone, then any sort of request like this can be considered an attack and the target would should inform the security team immediately. This way, you are programing your workforce to react defensively, which will both protect the individual but also serve as an early warning system for your business if the incident is reported.

■ **Tip**   Educating employees on how social engineers operate is something that should be built into your security awareness program. This could be delivered in the form of an online course or possible scenario-based classroom training where they will learn when to take third-parties at their word and when they should be reporting them to the security team. Teaching staff the difference between being trusted and trustworthy will help them see the difference, which is important when it comes to them making decisions as to what information should be divulged, over what medium (telephone, SMS, email, website) and to whom.

Teaching staff about social engineering during the annual security awareness review is certainly worthwhile. However, to make the messages from the training sticky with your staff, I would also recommend conduct drills of your own throughout the year as well, where you can potentially catch busy employees off guard. This is not to be confused with a so-called witch hunt, where you are seeking to name and shame employees who don't follow the rules, instead this is to be considered a learning exercise as a component of your security awareness program, where being caught out will be the wakeup call employees need to make the security lessons stick.

Common Attacks

Social engineering attacks are by far the most difficult attacks to protect your staff against, simply because your technical security countermeasures can't usually detect the threat. You'll need to find a way to explain to staff that they are actually being targeted and that the attackers are continually plotting how best try to dupe them. Let's look at a couple of good examples of the most common social engineering attacks.

Stealing Passwords

The attacker's primary goal (aside from getting money or access to your information) is to somehow own your systems. The easiest way to do this is to get hold of your username and password. Social engineers known that if they ask you for your password in a certain way, there is a high likelihood that you will simply hand it over. No way, you say, you'd never fall for it, but it happens and you need to remain vigilant and cognizant that people are not always who they say they are. Pretexting as a senior manager, system administrator or someone from your bank is a simple way to try and win your confidence. All they need to do is sound credible and use psychological techniques to make you believe you are talking to the person the purport to be. If they telephone you can claim they are from the bank, they may use your full name and date of birth to show they have prior knowledge about you. They might reinforce that with a statement of what you do for a living (cybersecurity dude) and even a couple of transactions from you last bank statement. This would effectively ID them as legitimately from the bank. However, you may have thrown away a few receipts from the coffee shop in a public bin, which started the attack. That way they know where you relax with your friends. It doesn't take a lot of effort to find out your name and a little bit about you. Next they hop on Facebook and LinkedIn to grab your profession and date of birth. Next they call you, however, they use all this information to ID themselves as your bank, hence putting you in a situation where you can either trust this person who seemingly knows who you are and has seen your bank activity—so they must be from the bank, right? Scary, isn't it, just how easy this is.

Email Attacks

If your email gets hacked, it's so easy for a criminal to pose as you and request any number of service escalations from that account. What I mean by that is, say you use Facebook and have this email address as your recovery address. All the criminal needs to do is click "forgot my password" on the website and send a reset to your email account. As long as he intercepts that email before you log in and see it (routing it somewhere else) he'll use the reset link and change your Facebook account.

Once he's locked you out, he can now pretext as you and launch a further attack on people you are connected to. This way you become either the final target or just an intermediary on the way to the final prize—that old school buddy of yours who happens to be a bank manager or pharmacist. Once the hacker has control of your email account, they'll have full access to all your contacts, calendar appointments, and all the emails you have left in your inbox.

This is one way that your account can be misused by an attacker, however, there are others. What if you hijacked email address is used as a springboard for a wider phishing campaign? Suddenly, you are now under suspicion as the guy who is behind the latest ransomware campaign hitting your network of friends and colleagues. No one wants to be that guy....

Further to this attack, you'll also need to consider the susceptibility of other messaging media, such as SMS, instant messaging platforms, like Skype and Facebook Messenger, and even faxing. They can all be duped.

Baiting

The premise here is that if you dangle a big enough carrot in front of the horse it will take the bait. Criminals will use a variety of clever incentives, such as a pre-release copy of a hot novel or movie, or maybe an unreleased album from a popular band, to convince the mark that they need to download the file. Nowadays these kinds of attack are not limited to email attacks or BitTorrent sites, they are also found through syndicated ad networks showing up on legitimate websites.

The old adage "if something is too good to be true, then it probably is," is accurate in regard to baiting attacks. If there is little way you can attest to the authenticity of the claims being made on a website, then don't trust it. It's as simple as that. It more than likely is malicious, and at best you are breaking the law, since most of these carrots are illegal pirate copies of copyrighted material.

Taking the bait will only serve to see you infected with malware, viruses, or worse, ransomware—where your systems will effectively be held at ransom unless you pay the fine you lose everything

Engendering Doubt and Distrust

Some of the best social engineering attacks focus on creating conflict and pitting multiple marks against each other. The attacker might use a technical attack (or some other kind of social engineering attack) to take over your Gmail account, and then build malicious emails that are sent from your account to their target. This could contain a phishing email, where they have tried to capture the target's systems too, but may be simply for fun, where they are trying to undermine and embarrass you.

An extension of this kind of attack is where the attacker pretends to be from the helpdesk of the compromised systems and asks for credential to log in and clear out the threat. Unwittingly, you are now giving additional credentials to the attacker, who can then either use them himself for further attacks or sell them to third-party hacking groups.

KEVIN MITNICK

One of the most notorious social engineering aficionados of the last century is Kevin Mitnick. He is infamous for being on the FBI's Most Wanted list for hacking into 40 major corporations—for nothing but the sheer hell of it. He is now the CEO of his own penetration testing company, Mitnick Security Consulting, LLC, where his team of security testers has the reputation of never failing to hack into their targets—of which many of the Fortune 500 companies have fallen victim.

Mitnick started young. His hacking escapades began at the age of 13, when he used social engineering to obtain a ticket punch for the Los Angeles bus company, claiming he needed it for a school project, which he then proceeded to use to travel free of charge. You can read more about Mitnick's early years on the Register's excellent series of articles at http://www.theregister.co.uk/2003/01/13/ chapter_one_kevin_mitnicks_story/.

In 1995, after a two-and-a-half-year manhunt, the Federal Bureau of Investigation finally caught him in North Carolina. His trial lasted four and a half years, resulting in a sentencing in 1999 of 46 months in prison, with an additional 22 months for not sticking to the agreement of his supervised release for his previous conviction of computer fraud back in 1989.

After getting out of jail in early 2000, Mitnick was prohibited from discussing any aspect of his personal story, but used his time to start working for the good guys, setting up Mitnick Security Consulting and authoring a couple of bestselling books on social engineering and hacking, called *The Art of Deception* (Wiley, 2003) and *The Art of Intrusion* (Wiley, 2005). Both of these are well worth reading. Eventually in 2011, after waiting the requested seven years, Mitnick published his life story in his bestselling book, *Ghost in the Wires* (Back Bay Books, 2012).

Details of all of Mitnick's books can be found at https://www.mitnicksecurity.com/shopping/ books-by-kevin-mitnick.

Building a Security Culture

A security culture is one where every member of staff actively participates in making sure the organization remains as secure as possible. This includes every member of the workforce, from the administration staff to the cleaners, all the way up to the CEO, including all contractors, partners, and even suppliers.

■ **Tip**   Consider drafting an operating agreement between your company and your suppliers that dictates what information security processes you expect them to adhere to. If they want to do business with you, they'll soon figure out that it's worth confirming.

Information security awareness programs can be procured from third-party specialist security training vendors, where they will provide the basis of the education and awareness campaign you provide to your staff. Clearly, you'll still need to design this yourself, to ensure that it meets your own particular organizational needs, however, having generic training material that can be customized to contain the details of your own policies, procedures, and requirements will shortcut what can often be a costly program to adopt.

Security awareness training will teach employees how items such as passwords and remote access token should be managed, what the corporate acceptable use policies require of employees, and how to identify and report security incidents. If you manage sensitive information, the security awareness training should also explain to staff how to handle this information, including how it's managed when emailed or printed out.

When new joiners enter your organization, the security training and indoctrination should be part of the induction process. This ensures that as soon as they are on board, the security awareness indoctrination begins. Metrics and feedback from the students should be recorded as part of the corporate record, and against each individual, so that at any point in time the organization will know what position it is in, in terms of security training. The frequency of this training should be determined depending on the levels of security required, as part of the overall corporate security policy, but in most cases where security has become part of the corporate culture, a yearly retake of awareness training is not uncommon.

Negligent Staff

Hackers know that we all have certain weaknesses that may make certain people susceptible to social engineering attacks. This is why the majority of phishing campaigns, which use spam email as their attack vector, come in waves. At tax time, for example, phishing emails will be cast as if they are from the Internal Revenue Service, while at election time they may look like political rhetoric.

In fact, without the initial attack being successful, where the computer user clicks on a dodgy link or opens an unsolicited attachment, the rest of the attack (the sophisticated payload) would be much harder, if not impossible, to get onto their systems. Spammers are setting up multiple campaigns, all over the world, where each campaign is tailored to a specific theme for that country or state. Furthermore, there are a number of persistent themes that the spammers use in their phishing campaigns, such as the scaremongering emails that claim to be from the police, suggesting you've been caught speeding and you need to urgently "click here" to ensure that you don't end up in court. With hundreds of thousands of these emails being sent every single day from botnets, it's little wonder that they are successful. Take a look at Figure 8-1. This is a recent email I received from what's purporting to be Tesco, a UK-based grocery store, that suggests I could win a gift card. Looking at the link (shown in the picture), you can see that it's nothing to do with Tesco.

■ **Caution**   Unfortunately, legitimate newsletter emails often use hyperlinks that contain third-party providers' addresses, especially if they outsource their email marketing services to another company. This means that some legitimate newsletters and marketing collateral from companies you are interested in may be misrepresented at spam by your technology and visual inspection.

Figure 8-1. *Phishing email purporting to be from UK retailer, Tesco*

A simple check of the URL in VirusTotal (`https://www.virustotal.com`) shows the link as a confirmed phishing site by Fortinet, shown here in Figure 8-2.

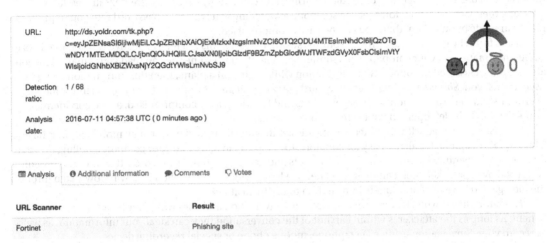

URL: http://ds.yoldr.com/tk.php?
c=eyJpZENsaSI6IjIwMjEiLCJpZENhbXAiOjExMzkxNzgsImNvZCI6OTQ2ODU4MTEsImNhdCI6IjQzOTg
wNDY1MTExMDQiLCJjbnQiOiOiJHQlliLCJsaXN0IjoibGlzdF9BZmZpbGlodWJfTWFzdGVyX0FsbCIsImVtY
WlsIjoidGNhhbXBiZWxsZWxsc2NpY2NidGWlsLmNvbSJ9

Detection 1 / 68
ratio:

Analysis 2016-07-11 04:57:38 UTC (0 minutes ago)
date:

■ Analysis ❶ Additional information 💬 Comments 🗳 Votes

URL Scanner	Result
Fortinet	Phishing site

Figure 8-2. VirusTotal identifies the target site as a phishing site

Addressing the issue is somewhat complicated since it takes a lot of retraining of people's behavior to remember not to simply click on anything that drops into the inbox. Oftentimes the only sure fire way of teaching people that this is a bad habit that needs to be broken is for them to suffer the pain of being compromised. However, there is one thing you can consider running in your organization that will ensure that some of your more susceptible staffers begin to see the error of their ways. In its simplest form, run a cybersecurity fire drill.

Cyber Drills

Many companies have started running cybersecurity drills. In the same way that safety teams regularly run fire drills to test evacuation of the building, this makes sure people know where the exits are, what the procedures for evacuation are and to make sure that the staff in charge in the emergency situation know what to do. Information security managers have started performing similar trials, where targeted phishing campaigns against your business are crafted, where you are the party behind the spam emails being sent.

There are a variety of software tools on the market that you can use to test your workforce's preparedness for a cyberattack. One such tool is the acclaimed, open source, Social Engineer Toolkit (SET). The SET is included in the penetration testing Linux distro called Kali Linux (available from https://www.kali.org) or directly from the authors at http://www.social-engineer.org/framework/se-tools/computer-based/social-engineer-toolkit-set/.

It is designed to allow security managers to craft a variety of advanced social engineering based attacks against your workforce, and is recognized as a standard tool within the penetration testing world.

■ **Note** SET was written by David Kennedy, with a lot of help from the open source community. Unlike many other testing tools, it relies on the social engineering aspect of the attack to ensure that the attack is successful, making this aspect of the testing much easier for pen testers who are not used to incorporating social engineering into their testing methodology. SET comes with a variety of attacks that are designed specifically to target individuals or organizations.

Shoulder Surfing and Eavesdropping

Attackers can use simple methods of shoulder surfing and eavesdropping to be extremely successful in attacking their victims. If you don't realize someone is watching you type your password into your laptop, maybe in a café or on a train, then you can be easily compromised.

Aside from the obvious capturing of your password, however, this is a really effective way for attackers to gather information on your company's personnel and operations. If someone can read your email while you are accessing classified or confidential information while sitting on a plane, then this information could be used against you. *Shoulder surfing* refers to a third party that steals information from you by simply looking over your shoulder. Information such as passwords and PINs are easily compromised, as are confidential forms that might be left open on your screen while you take a call.

The risks associated with shoulder surfing are significantly increased now that all mobile phones have a high-quality camera. It's all too easy for someone to video you logging into your computer, pulling up your email system, opening documents and spreadsheets and accessing company records. If your entire session is videoed by an attacker, then can refer to it later in a less obvious setting, when they will slowly step through the footage and have all that valuable information to use in an attack.

Eavesdropping is when someone listens to your conversation and uses what they hear for their own benefit. As long as the attacker is within earshot of the conversation they can steal your information, as well as record your conversation using a Dictaphone, mobile phone or special recording device.

Codes of Conduct

Codes of conduct are useful in assigning behavioral responsibilities to your staff members, contractors, temporary staff and subcontractors. The code of conduct describes many aspects of behavior, but for the purposes of information security management, you need to understand that it covers individual behavior that might compromise the confidentiality, integrity, and availability of company systems or information.

A typical code of conduct document might take the form of a simple list of statements that tell the employee not to openly discuss customer contact information outside the office. It also might include personal safety and integrity concerns, such as those connected with illegal drug use or the excessive consumption of alcohol. These are, after all, human vulnerabilities that could be targeted by an attacker at a later date, so they are weaknesses that you need to try and remove from the workforce if it all possible.

■ **Tip**　Activities that might lead to a staff member becoming a target for blackmail or coercion should be covered in your staff code of conduct document.

A variety of conduct-related matters are important in government departments where they may be acceptable in private industry. For example, corporate hospitality, gifts and improper customer relationships could lead to unwanted allegations of bribery and corruption. In a government setting this is extremely compromising and difficult to address, however, it's worth addressing this even in the private sector since these kinds of reputational damage, once surfaced and covered in the media, will certainly affect your ability to sign new large-scale customer up, at least in the short term.

Acceptable Use Policies

In support of your code of conduct document, you'll also want to draft an *Acceptable Use Policy*. These are directives for employees on how the business expects them to use corporate resources, such as the Internet and email.

Ask yourself, when should members of staff be allowed to access the Internet for private matters? Is it acceptable that they can access Gmail, for example, during their lunch break, to check their private messages? Gmail can pose a threat to your internal systems since it is highly likely to contain malicious attachments, so with an SSL protected session within a browser connecting through your company's perimeter defenses, there is a chance that this attack vector could see malware creeping through your DMZ unhindered via the web browser.

Maybe you have decided to allow employees the right to send personal email from their corporate account. If this is the case, what guidelines have you created to let employees know how often they are allowed to use corporate resources and at what times of the day is it permitted. The same question could be asked about sending joke emails to colleagues. Do you allow this or ban it? Will you be tolerant of this kind of activity to a certain degree and, if so, what level of usage is deemed acceptable?

All of these parameters should be analyzed and discussed with team leaders, HR advisors, as well as the C-suite management before enforcement, since their actions are equally under the same policy as lower level employees. Try to strike a balance between security and trusting your staff, since overdoing this kind of enforcement can be seen as authoritarian and causes more problems than it is worth. To exemplify this, it may be better to allow unlimited access to the Internet and trust your staff to get their job done, only blocking sites that are illicit or obviously unnecessary gratuitous, or where browsing these sites even accidentally could be illegal.

■ **Note**   One aspects of an Acceptable Use Policy you should always consider with the HR team is how you will consistently deal with a breach. If an employee attempts to bypass the security controls within your environment, for example, a measured and appropriate response is essential, as long as it's repeatable and applied to all employees equally.

It might be in the company's best interest to allow staff to access their bank accounts and sort out their weekly shopping, rather than having them rushing home to get to the supermarket. A compromise can usually be struck between good sense and being overly cautious. Again, like all aspects of employee behavior, letting them know what is expected of them is the best place to start. Only consider enforcing restrictive policies if they repeatedly breach your trust.

Every aspect of an acceptable use policy should be explained in detail and you make sure that all employees have the opportunity to acknowledge they have read it and understood it.

Employment Contracts

A contract of employment is a useful document that can be used by the information security manager to enforce aspects of the acceptable use policies and explain the obligations if staff with regard to conduct. The employment contract creates a legal relationship between the employee and the employer, ensuring that all parties are clear about mutual obligations.

As an information security manager, you should ask to review employee contracts, looking for security responsibilities to be documented in enough detail to make sure that there is no ambiguity and is something were to be contested in a tribunal or court of law, the legal connotations will stand up to scrutiny. You should take these kinds of contract to special employment lawyers and request they are reviewed against a number of potential scenarios:

- What happens if an employee purposely leaks sensitive information to a third party?

- What happens if an employee is caught misusing the company's IT systems (could be for pornography, gambling, or simply overusing social media)?

- What happens if an employee tries to hack the internal network?

- What are the obligations of the employee to keep their login details private? What happens if they breach this rule?

Your legal council should be able to help you craft a contract of employment that is good enough to cover all eventualities of misuse without being too specific. Try and include specific tasks for individuals in the terms and conditions for a particular role, which would be attached to the employment contract and referenced, without each contract being different.

Employment contracts should be written to be as specific as possible about what is expected from the employee in terms of behavior and conduct, but still have enough flexibility to be used in any other circumstance not directly referenced. Again, seek legal advice as to the best way to achieve this result.

Specific statements should explain to the employee what behavior will not be tolerated under any circumstances (use of company ICT for illegal activities) from the company's viewpoint. This can also include aspects of the employee's life outside of the company, such as use of illicit drugs. These kinds of Issues can lead to staff vulnerabilities that could see them targeted by an attacked and the vulnerability used as leverage. Issues relating to your company's intellectual property should also be covered, so that if stolen information ends up in the hands of your competitor or a foreign government (in the case of government workers) the contract can be used to explain mutual responsibilities during a tribunal.

All aspects of acceptable use for systems and knowledge picked up on the job should be referred to as the company's property.

Lastly, make sure that each page of the employment contract is signed by the employee to ensure that there can be no case of non-repudiation, where the employee claims ignorance of a contractual clause.

For boilerplate contracts that can be used in the event of you not having one, check out http://www.uslegalforms.com.

Personnel Security Life Cycle

The employment life cycle starts a while before any new employee comes on board, during the recruitment process. Your human resources (HR) team will undoubtedly have a methodology that they follow, something like the simplistic life cycle model shown in Figure 8-3.

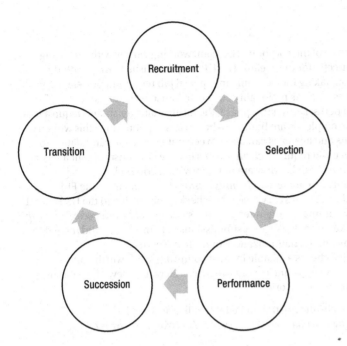

Figure 8-3. *The standard employment life cycle model used by human resources teams*

Each of these stages has its own set of security requirements and protocols that can be used to ensure that staff are who they who they say they are, that they have no criminal convictions that would discredit them and that they are trustworthy.

The rest of this chapter looks at this employment life cycle, including pre-employment checks, security vetting and through life assurance measures that employers can take to ensure that employees remain trustworthy.

Recruitment

The recruitment process is usually the purview of the corporate HR team, working closely with the hiring manager who requires the additional resource(s) for their team. The HR team will usually work with the hiring manager to create the role description, taking into account any special job requirements relating to skills, competencies, personal circumstances (such as nationality, locale or "must be willing to relocate") along with salary bands, titles, benefits and perks. During this phase, the hiring manager should request that any special security-related attributes of the employee are built into the job description, since this will serve as the first filter that recruitment consultants and agencies can use to weed out unsuitable candidates. You could, for instance, specify that the employee will require a clean driver's license and must present a recent police certificate that can attest to their identity and that they are not a convicted criminal.

In the United States, for example, citizens can request an *Identity History Summary* from the FBI (https://www.fbi.gov/about-us/cjis/identity-history-summary-checks). According to the US Federal Bureau of Investigation, an Identity History Summary—often referred to as a *criminal history record* or a *rap sheet*—is "a listing of certain information taken from fingerprint submissions kept by the FBI and related to arrests and, in some instances, federal employment, naturalization, or military service."

There are similar kinds of national police checks available in most countries, so it's worthwhile to include this as a standard requirement in every single one of your prospects. Here are a few of the national authorities for these kinds of checks from around the world:

- **Australia**. Checks are carried out by the Australian Federal Police and can be ordered at https://www.afp.gov.au/what-we-do/services/criminal-records/national-police-checks.

- **Canada**. The Royal Canadian Mounted Police can issue a Criminal Record and Vulnerable Sector check at http://www.rcmp-grc.gc.ca/en/criminal-record-and-vulnerable-sector-checks.

- **France**. The Ministère de la Justice is the French authority for national police checks. Their website is available at https://www.cjn.justice.gouv.fr/cjn/b3/EJE20c.

- **Hong Kong**. The Hong Kong Police Force is the authority for police checks in Hong Kong. They can be contacted at http://www.police.gov.hk/ppp_en/.

- **New Zealand**. The New Zealand Police are responsible for issuing police certificates and conducting criminal records checks. Their website is at http://www.police.govt.nz/faq/how-do-i-get-a-police-clearance-certificate.

- **United Kingdom**. The National Police Chief's Council is responsible for UK criminal records checks, which are issued via the website at https://www.acro.police.uk/police_certificates.aspx.

Clearly, there are equivalent organizations in every country that can carry out these kinds of checks, so it's a very easy request to make, no matter what the nationality of the individual is, that they obtain such a check.

For a full inventory of all of the countries that have this capability, there is a great resource on the Government of Canada's website at http://www.cic.gc.ca/english/information/security/police-cert/index.asp.

Selection

The selection process follows on from recruitment, where you weed out the candidates you are not interested in and begin interviewing the ones that, at least on paper, passed all the initial checks and balances.

The interview is an important step in selecting the right employee for the role. This is where you have the ability to test that what's written in the resume is accurate and find out exactly what role the interviewee played in some of the projects they stated they were involved in. From an information security management point of view, you should try and have some standard questions included in the interview that try to find out whether the employee has integrity. The following questions make for useful indicators as to whether the interviewee would make a good and honest employee:

- Can you tell us about a situation that saw you speak up for your beliefs over something you were expected to do, even if it was an unpopular decision?

- Can you tell us about a time when you made a critical mistake at work and admitted it to your manager?

- Describe a situation that made you uncomfortable in work and how did you resolve it?

- What aspects of your personality engender trust in your coworkers?

- Has your integrity ever been challenged and, if so, how did you deal with it?

- Describe a situation when you escalated something to management about a coworker.

The majority of these situations will have occurred at some time or another throughout most people's careers. If the prospective employee is a mature employee, they will have war stories that align with most of these questions. Listen carefully to how they are answered and use gut instinct and judgment to determine if the candidate is lying or embellishing the truth. If you have the ability to check references, speak to the referee about these answers if you can, as long as you have permission of the candidate. Personality testing and psychometric testing can be used to categorize people into certain groups, where you can then determine if that personality type is suitable for the role. If it's a high-stress, incident management role, then a passive personality may not be the best fit for the role, no matter how well they interviewed and how knowledgeable they were. The most famous personality profiling methodology is known as the Myers-Briggs Type Indicator, which can be researched further on the official website at `http://www.myersbriggs.org/my-mbti-personality-type/mbti-basics/`.

Once you have decided that a candidate is fit for the role, you should conduct all the background checks and request that the candidate obtain a criminal records check to make sure that they are who they say they are (they should already know this is a condition of employment from the job specification). If all of these check out and everything looks fine, you can proceed to the offer of employment, which includes a contract detailing all of the special information security, conduct and intellectual property clauses we discussed earlier.

Security Vetting

For some government jobs, especially in the federal government (in most countries), some level of security clearance will be required. This is a deeper check into a candidate's personal circumstances, used to determine vulnerabilities and risks that may be related to employing this particular person. For example, the Australian g Security Vetting Agency (AGSVA) is the central Australian office responsible for processing and granting security clearances for Australian government agencies, as well as many of the individual state and territory agencies. Suitability to hold a clearance is determined through a variety of assessments and checks into the background and individual circumstances of the candidate. Security clearances are also linked to the protective marking of the information or the systems an agency manage, and are graded in terms of increasing levels of depth into the candidate's life. Sticking with the Australian example, security checks are undertaken to ensure that people who are entrusted with access to classified government data are eligible, suitable and can be trusted to access them. The following are the levels of clearance available for government employees in Australia:

- Baseline clearance

- Negative Vetting 1 (NV1)

- Negative Vetting 2 (NV2)

- Positive Vetting (PV)

The difference in the process between each of the levels is determined by the level of trustworthiness that the agency requires in the individual. For example, a government worker that only handles unclassified information, who has no access to information with national security implications, may well only require a baseline clearance. Whereas, someone with regular and frequent access to TOP SECRET military intelligence would be significantly more at risk, therefore the positive vetting would be appropriate. The higher the level of clearance, the more invasive and probing the process will be. For example, moving from baseline clearance to negative vetting 1 requires a full exposure of financial matters, whereas moving from NV1 to NV2 also includes a lengthy recorded interview by a trained interrogator. Positive vetting is even deeper, but we'll leave the details of that process to your imagination.

The final point to mention about vetting is that it's not a one-off process. The initial process provides a baseline of the individual's situation at a point in time. Once clearance has been granted, there are a variety of terms and conditions, along with responsibilities and actions, that need to be adhered to. In most NATO countries where clearances are transferrable (or at least comparable), this post-clearance process is known as *aftercare*. If any of the circumstances of their clearance change they have a duty of care to the clearance authority to report these, allowing the authority to weigh up the risks and decide if clearance can still be held.

Finally, government security clearances expire. This means that the entire process should be repeated at regular intervals, usually determined by the level of clearance the candidate holds.

■ **Note** In the United States, the Office of Personnel Management (OPM) is responsible for security clearances. In 2015, the FBI reported that the OPM's internal systems had been hacked and alleged that the Chinese government had purloined the entire database of clearance details. This means that every single employee of the United States government, then and prior, have had this most sensitive information stolen by a foreign government. Read more about this hack here: https://www.washingtonpost.com/world/national-security/chinese-government-has-arrested-hackers-suspected-of-breaching-opm-database/2015/12/02/0295b918-990c-11e5-8917-653b65c809eb_story.html

---

Performance and Succession

The performance stage of the employment life cycle starts on the first day that the employee takes up office. The security background checks have all come back, the clearance has been granted and all the psychometric and personality tests have come back positive. From here, the information security manager's job is to refocus to monitoring this new employee alongside all of the other employees. There are three aspects of monitoring that should be considered:

- Monitoring for careless, sloppy security practices

- Monitoring for malicious intent

- Monitoring for changes in behavior

First, careless employees will undoubtedly be the most prevalent security risk you face. It's so easy to forget to follow a security process when someone is under pressure from their management to deliver an outcome, so corners are cut. This can lead to security vulnerabilities being exploited by external attackers, such as from the threat of phishing emails and ransomware. Education is the key to fixing this problem, as I said countless times throughout this book. Make sure that you have a security awareness program that regularly reminds staff of their security obligations and tells them what the threats are. Also, if you have a security operations center (more on this later in the book), have them monitor new staff to see what they are up to. Maybe heighten the level of monitoring for the duration of their probation period, just to make sure that they are following process, but don't use this as a means to reprimand them immediately, use it as a tool to educate them, so they know you are watching. As soon as the employee realizes he can't break the rules without being caught, he'll think twice about cutting corners in the future.

Malicious insiders are somewhat harder to identify. This is where a software system comes in useful. You should draft scenarios of how you think a malicious insider might operate, then configure your software systems to detect this. Also, baselining expected behavior is a good way of determining if people are acting in a peculiar way, so that if they deviate from that baseline you can investigate.

■ **Tip** Behavioral indicators are by far the best way to determine how likely someone is to cause a security incident. However, there is often too much data to be able to do this kind of monitoring manually for every employee. You should consider a software solution, such as ObserveIT, which can provide visibility to security operations teams into what users are doing, down to individual sessions. For more information on ObserveIT, take a look at their website at http://www.observeit.com.

Transition

The final stage of the employment life cycle is when employees are leaving, either because they are changing roles within the company, leaving under good terms to move to another organization, or being fired because of misconduct or a security breach. Whatever the reason, there are a few things that the information security manager needs to ensure:

- All systems access is revoked as soon as the employee leaves the post.

- Access badges, passes, or permits are taken back and electronic access cards are disabled.

- Uniforms are handed back, since uniforms could be misappropriated by an attacker and used to get into your facility past the guards.

- An exit briefing should be held, reminding the employee of their security obligations, even when the leave the company (related to intellectual property and working for customers or competitors).

Conclusion

This chapter has covered a lot of ground on personnel security; however, there is so much more that you'll need to consider when you start to lift the hood and look at the engine. The nuances of working with security clearances, for example, will confuse even the most robust of security managers if you've never been exposed to this sort of thing before. Some aspects of physical security, such as training staff to be on the lookout for social engineers, are actually great fun, since the cybersecurity drills we discussed earlier can be a real eye opener for everyone, including board members. The most important thing to remember in personnel security is that you are dealing with people and people are fallible. So, put systems and checks in place to make sure that your people are safe and secure, that they know what is expected of them and if you see them deviate, a gentle correction is often better than an official warning. As long as your staff knows that you have their back and you are monitoring them, they'll usually do the right thing.

CHAPTER 9

■ ■ ■

Protection of Premises

In the absence of orders, go find something and kill it.

—Field Marshall Erwin Rommel

There are many aspects of information security that have a direct effect on people, processes, and technology. As an information security manager, you will be required to become familiar with and start making sense of all of the physical security issues that affect your organization's ability to protect its information and systems.

As a minimum, you need to acquire enough knowledge of physical security controls to make sure your overall approach to defending your organization's castle is robust enough to fend off attacks, be them from intruders, terrorists or industrial spies. This chapter covers some of the most important physical security considerations that affect today's connected world. We'll look at the facilities from which businesses activities operate and explore some of the weaknesses that the information security manager can address as part of your overall security program of work. We'll also look at the typical threats and vulnerabilities that affect our everyday working environment, using a risk-management approach to address these in a cost effective manner.

What Is Physical Security?

If you have built castles in the air, your work need not be lost; that is where they should be. Now put the foundations under them.

—Henry David Thoreau

This quote from Henry David Thoreau is extremely pertinent, given today's shift to cloud-based technologies. Without a solid foundation, then your business in the cloud will be extremely vulnerable. So, let's start by looking at what physical security is and how we identify those weaknesses in the castle's foundations.

Physical security actually refers to anything that supports your security posture that might be tied directly to the environment around you. For example, when you consider how to implement secure access control, you'll need to factor in access to information through direct physical contact with the systems (potentially by a threat actor who wants to steal the asset).

You might have installed a variety of technical security controls that grant and monitor access to authenticated and authorized personnel, such as network access control lists, two-factor authentication, and system alerting to detect access attempts by unauthorized personnel. These alarms would typically trigger your incident response processes, allowing operational security teams to respond. However, what would you do if the server holding all of your critical business data was stolen? If all of your data stored on systems in your data center, where they have weak or broken security processes for physical access control, was accessible by an intruder who could simply walk into the facility, unplug the server, walk out, and drive off with your crown jewels. In addition, you also need to consider information in various forms, other than just network connected digital data. What if your information has been printed? What do you do with backup tapes or removable media? In each case, your data is in just as much danger as it would be in the digital world, even more so in some cases, so you will need to consider these threats and vulnerabilities and introduce controls to protect it. If this world of physical security threats and vulnerabilities is all new to you, don't fret, there are plenty of great resources out there that can help you once you establish a framework to manage the issues. The following standards and guidelines are useful examples of where you can start to get to grips with some of these physical security issues:

- ISO/IEC 27001 and ISO/IEC 27002

- ISO 22301

- NIST's Cyber Security Framework

- COBIT

Wading through standards can be somewhat thankless, especially if you are new to the role of information security manager or are more used to dealing with traditional information security controls, such as firewalls, IPSs, and anti-malware products. By following standards such as the ISO/IEC 27001 and ISO/IEC 27002, you'll find yourself asking, *That's all great, but how do I implement this and is this my job as security manager?*

And there lies the rub! Standards don't explain how to implement controls, instead they tell you what the objective is: it's your job to figure out how you meet that objective. Let's start by looking at the ISO/IEC 27001:2013 and ISO/IEC 27002:2013 standards.

Physical Security in ISO/IEC 27001:2013

ISO/IEC 27001:2013 is by far the most commonly referenced information security standard. It contains sections that cover technical security, physical security, organizational security, policies, governance, software development, and business continuity. By complying with the standard and meeting all of the control objectives, you'll be in a strong security position where you are protecting your information reasonably well. It doesn't necessarily mean you won't be hacked and it certainly doesn't stop you being a target, however, it does show that you've gone some way down the path of implementing a security management system that covers all the security requirements a business might be expected to have complied with. *What's the catch?* Take, for example, the list of physical security controls in ISO/IEC 27002:2013: it has eight pages of controls relating to physical security, many of which are so generic and high-level that they are meaningless in any practical way. They focus more on the management of people and their behavior than real facilities security, aside from a few high-level statements about perimeters.

ISO/IEC 27001:2013 offers a good place to start, listing each applicable control you'll need to evaluate in the context of your own organization. The following list contains the range of physical security control objectives contained in the standard:

- Building perimeters

- Access and entry controls

- Securing offices and rooms

- External and environmental hazards

- Working in secure areas

- Delivery and loading areas

- Media handling and equipment security

- Cabling

To reiterate, the main problem with the ISO standards is that they tells you what the control objective is (i.e., what you need to achieve, without telling you how to do it). For example, ISO/IEC 27001:2013 reference A.11.1.1 says: "Security perimeters shall be defined and used to protect areas that contain either sensitive or critical information and information processing facilities."

The question that all new security managers will have is, *How do I know what to implement to meet this objective and how do I know if good enough to meet my needs*? Should you be building a wall or a chain-link fence? Do you need razor wire or barbed wire on the top of the wall? What about dimensions? How high should the wall be? Should it be two bricks or one brick wide? What depth should the foundation be? Does it need additional defense-in-depth from an inner fence three meters inside the boundary perimeter to act as a demilitarized zone? What about additional CCTV camera surveillance or a guard tower?

As you can see from this list of questions, the ISO standards don't really help other than to set you running off in multiple directions without any guidance on implementation in your context. Nevertheless, this is exactly what we should expect from standards, given their international nature, as they can't recommend how any one company, government, or country should implement a control. What works for one organization might not work for another, simply because of the location or the nature of the industry. So, the question remains: *What next*?

Start with a Risk Assessment

Start with a survey. Just like any other aspect of security management, whatever you decide to do to mitigate the risk requires an assessment of threat and vulnerability to justify the investment in controls. In this case, your survey will focus on physical access control, surveillance and alarm systems (CCTV, smoke and fire sensors, and intrusion detection systems), perimeter defenses, and alternative building entrances, such as loading bays, roof accesses, and sub-basement accesses. These are all security *control points* where weaknesses will leave you exposed to any number of possible attacks.

During the risk assessment, you should calculate the potential business impact from successful attacks, where threat actors range anywhere from criminals to natural disasters and physical hazards. As the organization's information security manager, it's your job to coordinate this task across a variety of stakeholders so that you gain a number of vital perspectives on physical security that you are unlikely to be able to do on your own. For this reason, physical security risk assessments must be undertaken as a team effort, so make sure to include your facilities management team, external contractors used for providing services, such as security guards, alarm monitoring and maintenance technicians, especially those who look after security and safety systems, such as smoke alarms, HVAC systems, lighting, and CCTV equipment. You'll also need to include an assessment of the business's courier services, especially those used to transport sensitive or valuable company information from one site to another, such as those that transport your system backup tapes to a secure offsite storage facility. Furthermore, waste disposal services should not be overlooked as confidential information almost always ends up in bins when organizations don't pay attention to security practices or take them seriously. It's also advisable to consult with local law enforcement and emergency services during this preliminary phase of your risk assessment, since they often provide the best advice as to how to act under extreme conditions, such as how to deal with civil unrest, influenza epidemics, and criminal activities in the local area. There are overlaps, of course, with crisis and emergency management, as well as business continuity management, but these aspects of physical security design need to always be considered and the associated risks assessed.

■ **Tip** For your risk assessments, you need to calculate the value of the asset(s) that you are trying to protect and factor the cost of replacement into your assessment of the requisite security controls.

Threats and Vulnerabilities

The risk assessment will help identify potential risks to the business (loss of data, loss of key personnel etc.). Weaknesses in the security infrastructure would be identified by a vulnerability assessment and the measurement of the criticality level of these would be determined by the likelihood of them being exploited and the impact of doing so (both of which would be determined by the attacker). As the security manager you can roughly measure the risk using the methodologies we already have at our disposal, based on the framework we discussed in Chapters 4 and 5. The business can then decide whether to accept, transfer, reduce, or mitigate those risks as appropriate.

Start by communicating with the executive exactly what it is you are planning to do. You should ask the board what they believe the security posture of the organization is and have them tell you what they are concerned with. This should allow you to make well-considered decisions as to what to take back to them in terms of business cases for new or improved controls. If the business doesn't regard security as a board issue as yet, be careful not to appear as if you are trying to scare them into giving you more budget. This almost certainly will not work and you'll lose credibility in the process. If you are lucky enough to work in a business that gets security and risk at board level, such as in the heavily-regulated nuclear energy sector or chemical manufacturing sector, then your job as information security manager should be easier in terms of getting funding for controls. However, in these sectors, the corollary is that you need to do a much better job of protecting their facilities and systems, since the threat is much greater.

SECURITY OF NUCLEAR POWER PLANTS

In the United States, the nuclear energy industry is one of the most rigorously regulated and hence safest industries. Each nuclear power plant has to be protected by a series of resilient backup systems that add layers of additional safety protocols. They are required to provide high-grade physical defenses and each individual nuclear power plant will have its own highly trained and drilled security force.

There is a real threat from terrorist attacks on these kinds of critical national infrastructure facilities, where the impact of damage could fall into the extreme range, potentially involving high loss of life and widespread damage. As a whole, the industry has improved its overall approach to security in preparation for dealing with these kinds of threats, such as direct assault, car bombs, and commercial airliner attacks. Nuclear power plants are now all equipped by law with security systems that help protect them from intruders and protect the public from radioactive releases.

The Nuclear Regulatory Commission (NRC) has stated that power plants are now "among the best-protected private sector facilities in the nation." They impose high security standards, and especially since September 11, 2001, the NRC has significantly raised security requirements through the publishing of formal requirements, which are audited by them as the regulator.

The US Department of Homeland Security published *Nuclear Reactors, Materials, and Waste Sector-Specific Plan* in 2015 as a component of their wider *National Infrastructure Protection Plan (NIPP)*. The NIPP provides guidelines for all agencies and national critical infrastructure providers on how to identify security requirements and deal with identified threats. The NIPP includes specific guidelines aimed at the chemical sector, communications sector, dams sector, nuclear and traditional energy sectors, as well as food, agriculture, water, and transportation sectors. They claim that by following the guidelines, participants are able to implement security measures that "support the local and regional jurisdictions where facilities and systems are located and events take place."

An index of all the NIPP sector-specific plans can be found on Department of Homeland Security's website here: https://www.dhs.gov/2015-sector-specific-plans.

To start with, make a list of all of the threats and vulnerabilities you discover as you walk around your facility. Take any input you gather from your discussions with site stakeholders then ask the questions as to what any given threat has to gain by attacking your facility.

You'll need to identify how probable an attack might be to result in a real security incident and each risk should be associated with a likelihood rating, backed up with evidence you glean from your discussions with local governments, law enforcement agencies or other authoritative bodies you consult.

■ **Note**   FedStats is the portal that supports over 100 US government agencies that produce and disseminate official federal statistics. FedStats can be consulted in a physical security assessment when you want information on a variety of useful information that can factor into your security risk assessment. For example, you might look at the rates of crime in your local area, drilling into the statistics to see that you are in a locale that is highly subject to burglary. If this is the case, you can determine that there is a high likelihood that your facility might be targeted by local crime gangs. From that you can determine that they are unlikely to be well-funded or sophisticated in their methods, so you will need hard barriers that will keep out these kinds of attackers, with enough deterrents in place, such as highly visible alarms and CCTV equipment, to put them off. FedStats can be found here: `https://fedstats.sites.usa.gov/agencies/`.

Make sure you include a survey of any existing control systems you have in place. Look at your building's access control systems, perimeter systems and internal door systems. You should also look at existing surveillance and alarm capabilities, such as CCTV cameras and infrared detectors, smoke detectors and fire detectors and suppressors. Fences and alternative building entrances, such as the loading bay, roof access, and sub-basement access also need to be considered in your survey. Further to this, you also need to consider leakage from your physical infrastructure of key technical systems and controls, such as understanding how far your Wi-Fi signals leak beyond the perimeter fences and checking to see if power cables or network cables are exposed in high-risk public areas. Ask whether your building management systems (BMS) are accessible remotely, as a convenience to allow for ease of support by vendor, and assess the risks of that being compromised or misused.

All of these building security measures either protect you or leave you wide open to intruders if they are not meeting the objectives of their purpose. Your risk assessment needs to be thorough enough to identify where the weaknesses are so that your overall risk assessment addresses them adequately.

Identification of Physical Threats

You will be required to undertake a threat assessment that considers all of the threats that affect your business, both today and in the future.

Begin by listing the threats actors that might have the potential to attack your facility, including what they have to gain. A list of threat actors, such as follows, might be what you come up with, but there may be more when you consider the industry you work in and the value of your information to an attacker:

- Common thieves
- Organized criminal gangs
- Journalists
- Competitors
- Terrorists
- Industrial spies

Next take a look at the neighborhood your facility is in and assess the potential of social unrest, riots, demonstrations, and general crime affecting your ability to do business.

■ **Tip**   Physical hazards don't have to directly affect your own facility to be negatively impacting on your business. A power cut or volcano at your datacenter site hundreds of miles away will likely still cause massive disruption. It is critical to understand the locations of all of your assets, and critically assess the real risks to all of them.

As most of us do, using Google is the best place to start; however, you can also take a look in your local library or contact the government to see if you can glean historical information that helps you determine the likelihood of a threat resulting in a real impact to your business. If you are based in Los Angeles, for example, there is a very good change that at some point you will have to deal with an earthquake. You will need to consider what happens during an earthquake as well as what happens afterward. If your business is disrupted an all your staff are working from a backup facility, is the primary facility now less secure and could it be the focus of a criminal attack? You also might want to consider military and policing issues, as some international locations may have threats that local facilities are not subject to (martial law, for example). Now, move on to a list of all the physical hazards you may face, such as:

- Tropical cyclones
- Floods
- Earthquakes
- Tornadoes
- Heatwaves
- Bushfires
- Cave-ins
- Collapsing sinkholes
- Crashes (planes, trains, and automobiles)
- Staff illness (pandemic flu, Ebola)
- Volcanoes
- Explosions (either on-site or in the neighborhood)
- Toxic chemical releases
- Nuclear power plant meltdowns
- Landslides
- Power cuts

When you consider the impact and likelihood of threats to your operations, ask yourself what your staff will do during an attack or natural disaster. What happens if the roads are closed or inaccessible due to excess rubble or flood waters? What if a hurricane completely obliterates one of your offices? In this case, you will need to fail over to an alternative facility and a allow staff to work from that, or a different, location.

■ **Tip** Try to subscribe to as many alerting systems as you can to receive alarms when natural disasters strike or are imminent. However, you need to tune these alerts to make sure you aren't swamped and forced into action based on a false positive. Alters can help you enact your emergency management plan on time to minimize the impact of a disaster or attack. For example, you might receive a warning that pandemic flu is now affecting your locale. If you get such an alert from the CDC, for example, you can now inform your workforce to work from home, get inoculated or whatever other mitigations you have in place.

Identification of Physical Vulnerabilities

> *A weakness of an asset or control that can be exploited by one or more threats. (ISO/IEC 27000)*

When you finish assessing threats, you need to begin the vulnerability assessment in earnest. This is where you evaluate your systems and facilities, looking for weaknesses in existing systems. Vulnerabilities offer threat actors the ability to attack your systems and facilities in order to achieve a desired outcome (the business impact).

■ **Tip** Threats can be either man-made or natural hazards, so make sure that you identify both types and evaluate the vulnerabilities that they could exploit to achieve a negative business outcome.

To illustrate this point further with an extreme example, if you identify a threat to your operations whereby your datacenter is located under the primary flight path from the local airport, the likelihood of a plane crashing into your facility is higher than it would be elsewhere in the city. If your building's exterior wall's construction is insufficiently strong—that is, not built with reinforced concrete—then this could be considered a major vulnerability. The risk, while unlikely, may still be evaluated as extreme, given the fact that you manufacture hazardous chemicals and therefore the business impact of an accident is extreme. Clearly, a plane hitting your building would be a major issue, whether you had reinforced concrete or not and in this scenario, if there was a real risk due to the location under the flight path, you'd be liaising with the airport and aviation authorities to understand their own emergency procedures and find out how malfunctioning or commandeered planes would be rerouted to safer flight paths in the event of any incident.

When you begin the vulnerability assessment, try evaluating your building's architectural schematics and floor plans, looking for entry points and potential blind spots in your existing controls. Ask the facility owner what materials were used in the construction of all aspects of the building, such as internal and external walls, floors, and ceilings, since some materials won't meet local building standards. Having incorrect or underrated construction materials could even hamper you in keeping your compliance certificate to operate, so this is of critical concern. To find out more about building regulations, contact your local authority. If you work in a government department, you should consider reading any national or local guidelines relating to security and safety, since there may be construction standards you must adhere with, especially if you handle classified data.

Complete the Risk Assessment

Agencies are to employ a risk management approach to physical security that conforms to the protective security principles. Agencies are to determine the appropriate level of physical protection for their functions and resources, including their employees, information, assets, and clients. These decisions require a rigorous analysis of security risk. (Australian Government, Protective Security Policy Framework)

Risks are calculated as a factor of threat, vulnerability, and impact and are almost always categorized in the same groups, relating to loss of reputation, loss of life (safety) or loss of cash. Deciding how you determine the risk rating of any given risk depends entirely on your organization's own approach to risk management, which you may already have identified, based on the discussion we had in Chapter 4.

For physical risk assessments, make sure any risks you raise are explained as a statement of likelihood and impact so that the executives or managers understand what they are accepting or mitigating. This allows you to see investment funding to fix the problems and allows managers to decide on the course of action they want to take, based on having all the facts. For example, if you tell your CEO that the building's security infrastructure is weak, given there is no alarm and the windows have only got simple locks, and then a burglar could break in and steal *all* of your desktop production systems (of which you have 20). These systems are $3,500 each (being Apple iMacs) so the total value of loss to the business amounts to $60,000 to replace all of these systems. Furthermore, the disruption to productivity could set the business back by 10 days of product development. You have 20 product developers who will lose ten days' worth of development, which amounts to a further loss of $100,000. The executive understands this, but the marketing team also has some input: by not getting to market in the week you intended, you could also lose valuable market share, adding another $50,000 onto the total financial impact of the theft. Given all of the threats and vulnerabilities you have identified, burglars and weak building security, the likelihood of attack is rated at high—you are in a high-crime area too!

The risk is therefore assessed as a high likelihood (80% chance over the next 12 months) that you will be burgled, resulting in losses of approximately $210,000 to your CEO's bottom line. A new building alarm system will cost in the region of $40,000 and a fully monitored CCTV system will cost an additional $10,000. You also suggest grills on the windows at a cost of $10,000 and Kensington locks on all the desks for the PCs to be connected to the building infrastructure will cost an additional $500. The total mitigation costs amount to $65,500. You present this risk balanced case for security investment to the CEO who can now decide as to whether he'll pay the $65,500 to mitigate the risk, accept the risk (and maybe take out a better insurance policy), or just deal with the consequences. Insurance might cost $5,000 per year, but the business will still have to deal with the disruption, costing in excess of $150,000 (lost work and market share), so insurance, while one option, really just mitigates against tangible asset loss and not the reputation or market share risks. Furthermore, don't forget that the insurance company will want to manage their own risks and may insist that you deploy approved locks on windows, CCTV and Kensington locks to prevent systems theft before they will accept the risk and insure you.

In order to evaluate each of the controls you want to invest in, you should perform a before and after risk assessment that shows the impact each one has on reducing risk. Any risk left over after you implement your controls is called *residual risk* and this is what the CEO will be accepting once he's decided how he wants to proceed.

```
┌─────────────────────────────────────────────────────────────────────┐
│        AUSTRALIAN GOVERNMENT CONSTRUCTION STANDARDS                   │
└─────────────────────────────────────────────────────────────────────┘
```

The Security Construction and Equipment Committee (SCEC) is an Australian Federal Government organization that evaluates a variety of security equipment for use by all Australian Government agencies and departments. SCEC publishes a catalog of equipment that has been independently tested against rigorous assessment guidelines, called the *Security Equipment Evaluated Product List* (SEEPL). SCEC also maintains a list of registered, trusted locksmiths who have been assessed as trusted by the Australian Federal Government, and provides briefings and how-to guides for government departments for installing security controls to meet a variety of control objectives. Additionally, SCEC endorses national courier services as being fit for handling sensitive Australian government information that needs to be delivered to an individual within another agency or department.

Most countries now have an equivalent of SCEC to offers guidelines and assurance services in relation to physical security matters. If in doubt, check with your local government representative.

Perimeter Design

[It] should be physically sound (i.e., there should be no gaps in the perimeter or areas where a break-in could easily occur); the exterior roof, walls and flooring of the site should be of solid construction and all external doors should be suitably protected against unauthorized access with control mechanisms, (e.g., bars, alarms, locks); doors and windows should be locked when unattended and external protection should be considered for windows, particularly at ground level. (ISO/IEC 27002)

The first line of defense any building has is its perimeter. The perimeter comprises the external walls, doors and fences, gates and bollards that act as both a psychological and physical barrier to intruders, while permitting those who are authorized to enter the facility to pass through with minimal inconvenience.

Beyond this external perimeter, legitimate visitors usually make their way to your building's reception area, where they are greeted by your receptionists or security guards who check their ID and check them in as visitors, often issuing visitor ID badges that clearly show employees that this is a guest that should be escorted at all times by a member of staff. The reception area also serves as a second layer of protection, working as a soft access control point to deter potential opportunist intruders from entering the internal office space without authorization. Let's first start by looking at the exterior perimeter which offers ingress/egress points for staff and visitors, but may have weaknesses that are leaving you open to potential attack.

What is a perimeter? This might seem like an obvious question, especially when it's the outside edge of the area that you control, typically defined by a wall or a fence. However, a less obvious perimeter might exist, such as an open car lot or landscaped garden. If you share a facility, potentially in a managed office, then the perimeter might be the entrance to the facility, while the internal perimeter you have control over is inside the building on the floor where you do business. As you can see, there are multiple perimeters of different forms that you need to consider before making any decisions on how to protect them and add in controls. You'll find that in some instances you have better control over perimeters than others, depending on what kind of facility you own or operate. In a managed office, for example, you may not be able to influence the building's owner to modify their infrastructure to meet your specific needs, so you'll have to focus your control efforts more on other kinds of security measures.

■ **Note**   The ISO/IEC 27002:2013 definition of a perimeter, while accurate, doesn't offer any guidance on how to secure it. How easy is it to ensure there are no gaps in your perimeter? Do you know where a break-in might occur? Can you gauge how easy it might be to defeat whatever measures are there? How can you make sure you've done enough? What is the competency level of the average thief or intruder, since you'll need to understand this to allow you to determine what's easy and what isn't for the local criminal contingent?

If you have any doubt as to which approach you should be taking in designing your perimeter, I'd recommend calling in an expert physical security consultancy that has the expertise to give you a proposal with various options and costs. Most modern penetration testing companies worth their salt have all of the skills needed to assess a company's physical security, similar to the way they assess the technical security posture we are more familiar with. Penetration testing companies should be offering a blended approach to their testing method that includes both physical and technical assessments, as well as a comprehensive review of security processes relating to how staff work and react to threats—that is, assessing the workforce's susceptibility to social engineering. The reality is that most penetration testing companies will subcontract specialisms to experts, so make sure your selection of your preferred testing company has subcontracts in place with experts who provide relevant references and documented experience.

If your business doesn't have the funds to outsource a physical assessment, there are a few things you can assess by yourself to see where the vulnerabilities might lie. Run through the following list of questions and see how you fare:

- Is your perimeter equally as strong all the way around your facility? You might find that the fence at the back of your property, as it backs onto a road or railway, is of a different construction to that of the front. However, these are still ingress points for intruders and can't be considered secure simply because they are not publicly accessible.

- Does your perimeter provide an adequate *deterrent* to potential intruders? You should assess the answer to this question from the perspective of an attacker. This method of assessment is known as Red Teaming, where you and your team assume the role of the attacker and try to figure out what the weaknesses might be. When you Red Team a problem, you need to be careful not to discount any ideas your team comes up with. Sometimes, the most outrageous ideas in one person's eyes are the most obvious in another's. There are no bad ideas!

- Do you have additional security controls, such as CCTV and intrusion detection systems, protecting your existing perimeter? These compensating controls can act as further deterrents to intruders since they are highly visible and work both as a psychological barrier and a security enforcing function (as long as they are actively monitored).

- Does your property have any adjoining buildings that are not in your control? If so, these also need to be assessed as you would for the rest of your perimeter. Sub-basement access from a drainage system that spans both sites might leave you vulnerable to intruders breaking through your neighbors defenses and accessing your facility though that weakness.

- Look for measures that might delay an intruder so that your compensating systems have time to detect the attack and respond. You might have a man-trap inside the guard room that all staff has to pass through, that way making sure that every staff member and visitor must cross your perimeter one at a time. Having a surveillance system (CCTV) within this perimeter control zone will further bolster your defenses.

- Do you have adequate signage showing where your facility is, stating that it's private property and advising potential intruders that they are being monitored and thieves will be prosecuted? These signs can act as a deterrent, especially to opportunists who might simply be put off by your drawing attention to your security controls.

■ **Note** The majority of modern security breaches include a blend of physical, social engineering and technical attacks that work together to make the attack exponentially more likely to succeed.

Barriers, Walls, and Fences

There are a variety of barriers you can use in perimeter design, depending, of course, what kind of facility you own or occupy. The key function of a barrier is to prevent unauthorized access and delineate your property from other businesses or public areas. Some barriers are installed to defend against environmental contamination, while others might be built to publicly demonstrate the business's commitment to security or secrecy (government buildings, nuclear power plants, etc.).

If you have a standalone facility rather than a shared or managed office, you can install a barrier at the edge of your property to act as a deterrent to intruders. Fences and walls are the most obvious perimeter defense, where the need becomes apparent from your risk assessment. The level of protection that a fence or wall can provide depends on the materials used in construction, as well as its height, width and any additional compensating security measures, such as barbed wire on top of a wall or fence. You might also consider security lighting and alarm systems mounted on the fence or wall to provide an additional level of protection, which can also be linked to the CCTV system and a response unit (triggering a security guard to visit the site of the alarm sensor that was triggered).

■ **Note** A variety of standards can be checked to help you decide what kind of perimeter defenses you want to install (maybe relevant for the facilities manager but it doesn't hurt to understand this from a security management perspective. For Australian Government buildings, for example, the Security Equipment Evaluated Products List (SEEPL) (https://scec.gov.au) is a good place to start, while BS1722-12:2006 and AS 1725:2003 both provide specifications for fences built using open mesh steel panels.

For vehicular barriers, you can reference PAS 69:2006 as a specification of the kinds of security barriers that can be considered for fixed barriers.

Access points will need to be built into the outer perimeter need to provide access to and from the facility. These access points need to be considered as security controls that are as strong as the rest of the perimeter defenses; otherwise, they become the target of attack. You will need to consider both pedestrian and vehicular barriers, depending on the entrance or exit from the facility in question. It may be that you have a pedestrian entrance at the front of the building but a loading bay at the back, where access is predominantly granted to vans and couriers.

If your risk assessment doesn't demand a fixed fence or wall, you might need to consider the threats from illegal vehicle access. This can be mitigated using bollards or other kinds of fixed impedance that will allow pedestrians free access while prohibiting access cars and vans. As an alternative, you should consider trees and hedges as a way to define your perimeter, which provide more of a psychological barrier than a hard barrier but will stop a fair proportion of inadvertent trespassing simply because it's clear where your private property starts and public areas stop.

US ARMY FIELD MANUAL 3-19.30

The US Department of the Army publishes a collection of useful documents, known as *field manuals* (FM), that offer guidelines to army personnel on how to deal with a variety of challenges they will encounter in their work. FM 3-19.30 provides guidance on physical security matters, with chapters on physical security design, protective barriers, security lighting, electronic security systems, access control, locks and key systems, security forces, in-transit security and inspections and surveys. With regards to protective barriers and fences, for example, FM 3-19.30 is quite prescriptive in suggesting three different kinds of fences that are authorized for use in protecting restricted military areas. The document is very clear in suggesting that the type of fence used should be selected based on the threat and the degree of permanence required for the fixture. This follows the same basic premise we've looked at throughout this book, basing all our decisions on risk and ensuring they meet but don't over exceed the requirements. These guidelines are descriptive and highly prescriptive. The following quotation is taken from this document and shows the level of detail. This document is well worth reading if want to see the level of detail the military goes to in order to secure its facilities.

Standard barbed wire is twisted, double-strand, 13.5-gauge wire, with four-point barbs spaced an equal distance apart. Barbed-wire fencing (including gates) intended to prevent human trespassing should not be less than 6 feet high and must be affixed firmly to posts not more than 6 feet apart. The distance between strands should not exceed 6 inches, and at least one wire should be interlaced vertically and midway between posts. The ends must be staggered or fastened together, and the base wire must be picketed to the ground.

Mailrooms and Loading Bays

Some of the riskiest and most vulnerable locations within a building are the delivery rooms and loading bays. Most buildings have a dedicated mailroom that handles incoming and outgoing mail, parcels and even inter-site mail, all of which is passed to a courier to take to its destination. Let's take a look at some of the issues with these sorts of vulnerable areas in your building's perimeter.

Mailrooms

The mailroom is often situated just inside the front entrance of the building, or possibly at the rear of the building near the loading bay. Its location is such that it provides easy access for couriers and postal workers to drop off and pick up parcels and post without them having to enter the inner office space in the building.

By considering the sensitivity of the kinds of information that potentially transit through the mailroom, such as employee pay slips, confidential management briefings, products, partner or supplier contracts, or even legal and compliance related documentation, then the risk posed to the organization by a threat actor attacking this room is greater than some of the other areas inside the building, where you have tighter control.

Delivery Areas and Loading Bays

Delivery areas and loading bays are quite often targeted by criminals and intruders as locations where high value items are handled, yet lesser security controls are often present. These external features of your facility are typically situated away from the main entrance to your offices, maybe at the back of the building, or even remote from the main workplace in a warehouse facility.

Burglary, compliance penalties, insider theft, data loss, and accidental damage are just a few of the threats faced by the business, all of which are the responsibility of the information security manager, given the role of assurance across the whole of the business. You'll need to consider personnel security and safety as well as the physical security controls you can use to improve the overall security posture of these delivery areas, including any technical controls you might consider implementing.

Reduce the Risk

To reduce the risk that these areas become your biggest vulnerabilities, start by considering which personnel are manning your postal rooms and delivery areas. They are often junior or administrative staff, who don't tend to be as security conscious as the rest of your professional workforce. These employees could well be contract or casual staff and, in some cases, might even be warehouse laborers, employed to do nothing more than shift boxes and handle simple administrative tasks.

Jobs undertaken in the loading bay might also include direct liaison with postal and couriers, facilities management companies and utilities companies, such as water supply, electricity supply and even vending machine engineers. Cleaning companies might also use these building entrances rather than the primary front entrance, especially where the image of the front of house is important to the business. Physical risks in these areas can be mitigated by migrating information into electric systems, but you need to consider what's riskier: working with information electronically or physically.

From a safety perspective, rather than a security perspective, *manual handling* is an important consideration for health and safety representatives. Any postal staff members who handle sensitive mail should be sufficiently security-vetted to ensure that they are trustworthy. Security procedures should be written for registering all deliveries and parcels transiting in and out of the facility.

■ **Warning**   Don't rule out employees using the internal postal service to bypass security at the front desk to steal documents or equipment. Postal staff should be taught to be vigilant in their awareness of suspicious activity or packages. Teach them about security threats and what to look for.

In some cases, organizations mandate that this part of your facility is the primary main entrance for facilities staff, such as maintenance workers, maintenance engineers, and even staff. Precautions should be taken to ensure that walkways are safe for people coming in and out. Ensure that boxes and packing material are not strewn around, since this is an invitation for an accident to occur, leading to a subsequent lawsuit.

If your business relies on vetting staff, consider what the vetting requirements are for your facilities staff and your suppliers. It may be that it's commonplace for postal workers to be handling company secrets, so what happens if that worker opens a confidential document, reads it or copies it? Could it be valuable to them to put it up for sale to a competitor? You might not consider a full-scale security clearance check is needed (akin to the Federal government security clearance checks, carried out by the Office of Personnel Management), but you can still apply to your local criminal justice organization or police force for a standard criminal records check.

It is also worthwhile having regular reviews of your employees' clearances, no matter what part of your organization they work in. Have management trained on how to ask leading questions about the worker's life, personal situations, and financial situations to see if there is any possibility of them being prone to bribery or coercion. If you are suspicious, dig a little deeper or post them to a less risky role. The management should be trained in identifying issues with workers' trustworthiness, in terms of telltale signs that someone's life situation has changed. For example, if a worker becomes increasingly late into work or smells of alcohol most mornings, it may be an indication of trouble at home. If they seem anxious or worried and look like they are tired, they may be having money problems. If you spot these problems early, you can see what the organization can do to help, before they resort to extreme tactics to solve their problems.

Security Guards and Dogs

Security guards can be given a variety of responsibilities in support to your staff and management. For instance, you might mandate that a security guard oversees all deliveries handled by your facilities workers in the loading bay and postal room. This becomes the second person in a *"two-person rule"* policy for handling of all mail and shipments.

■ **Note**   The two-person rule is a way of mitigating the risk of a malicious member of staff or contractor being able to physically attack a system, since they are always accompanied by someone else. It would therefore require both people to be malicious, which is less likely.

Security guards can be used to help mitigate the risk of theft and fraud, should one of your lower paid facilities staff be colluding with an external threat actor from a delivery company. Guards can monitor these vulnerable locations in your building for intruders, either in person or using CCTV and intrusion detection systems. Security guards can also be rostered into patrolling the outside of the facility, looking for suspicious behavior or persons. The term *casing the joint* sounds like something from the Sam Spade stories, but it describes the activities of criminals observing the behaviors of a target, prior to planning a crime. By looking for vans or cars parked outside your building for prolonged periods of time, or potentially strangers loitering nearby who appear to be watching traffic coming and going from your delivery area, security guards not only act as an early warning for you, they also become a deterrent, simply by being seen by the criminals.

When you plan the rosters for manning your loading bay, both with facilities staff and security guards, if needed you could keep a skeleton staff on at the weekend, especially if deliveries or shipping occurs outside normal business hours. Weekends and evenings are when criminals more often strike, for the simple reason that your guard is down. In this case, add additional security measures so that you have coverage 24x7x365, such as CCTV and remotely monitored alarms.

Guard dogs can also be used to patrol the inside of your perimeter, especially in and around the more vulnerable loading areas. Dogs can be used to provide both a deterrent and a detective security controls, however, bear in mind guard dogs are expensive and require careful handling.

■ **Tip**   Consider providing your security guards with an anti-duress capability and a way to call for help should an emergency arise. One touch alarms are common, where an accessible button can be depressed to raise the alarm with a remote command center. From there the police can be called. Sometime a mobile phone is supplied with speed dial numbers preprogrammed into the handset, or a special app installed on the device that sends a silent call for help. Whatever way you achieve this result, make sure your processes are well documented and socialized with all members of your security force so they all know how to use the system.

Crime Prevention through Environmental Design (CPTED)

One last thing to consider in evaluating potential external security controls is that not all barriers need to be overt or based on the traditional "stronghold" approach of unsightly walls and intimidating fences. You can use a beautifully manicured, tiered garden, for example, as a barrier between the road and the building that has enough hard landscaping built into it to stop a ram raid on the front of the facility. CPTED has become a major consideration in the design of buildings, typically from an architectural standpoint, to control and mitigate security threats. Trees, hedges, seating, along with the strategic use of color and lighting, can show people where the perimeter is, while looking aesthetically pleasing but still mitigating the risk. You can have thorny hedges instead of fences, which bloom into beautiful flowers or fruit, but will still keep intruders from squeezing through, along with sloping window ledges that prevent an intruder from using them to climb upward. There are a huge number of design initiatives you can investigate in this space.

■ **Note**   Crime Prevention through Environmental Design is extensively covered by the Queensland Police. More information can be found here (http://www.police.qld.gov.au/programs/cscp/safetyPublic).

CCTV

Many CCTV systems are not installed properly, have not been maintained, provide poor quality video footage or are switched off/broken at the time of the incident. If evidence is gained from a CCTV system in such cases, it may be excluded by a court. A poorly installed, maintained, or functioning CCTV system is only marginally better than having no CCTV system at all.

—Tasmania Police

Closed Circuit Television (CCTV) systems are used for surveillance. In some cases, fake cameras have been incorporated into security design to provide a psychological deterrent to intruders who may simply be looking for weaknesses in your overall security model. You should deploy functional cameras in high-risk areas, with fake cameras mounted in high-visibility areas to act as a deterrent.

Cameras can either operate in a proactive, fully monitored mode, where the output is observed in real-time and acted upon by security guards within a manned security operations center. In this mode of operation you will need to consider shift rosters for guards and ensure there are enough staff to monitor the cameras and react to incidents should they occur. It's no use having a set of cameras displaying a continuous feed in an operations center if all your guards are out walking the floors or doing a perimeter sweep. The second mode you can run your cameras in is audit mode. This means you are continually recording the feeds from the cameras but you only review the footage if an incident occurs. Both modes together will give you the best outcome—that is, you keep the footage for a predefined period of time (say, six months) but also monitor the live feeds for any real-time incidents that you may need to react to.

The following are considerations that you'll need to review when you design your CCTV solution:

- **Cost**: What budget do you have to work with for surveillance?

- **Camera quality**: Lens type, resolution, night-vision capability, sensitivity, weather resistance, and so forth.

- **Timestamps**: These are useful for evidential weight.

- **Siting**: Coverage, viewing angle, lighting, vandalism and potential attack, and height.

- **Cabling**: Cabling needs to be hardy and weather resistant, as well as attack proof. Cutting cables should send an alarm to the security operations center.

- **Recording equipment**: When you record CCTV footage, ensure the system can meet the evidential requirements you might have to adhere to should the footage ever be required in a court of law.

USING CCTV IN COURT

CCTV footage can be used in court to help prosecute an intruder, however, there are a number of factors that need to be considered as CCTV can also cause problems if the footage is deemed corrupted by the defense council. For starters, you need to make sure that the installation of the cameras is undertaken by certified installers and that the products supplied are sound and reliable, meeting all of the necessary standards and legislation. The quality of the footage needs to be sufficient to identify intruders' faces and record car number plates, make, and model. When it comes to management of the footage, mishandling or inappropriate access can end up with evidence being deemed inadmissible because it can't be relied upon. The Tasmanian Police's Crime Prevention and Community Safety Council have published guidelines that offer some excellent advice to help anyone looking to integrate CCTV into the physical security solution.

More information can be found here: (http://www.police.tas.gov.au/services-online/pamphlets-publications/closed-circuit-television/).

Lighting

Security lighting is the final consideration of this overview of physical security. Lighting's primary function is to assist us or our surveillance systems observe security threat in areas that are hard to observe due to a natural lack of light, be it in shadows, within the building, or around the perimeter at night. Lighting also needs to be considered in safety discussions where regulations relating to working in low-light conditions may need to be met. This will require you looking at your local working practices and obtaining the guidelines from your local government as regulations and safety requirements can vary considerably. There are many different kinds of lighting systems that can be used to address security concerns. There are many features and requirements you'll need to consider prior to buying a lighting system for your facility, such as:

- Purpose
- Budget
- Coverage
- Power supply
- Redundancy
- Attack resistance

The best advice for designing your lighting solution is to contract the design to a specialist who understands the best way to integrate the system into your facility, can recommend a variety of options that reduce the risk to an acceptable level and ensure compatibility with the rest of your security design. You'll need to make sure that the system properly complements your CCTV solution, ensuring it doesn't lead to image burnout or over exposure, when the high-lumen security light trips on.

The Australian Government suggests that security managers and facilities managers use the Illuminating Engineering Society publication *IES-G-1-03 Guidelines on Security Lighting for People, Property and Public Spaces* as the reference for designing lighting systems for facilities.

Administrative Security Controls

The security policies and procedures you publish for your organization flow down to all members of staff, including those in the loading bay or postal room. Make sure that your policy decisions can be implemented and tested in all circumstances. It's no use if your policies and procedures work just fine for office workers, but are untenable in these less-common circumstances.

Conduct "fire drills" for all aspects of your security procedures and emergency preparedness, maybe calling in your preferred penetration testing company to attempt to breach your security. As a more costly, but insightful review, perform this as a blind test, where you provide no documentation or insight to the pen testers, so they act as a criminal would have to if they want to gain entry, otherwise the business hands over the information up front, allowing an often limited budget to be invested in actual testing rather than reconnaissance. Use this test to also see how effective your surveillance is, or test how your security guards or dogs react. Educate your staff on how to deal with incidents and ask them to look for improvements in the processes during drills.

Provide your staff with emergency powers, whereby, under certain extreme conditions, they are permitted to act beyond their normal roles. An example might be for the postal workers to close down the facility if they suspect an attack is imminent. You would not normally expect the postal worked to do the job of the security team, but in some cases they are your first and last line of defense.

Finally, plan for the worst. For example, there is a fair chance that a robbery will take place at some point in the future, so make sure the safety of your staff is paramount. Explain how they should act when confronted or threatened with physical violence. Instruct both staff and security guards to stand down and wait for the robbery to finish before calling the authorities; reckless behavior can spook a criminal and if they are armed it can end in serious injury or death. Armed gangs are often carrying guns, knives, or baseball bats and under stress are not afraid to use them.

Internal Building Security

Once inside your facility, visitors and staff will typically pass through another control point, such as a reception area or guard room, into the inner protected area of the building. These internal areas often fall outside the direct scrutiny of the front-of-house security guards, since their remit is normally focused on mitigating the risks and threats posed by intruders. Let's take a look at some of the concerns related to the inner workings of your facility and some of the more important considerations that the security manager should address when assessing threats and installing controls.

Reception Areas

Inside the front entrance of your facility you'll more than likely find a control point for processing visitors and registering guests. In most cases this is your building's reception area and provides a number of security controls that can't be overlooked. You'll find two kinds of staff in a reception area: administrative staff (receptionist or clerk) and security personnel and while there are crossovers in the kinds of functions these staff perform, receptionists will never provide some of the more robust security functions, such as man-handling, patrols and enforcement.

Design of your reception area should focus visitors to report to the desk as their first port of call once inside the facility. The desk should be sited to have full oversight of the entrance to make sure the guards or receptionists can see every visitor. It's common to have a CCTV system monitoring the entrance and the engagement with the reception staff, so that an audit can determine if all visitors have signed in prior to accessing the rest of the building. Most of the time this will involve checking a predefined list of expected visitors, then issuing a visitors pass, while calling through to the authorized requestor who informed the reception desk that the visitor was coming. If this process doesn't exist, it's a control that is worth adding in as it ensures social engineering can't be used by an intruder to bluff his or her way into the facility by simply saying the name of an internal member of staff. The reception staff should also contact the requestor to escort the visitor, since the visitor might say they will call through, without actually making the call. Visitor badges should not provide door access unless the identity of the visitor is proven and they have suitable authorization or clearance to access the building without an escort.

Be careful about overusing the reception area for things that should be tightly controlled, such as management of keys to secure rooms or handling post. If you can't guarantee that the reception desk will always be manned, ensure that visitors know how to get the attention of someone who can provide access or answer their query. In some cases, depending on the needs of your risk treatment, reception areas can be supplied with lock boxes to securely store visitors' smartphones to prevent them from taking pictures of sensitive information or systems while on site.

Access Control and Identity Management

The requirement fulfilled by the installation of access control systems and identity management systems is that you want to only permit authorized staff to freely enter certain zones within the facility. Each internal zone within the building has its own security requirements, based on the classification or sensitivity of the information contained within, so for that reason, the security mechanisms should be selected to provide adequate risk reduction against the assessment carried out in the first step of this evaluation process.

Simple access control systems provide a single security control, which is tied to the user having something in their possession. Most modern systems use a smartcard or proximity card that is presented to a reader, which unlatches the door. However, if one of these is lost or stolen, there is no way to confirm the identity of the staff member presenting the card. In essence, it reduces the risk of anyone without a card getting in, but a determined attacker will easily find a way.

You could use a combination of process and security awareness training to mitigate this threat further. If the pass card doubles up as an identity card, with the owner's picture, name and even clearance level shown clearly on the front, and your process says that all staff and visitors must wear their ID badges at all times, then anyone not displaying an ID badge should be challenged by a member of staff, as long as they know to do so. You will definitely need to educate your staff that they need to remain vigilant at all times and any unusual activity or staff continually refusing to wear badges should, under most circumstances, be formally warned.

However, a determined attacker will still be able to knock a staff member out, stick them in a cupboard, and use the access card to gain access to your facility, especially if it's a swift attack and they don't care about being spotted (they may have a gun, for example). To respond to this threat, you can select an access control system that has a second factor of authentication, such as a pin number. The underlying principle behind multiple factors of authentication is that they should be selected out of:

- Something you have (the access card)

- Something you know (the pin number)

- Something you are (a biometric, such as fingerprint or iris scan)

Having two of the same factor does not reduce the risk as much as having two different ones, so be careful of systems that sell themselves as two factors when in fact they are not. Having a picture on the card is not a factor of authentication, all it does is support the initial one, but provides no enforcement at all.

Intrusion Detection Systems

Intrusion detection systems (IDS) alert someone (either an internal guard room or an offsite security firm) that an unauthorized person has entered a controlled part of your facility. You need to be careful about selecting an IDS without due consideration. They should only be used when you can guarantee they will provide a good level of detection without triggering regular and costly false positives. What I mean by false positive is, if you have a cleaning company or landscaping company that regularly visit your premises out of normal business hours, which you have no real control over, and then you need to be careful not to be trigger alerts based on their presence. You can use an IDS in any of these cases, but it may be better to link it to a CCTV monitoring system, where a guard or offsite monitoring company can check the activities of the personnel that triggered the alerts.

TYPES OF SENSORS

There are a variety of different IDS systems on the market, but the feature that is most important in terms of design is to select the right kind of sensors to detect the threats you have identified in your risk assessment. Some sensors trigger on an electrical contact (or breaker) basis, such as the magnetic contacts that are often found in home alarm systems. Some IDS sensors are based on photoelectric cells where they are triggered by light falling on them (maybe from a torch) or in an opposed photoelectric system, they trip when a continuous beam of light is broken. Sound can also be used to trip a microphone-based alarm, and the software behind these systems is clever enough to take a baseline of ambient noise and only trigger on threshold breaches. This helps reduce false positives. The last type of sensor we'll look at here is related to monition, either on a large scale or small scale. Large scale motion detectors, akin to the internal alarm systems in your house or linked to security lighting outside your home, can use infrared detection to detect movement, even at night. Vibration sensors measure small amounts of energy when an ambient pattern is affected. If the room you are protecting is next to a noisy electricity generator, for example, it will create vibrations all of its own. However, the sensor can be tuned to alert only when it detects variations over the generator's ambient levels of vibration. You might set the tolerance to 30% so that a lorry passing by outside doesn't compound with the generator vibrations to trip the alarm.

Alarms and Sensors

A burglar alarm is designed to detect when unauthorized persons attempt to enter a facility or go into an internally protected room that has additional security measures over the rest of the building.

As with household alarm systems, the facility's alarm sounds when a control switch of some type is tripped, such as a contact point on a door being shorted, or an impedance circuit in a window being broken as the glass is smashed.

Motion detectors, commonly based on infrared sensors, can also be used in conjunction with heat sensors and weight sensors to protect against a variety of threats. Alarms can alert and notify in a variety of ways, depending on your requirements.

Alarms should be configured to notify your security guards that something has occurred. Less sophisticated alarm systems will typically make a loud noise, such as a claxon or bell ringing to alert anyone in the vicinity that a breach may have occurred. More sophisticated alarm systems will signify where the breach has occurred and send electronic alerts to security control rooms, business owners, or even law enforcement.

POWER SUPPLIES

Power supply failures are a massive problem for businesses that rely a lot on technology. Issues come in the form of power cuts, from the substation, glitches in your building's power supply, spikes due to atmospheric conditions, or even mistakes from contracts (imagine the water company digging through the power cables in the street outside). Computer systems, especially high-end server systems, don't fare well when switched off without a proper shutdown procedure being followed. Ensure that your building has adequate power backup available that allows your IT team to shut down systems elegantly, otherwise you'll find yourself with a significantly bigger problem when the power returns: crashed hard discs, services that won't start and database corruptions. If you require your IT services to work under all of these circumstances, you'll need backup power generators, voltage regulators, smoothing circuits and UPSs. As you required more and more power failure protection, costs will go up as the risk is reduced. You need to provide a balanced, risk-based approach to power management, which the executives in your organization can sign off.

Clear Desk, Clear Screen

Clear screens and desks may seem somewhat draconian, not in keeping with the way your staff is used to working. However, enforcing this will not only serve to keep your work environment neat and tidy, it also help prevent serious security threats related to loss of confidentiality, integrity and availability of information.

Most office work is conducted on computer systems, so it's plausible that there are times when systems are left unattended, potentially with sensitive information shown on the screen. There are reported cases of staff rushing for a toilet break and not locking their systems, or forgetting to lock them when they go for coffee. This can leave sensitive information displayed on the screen for a passerby to read. It also leaves the network open to access from that unlocked system, where an attacker would have the full logged in privileges of the user. Any malicious activity would also be traced to that user, further compounding the issue.

Open plan offices are somewhat to blame for this issues as there is more risk of unauthorized members of staff seeing screens than they would have be able to should each member of staff work in a closed office. As such, it's important to consider both technical controls, such as screensaver lockouts after a short period of inactivity, as well as siting of screens and the installation of protective filters that help reduce shoulder surfing and casual overseeing of screen from an open plan office, so that documents cannot easily be read by visitors or cleaners who are working behind the users.

The risk of someone overlooking your screen and seeing information they are not permitted to see is high. Desktop monitors are, by their nature, prominent features on your desk, and with bigger and brighter displays, the ease of shoulder surfing (as it's known) is increasingly problematic. All staff should be made aware of this issue through security awareness training and they should be advised to look around and be vigilant when working, especially if they are working on sensitive information.

■ **Caution**   It's not always obvious that you are being observed. Have you considered where your CCTV cameras might be? Maybe a security guard in the control room is looking at sensitive corporate information, which he should not have access to. Maybe your PC is facing the window and there is a hotel on the opposite side of the street. Could an attacker have taken a room in the hotel and be looking at your corporate secrets using high power binoculars or a telescope? These might seem like James Bond style threats, but they do happen and corporate espionage is as rife in industry as theft and electronic attack.

Your security policy should include a section on managing the threat of shoulder surfing and accidental data breaches through leaving systems logged in when the user has taken a break. This should be included in what's known as your *clear desk policy*. Further to this, you would typically create security operating procedures that include details on how members of staff manage their working areas. Staff should be encouraged to be aware of these security concerns and to question people who do not have clearance to see data.

Clear Desk Policy

The old adage of a cluttered desk meaning a cluttered mind may well be true. However, a cluttered desk also presents a major security risk. Users can inadvertently lose classified documents in a pile of unclassified information and forget that it's even there. Even if you have security policies that call for sensitive information to be locked in a secure cabinet, if desks are untidy, users may still forget to do this. At the end of the day, when users are heading home, there is a high likelihood that they won't through everything on their desk to see what should be filed.

The security policy should include guidance on staff clearing desks of clutter each day. If you are planning to introduce such a policy, make sure that staff has the necessary lockers and filing cabinets to lock classified information away when not in use. Make sure they have the necessary facilities to store personal items too, such as notebooks and textbooks. A clear desk should means just that—completely clear of all items.

Lockable desk drawers or plinths can be made available to users that need them. This comes with cost, but it should be justified as part of your risk mitigation strategy. Cabinets can be assigned to teams, allowing them to store protectively marked information, with the whole team sharing the combination to that cabinet. The facilities management team should retain the master keys, recording the combination codes in case of an emergency.

MANAGING NOTEBOOKS

You might think that a sidebar on managing notebooks is excessive. However, there are risks associated with what your workforce writes down, maybe as notes from a meeting or engineering notes related to systems or formulae. Notebooks can contain a plethora of useful information to an attacker or social engineer, which could be used to mount a full-scale attack. Personally identifiable information might also be jotted down in a notebook, along with the names and addresses of customers. This is also valuable information to an attacker. Users might also write down things they don't want to forget, such as complex passwords for administrate accounts. This non-technical weakness can instantly circumvent all of your expensive security access controls and leave you entirely owned by the attacker.

So, how do you prohibit users from writing things down? Unfortunately you can't however you can make sure that if they do commit something to paper, they pay attention to the classification and handling of the notebook. For example, it be required that they write down all the admin passwords for network switches, since this is the only record of the passwords anywhere and they need some way to pass this information on to other technicians. So, the policy will say, the notebook should be locked away in a safe, where the combination is known only to the security guards. Each time the book is accessed, the security guard records who accessed it and what their reason was, checking their ID and authorization at that time. In essence, as the information security manager, you are allowing these things to happen, just adding in corporately enforced and endorsed procedures to make them more secure.

Security of Equipment

When you look at the threat of equipment being taken offsite or stolen by members of staff or contractors, you'll need to look at the measures you have in place to protect these physical systems from theft, as well as the measures needed to protect the information they contain. For the purposes of this section of the book, consider the information asset as already protected on the device (potentially using encryption or some other security control) so the focus here is more on protecting against physical theft. The physical security risk assessment undertaken across your facility will tell you what the financial impact of such an incident occurring might be.

Loss of equipment can lead to reputation damage as well as financial loss since it can impact your ability to delivery services or conduct your business. It could also put the health of your workforce at risk, especially if the equipment in question is an air filtration system or cooler for the data center.

You need to put anti-theft countermeasures in place to help manage all of these kinds of equipment related risks. Desktop computer systems, laptops, and computer monitors can all be secured to your office infrastructure when left on the premises. You can use specialist locks, such as Kensington locks, to connect the chassis of the device to the fixed building infrastructure, such as water pipes, furniture, or special steel loopholes provided in the concrete floor. Laptops have all been designed with physical security in mind and almost every model from every manufacturer comes with a special connection port on the external chassis that will connect to a Kensington-style lock. You can obtain a master key from your lock provider so that individual users can open locks, as can the security manager or guards, should that be required.

The methods and requirements imposed on your users for securing equipment should start in your corporate security policy and flow down into local site security procedures that a responsible site manager can enforce. For example, a policy might state that all equipment needs to be appropriately secured. But what does appropriate mean? The procedure for laptops will then dictate that any laptop left overnight on a desk in your open plan office or overnight in the trunk of a car must be appropriately secured. Critical equipment, such as air conditioning systems and water filtration systems and should be regularly maintained by the vendor and you must ensure that the maintenance contract covers you for emergency callouts in the event of a failure.

■ **Warning**   The impact of an air-conditioning unit failing can be catastrophic for computer servers in your data center. Modern servers consume a lot of energy and give off a lot of heat, so a failure of the ventilation systems can lead to a critical system meltdown that can have significantly costly and disruptive consequences to your business. It is recommended that you monitor the temperature inside each of your computer racks and send an alert to your operations center should the temperature creep up over a certain threshold.

Security Considerations when Relocating

The control of an organization's property during a site move is of critical concern to the information security management. There are myriad stories in the media of lost USB storage devices, laptops and documents being left on a train or in the back of a taxi. These stories serve to reinforce the fact that an organization's property is not only a concern within the walls of the facility, but anywhere the property is taken. So, how do you mitigate the risk of thieves intercepting equipment as you relocate it to another building?

■ **Tip**   Relocation to a new office offers some great opportunities to undertake housekeep activities and uplifts in security that you might otherwise not have been able to do. You can ensure you securely dispose of old paperwork and demand that the new facility has the systems that may not have been available in your previous premises.

As usual, start with a risk assessment. This will help you determining which countermeasures to implement to protect your assets during transit. The risk assessment is used to assess the value of the items being transported and to take into consideration the ease as to which that item could be replaced. For example, if a particular technical gadget is stolen, something that was custom made for your special manufacturing factory, the value of the item is not just its replacement cost. It's also the loss of productivity during the time it takes to get a new one, the cost of shipping, installation, and so forth. If the item is a simple USB storage device, then the value should be considered more from the perspective of what's stored on it rather than the replacement cost. The market value of the secret recipe for your special black, fizzy drink are worth a lot more than a $50 thumb drive. When you perform your risk analysis, consider the likelihood of the incident actually happening, and be realistic about it. You will have competitors and ex-employees who'd like to potentially see you fail. These need to be factored in as threat actors when you estimate the likelihood of an attack.

Mitigations

There are many reductive measures you can use to mitigate the risk, ranging from simple to extreme. The information security manager must take a considered approach to selecting the most appropriate controls, to ensure the cost of mitigation is not excessive.

Start by marking assets with indelible ink, uniquely identifying them as your property. You can use barcodes, RFID stickers, and other kinds of physical tags to help you trace stock and monitor serial numbers. This will help with the recovery of the asset and if labeled as such may reduce the risk of it being stolen, especially by an opportunist thief.

When moving sensitive equipment or information from one place to another, select a trusted, potentially security vetted courier service that provides a level of assurance around its capability. Government departments often have preapproved special courier services to move classified documents and assets from one building to another.

If you are the information security manager for a government department, make contact with your national authority (such as the NSA or FBI) to see which couriers can be trusted. You should always consider the route that your courier or transportation service will use, since some neighborhoods are rife with crime and could be used as a front for hijacking your truck.

There is also a risk that computer systems could be intercepted and powered-up by someone in the transit company, inserting a USB hard disc and stealing all of your confidential information. Even if you don't encrypt information normally, now that your systems are leaving your premises, it may be time to consider adding in this technical security control. Nevertheless, it's possible that with enough resources or developments in cryptanalysis that even our most trusted encryption schemes will be useless for protecting confidentiality of information tomorrow. If your information is highly sensitive, consider wiping the physical systems and sending the data encrypted over a secure network.

Tamper resistant seal and tamper evident labels can be used on equipment to help notify you of unauthorized access. Seals can act as barriers, which, if broken, render the equipment useless or provide an indicator that someone has tried to break into it. For example, if all USB sockets have tamper evident seals covering them, the simple act of peeling them off will prove someone has tampered with them. Once the equipment has been transported to its destination, you should inspect the seals to determine if anyone has attempted (or succeeded) to break in. Take a look at http://www.tamperevidence.com/voidtec-nr.php for more information on tamper resistance.

Conclusion

Physical security is a massive subject and risk and controls are changing all the time to deal with modern security threats. Information security managers should become familiar with the physical security domain, however, and equally as important, you should establish relationships with external testing companies and physical security experts since certification, technical standards and compliance is very important. As with most aspects of information security management, you become the coordinator of subject matter experts who help you gain visibility of the issues, assess the risks and them express those risks in meaningful language back to the executive management team so that they can make a decision as to whether they accept, treat or transfer the risk to someone else (such as an insurance company). I personally know a few security managers that have started in the technical security domain and moved to being physical security domain experts as they found this an interesting and varied career opportunity. What's nice is that you can see and feel the results of your efforts, so in many ways it's one of the most satisfying aspects of implementing a security program for your business.

CHAPTER 10

■■ ■

Protection of Systems

This chapter is the one that gets technical. If you want to be in information security, you have to accept that you will be dealing with technical systems, working closely with technical people and the majority of things you are protecting relates in some way or another to the protection of systems. Over the next few pages we are going to look at the various categories of malware in circulation today, including some detail of how these malicious programs are used by hackers to attack your systems. We'll also look at ancillary attack modes used by criminals to ambush unsuspecting end users, such as the modern triad that has become the scourge of the Internet: spam, phishing, and ransomware. In the second half of this chapter, we'll pivot to the aspect of system protection, looking at the defensive countermeasures you can use to secure your networks, protect your computers, and keep your applications and information safe.

Introducing Malware

When we read about hacking in the news, we usually hear that massive corporates or government departments have been breached and some kind of corporate database has been stolen. We truly live in the age of the *data breach*, were hackers break into an organization's infrastructure and purloin millions of records of personal information, either from their customers or internal staff.

Some of the biggest breaches of recent times, such as Target, Sony, Anthem, and the US Office of Personnel Management, have garnered massive media attention, however what we don't normally usually hear in the news coverage (or at least without digging a little deeper) are details relating to how the hack occurred. How did the attacker infiltrate the company network, what vulnerabilities were exploited, what flavor of malicious software (malware) was employed by the attackers and what countermeasures were in place that may have been bypassed or failed? These questions are the kind of questions that security managers and security staff need to be asking, since putting yourself in the role of an attacker is by far the best way to ensure that you see how your organization could be attacked.

Viruses, worms, Trojan horses, rootkits, spyware, adware—the list goes on. In our modern computing environment, especially when hooking into the Internet, you'll be bombarded by an expansive collection of technical threats, each of which is ready to strike at the heart of your computer system, preparing to steal your information, take control of your computer, or deny you of its service. To remain productive, these threats need to be kept at bay; however, the landscape is confusing. How do you know if you've plugged all the holes, bolstered the network, fortified the servers, and made sure your users are safe? Furthermore, what are all these different kinds of malware and how do they operate? Do they act autonomously or can these malware types integrate with other kinds to collaborate on making the threat greater than any individual hazard? Let's start by looking at the different classes of malware and how they operate.

© Tony Campbell 2016

T. Campbell, *Practical Information Security Management*, DOI 10.1007/978-1-4842-1685-9_10

What Is Malware?

You will undoubtedly have heard of the three most commonly understood malware types: viruses, worms and Trojan horses, however, do you really understand the fundamental differences that make one different from the other? If you want to make sure that your systems' defenses are strong enough to keep out the bad guys, then it's important that you understand the differences between a virus and worm, or a logic bomb and a rootkit, so that your technical countermeasures are mitigating the right risks.

POLICIES AND RISK MANAGEMENT

Irrespective of whether we are dealing with people, processes, or technology, we still need to remember that policies are required to ensure that cybersecurity is delivered consistently across the enterprise. For example, if you are building a network, then you'll want to build your services to align with a network policy that contains all the standards that must be adhered to and any principles that must be followed, such as, "Network devices must be identified prior to allowing them to connect to the corporate environment." You might immediately conclude that this means you need Network Access Control or Network Access Protection services installed on your infrastructure. However, another way to make sure that this is controlled might be to retain complete control over all user access devices, where they are booked out of an inventory held on site and booked back in before the user leaves. That way, only systems that are supplied by the network manager will access system resources. Which is the right answer? Well, it depends. Both serve the needs of the policy. The answer lies in the business and technical architectures selected to meet the requirements, with the solution based not only on cost but also on the effective management of risk. Now, you might be thinking that the policy needs to be clearer, but this is where you'll slip up. Policies should never be dependent on the solution, but they do need to state the intention.

Security policies should also focus on what is acceptable and what needs to be achieve rather than what's prohibited. From a networking and technical viewpoint, your security policy should cover some or all of the following:

- **Use of software**: Downloading, installation, and distribution.

- **IP protection**: Unauthorized use of confidential or copyright materials.

- **Hacking**: Intentional introduction of malware into the infrastructure.

- **Secrecy**: Account details and passwords must never be shared.

- **Timeframes**: Requirement for changing passwords, reviewing access, and so forth.

It's common practice to discharge certain responsibilities to staff through the security policy, so you should expect to document the people and roles that can use and manage the network.

Classifying Malware

One common misconception is that Trojan horses, worms, and viruses are the same thing, with the terms being used interchangeably both by practicing security professionals and the media. However, each kind of malware operates and executes in a very different way, so it pays to be clear and concise when you categorize any given sample.

Malicious software is a vast and extremely complex subject matter and researchers spend their entire career understanding the theory and practice of this insidious threat. In this book, we can only go so far in showing you what kinds of malware are out there and how they operate, however, by the end of this chapter you should be able to classify different kinds of malware from their behavior and determine which defenses should be deployed or configured to mitigate any given threat. Furthermore, it's unlikely that an attacker will use just one kind of malware in an attack. Typically, attackers will layer a variety of technologies on top of each other, in part to disguise what they are doing, as well as to affect some kind of change on the end system, maybe to extract data, maybe to open a backdoor, or simply to cause disruption through a denial-of-service.

At the highest level there are a few broad categories that contain most kinds of malware. Over the next few pages, we will look at the following:

- Types of malware

- Spyware

- Botnets

- Denial-of-service (DoS) attacks

The first thing we need to do is look at what malware actually is, simply because it can be quite confusing to anyone relatively new to information security. Malware, as you may have guessed, is a contraction of *malicious software* and has become the generic name for any nefarious software that runs on a computer system with ill intent.

If you were to look at the information security taxonomy, malware would be the family name for all of the kinds of bad software, more often than not wrongly labeled as viruses, such as Trojan horses, Spyware and Adware, key loggers, rootkits, ransomware, scareware, backdoors, as well as any other program that will do you harm.

Malware can disguise itself as a legitimate application on your computer, in some cases attaching itself to legitimate software in the same way that a biological virus attaches itself to healthy cells. Furthering the analogy to diseases that infect living organisms, some malware needs a host in the same way a parasite does. These programs operate without infecting another application as they tend to be standalone applications which exist and propagate independently. The reality is that there are dozens of ways that malware can infect your systems and each kind of malware can have a variety of ways that it will propagate from one system to another.

Figure 10-1 shows a high-level family tree of the malware we will discuss in this chapter. The following are the key characteristics of each category:

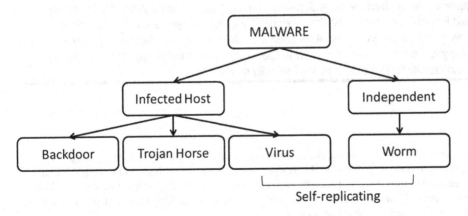

Figure 10-1. *Rudimentary taxonomy of malware*

- A virus is computer code embedded in another, possibly legitimate file or program.

- Backdoors and Trojans are malicious inclusions within software applications that can be exploited by a threat actor without the user knowing of their existence.

- Viruses and Trojans rely on human intervention.

- Worms are self-contained and may spread autonomously.

- Viruses and worms are self-replicating.

Rootkits are not shown in this diagram since they deserve a special mention of their own. Rootkits are in fact designed as supporting programs that hide both themselves and their malware counterparts on computer systems.

■ **Note** Most attacks these days combine the efforts of multiple pieces of malware. A single attack might propagate by using a worm while it installs a rootkit on each machine that it infects, and then opens a backdoor for a remote attacker to access the infected systems. Combined attacks are known as *blended attacks*. Each flavor of malware has its own strengths and weaknesses, with advanced attackers customizing each campaign to be as efficient as possible and to avoid detection, thus ensuring they have the best possible chance of success and extending their malware's lifespan.

ZERO-DAY ATTACKS AND EXPLOITS

There has been a lot of negative press using the term *zero day* to denote the worst kind of cybersecurity attack. There is no doubt that these are the worst kind of vulnerabilities in our systems (i.e., ones we don't know about) and if attackers manage to detect one and build exploit code that leverages its weaknesses, then all bets are off.

Nevertheless, we need to be careful of overusing or misusing this definition. Zero day refers to an attack on a vulnerability that is, as yet, unknown to the vendor or security industry. The downside is that there are no patches or mitigations when the vulnerability is publicly discovered, so there is no means of preventing a direct attack. Some anti-malware products can assist with zero-day protection, such as Intrusion Prevention Systems (IPS) since they use behavioral analysis and traffic analysis to map normal activity and can report or even block when something looks out of the ordinary. Clearly, however, building your defenses around the ability to spot anomalies is a better approach, so zero-day vulnerabilities and exploits remain a concern for IT security professionals

Viruses

Let's start with the most well-known yet misunderstood malware category: viruses. The term *computer virus* is entirely appropriate since this kind of malware operate much like its biological counterpart. A virus usually attaches itself to a legitimate software application in the same way that biological viruses attack our cells. Once the host is infected, the virus carries out its malicious activity, while replicating itself both within the host and to other hosts through a variety of vectors.

Unfortunately, since the term has been used throughout the growth of the malware industry from the early days of the Internet through to today, it has become synonymous with a variety of other kinds of malware, such as worms, rootkits, Trojan horses, and so forth. However, it's only truly a virus if it infects its host by attaching itself to a legitimate application since any other kind of modus operandi is the signature of a different malware category. There is a standard definition of viruses that can be found in RFC 1135: "A virus is a piece of code that inserts itself into a host [program], including operating systems, to propagate. It cannot run independently. It requires that its host program be run to activate it."

Interestingly, beneath the heading of virus, there are also a number of subcategories that you need to be aware of. One such category is the macro virus, which is a virus written in a macro (scripting) language, such as Visual Basic for Applications (VBA), which is incorporated into the Microsoft Office suite of application for Microsoft Windows based computer systems. Macro viruses became a common way of attacking computers back in the mid-1990s. The most infamous macro virus that is most often referenced in security texts is the Melissa virus. If you were infected with Melissa, you would open an infected Microsoft Word document, which would run the macro code, which in turn emailed a copy of itself to the first 50 people in your address book. Melissa spread quickly and easily around the world jumping into organization and infecting their internal systems so rapidly that many organizations had to shut their entire email systems down while engineers figured out how to solve the problem.

■ **Note** It's interesting how attack vectors and exploits go out of fashion, then when the countermeasures catch up and make the cost of exploitation too much against for the criminals, they reintroduced an old threat in a new context. In the most recent Ransomware campaigns, we're again seeing documents with embedded malicious macro code being used to attack their victims.

Worms

Like viruses, worms get their designation from their biological counterparts, parasites. A worm propagates from one computer to another, just like a virus might, however the difference is that worms operate independently of host applications. They don't require host applications to execute; instead, they operate as self-sustaining applications, leveraging host system services such as email and file sharing to propagate to other hosts. The term *worm* has also been defined in the standard, RFC 1135: "...a program that can run independently will consume the resources of its host [machine] from within in order to maintain itself and can propagate a complete working version of itself on to other machines."

The threat from the activity of a worm is that it will replicate, just like Melissa did, to as many neighboring computer systems as it can reach. The impact of a worm passing through your infrastructure is that it will consume vast amounts of network and system resources and potentially cause a denial-of-service outage to critical communications systems before you can eradicate it. It is therefore common practice for servers and networks to slow down and even halt due to the excessive replication load. This leads to a denial-of-service. The first time a worm was identified as an independent class of malware was back in November 1988, known as the Morris worm. Named after its author, Robert Tappan Morris, the Morris worm was released by the MIT graduate student from Cornell University and quickly caused havoc as businesses and systems crumpled under the excessive processing power it consumed.

■ **Note** Robert Tappan Morris was the first person to be tried under the Computer Fraud and Abuse Act of 1986, 18 U.S.C. Section 1030(a)(5)(A). Morris was tried, convicted and subsequently sentenced to three years of probation, 400 hours of community service and fined $10,050.

Trojan Horses

The term *Trojan horse* comes from Greek history, referencing a story from the Trojan War, where the Greeks were purported to have hidden a small army of warriors within a massive wooden horse that was offered to the people of Troy as a gift. When the people of Troy accepted the gift and brought it within their city walls, the Greek warriors emerged from the horse's belly and sacked the city, thus ending the ten-year siege of Troy.

A Trojan horse will appear as a normal application, but within it hides malicious code waiting to be activated. Some Trojan horses are designed to be annoying, doing this such as changing desktop backgrounds or displaying threatening messages to the user, even though they don't actually do any harm. Some Trojan horses, on the other hand, cause serious damage by really going through on these kind of threats. Some will delete your files, some will encrypt your files, while others have been known to create backdoors on your systems that give malicious users access to your system. Without you realizing it, attackers would be accessing confidential or personal information on your network.

Unlike viruses and worms, Trojans don't propagate by infecting other files. Instead they operate and execute independently on your computer. Trojan infections can come about through execution of code delivered via an email, maybe as a download from a website or wrapped up in some other guise, such as in a PDF or in a ZIP file. Trojans are frequently used as the so-called *zombie endpoints* in a network of botnets; we'll discuss this later.

Rootkits

A rootkit is a malware program that uses stealth to maintain a persistent and undetectable infection on a computer system. Rootkits often have full and unfettered access to the entire computer system, usually installed with full administration privileges. They use techniques to hide themselves, therefore it may be running as a process on the system, but not appearing in the list of running processes when you open up Task Manager (on a Windows machine). When you look on the file system, the rootkit code is hidden; it may be protected using access control lists so that users cannot actually get to it.

Rootkits sometimes hide in alternate data streams, which are hidden from normal directory listings— these are a fascinating aspect of the Windows file system that not many people know even exist.

Think of rootkits as malware that infect the core of the operating system, becoming inexorably intertwined with it. One important thing to note with regard to rootkits is that they are very difficult to detect and even harder to remove. You will need special software to look for rootkit indicators of compromise and specialist help to remove the infection.

■ **Tip** Alternative Data Streams (ADS) are a relatively unknown feature of Microsoft's NTFS file system, available on all modern Windows operating systems. ADS offers hackers a means of hiding malware, such as rootkits, hacking tools, and other useful resources, allowing them to be accessed without being visible to security guys and administrators. For more information on WindowsSecurity.com and accessing and using ADS, refer to the article at http://www.windowsecurity.com/articles-tutorials/windows_os_security/Alternate_Data_Streams.html.

Backdoors and Logic Bombs

Backdoors (also known as *system trapdoors*) are entry points to code within a program that take an abnormal input and use the action of the software to achieve an unexpected result—this could be data collected from an input via a website or from a message received over the network.

These kinds of unwanted code features are commonly found in commercial software products, sometimes intentionally included in the release of the software by the developer. One such notorious backdoor application that you might have heard of was discovered in early versions of Microsoft Excel. Chunks of unnecessary code were embedded in the Excel installation that did unusual things if a certain sequence of input triggered them: when these kinds of backdoors are included in commercial software as a "fun" addition rather than as intentional malware, they are known as *Easter eggs*.

Sometimes, Trojan horse systems use backdoors to attack their host. For example, if you were to accidentally download a Trojan horse onto your system, it may appear benign to begin with, and then open a backdoor when it receives an instruction from the attacker via the network. This is the technique that attackers use when pushing botnet infections.

Logic bombs are in many ways similar to backdoors. As a malware category, the main attribute that differentiates a logic bomb from any other kind is that it sits dormant on a computer system until a specific condition is met. Once that condition is met, the malware springs into life, performing whatever malicious activity its author intended. The conditions could be anything from a simple date which the malware is primed to detect, through to a particular set of circumstances relating to users, software, patch state, and so forth. Pretty much any logical condition you can imagine can be programmed in, which is why these dormant, sleeping threats are so dangerous. A logic bomb can even exist as a stored procedure inside a database, only executing when a specific database condition is met, such as a specific record is accessed or a specific user is running a query.

Spyware

Unlike the other categories of malware, spyware and adware are not programmed to cause damage, instead they lurk in the background and either provide information to a remote third party, or exploit your system resources to push unsolicited advertising to your desktop. Often the spyware of adware gets onto your computer system by one of the other malware vectors, such as a worm, where the worm executes on your system, installing the spyware or adware, then replicates to someone else's computer. In particular, spyware can employ a variety of functions, running key loggers (which recording all your keystrokes and sending them to the attacker) screen grabber (actual pictures of your screen, which may contain sensitive or confidential documents) or remote video or listening devices.

Botnets, Phishing, Spam, and Ransomware

Most people have heard of spam, universally accepted as junk email that clutters our inboxes. Something that most people don't appreciate is that the ratio of legitimate email sent on the Internet every single day to spam is 1:10. When you consider there is an average of 70 trillion emails sent every single year, that's a lot of spam.

Spam poses a number of threats from a variety of perspectives. Primarily, it clogs up our systems with unwanted messages, which consumes bandwidth and system resources as it goes. However, our systems are largely able to cope with that, but the real damage comes from the message content.

Most spam messages are trying to entice you to click a link or open an attachment that has a malicious payload. This makes spam the medium for infection from any number of other kinds of malware, which is why it's so dangerous. When you receive an email that tries to entice you to click a link or an attachment with a carefully crafted message that seems targeted at you, the mode of operation that it's using to attack you is known as *phishing*.

Spear phishing is an even more targeted attack, usually after doing some background research on you via social media.

A botnet is a collection of compromised computers under the control of an attacker. Each node is known as an *individual bot*. When a new bot joins a botnet, some malware will be installed and it connects to a central command server known as a *botmaster*. This is how the criminals instruct the bots to undertake certain functions, such as sending spam, used for phishing purposes, or installing other kinds of malware, or even launching denial-of-service attacks on online targets.

Ransomware

Ransomware has become one of the most prevalent attacks of today. Ransomware is most commonly installed after a user opens a malicious email attachment or clicks on a link to a malicious website contained within a phishing email. Once the malicious code is executed on the user's computer, it reaches out to the Internet with personal details relating to the user's machine that was perhaps seeded from its IP address, user name, or other user information, to generate a special encryption key that is specific to that system.

Then, when it has the encryption key downloaded, the payload sniffs out all the user's documents, photographs and even network shares, and then encrypts them using the individual key. Finally, the user is presented with the ransomware screen, saying that the user must pay the ransom to get their files back. These days, criminals are getting more and more sophisticated in the way they craft their malware. The Petya ransomware variant is especially nasty as it does not require an Internet connection to generate its encryption key and overwrites the system's master boot record (an essential component of a computer system that loads the operating system) before attacking the host and encrypting the file system. You can read more details about Petya ransomware at `https://blog.malwarebytes.com/threat-analysis/2016/04/petya-ransomware/`.

■ **Note** Most of the time, criminals honor the terms of the ransom note, sending the decryption key to users who pay on time. The reason for this is simple, if word gets out that the user will not get their files back even if they pay, people will simply not pay, since they know they have lost their files. But a cunning ploy of being a relatively inexpensive payment (a few hundred dollars) and an assurance that they will honor the agreement means more people are inclined to hand over their cash.

Denial-of-Service Attacks

You'll not have missed the media coverage of various big Internet companies having their websites "taken down" by hackers. In most cases the website has been subject to what's known as a distributed denial-of-service (DDoS) attack. A denial-of-service (DoS) attack occurs when a service, such as a website, becomes non-operational due to a malicious attack. This is typically because it cannot function under extreme loading placed on it by attackers. In many cases, a website will simply stop being responsive to user requests and appear to hang. However, in some extreme cases, the website may crash and show error codes to the user when they browse to that location. A DDoS attack is a special form of DoS attack where many sources are responsible for the extreme loading on the target.

More often than not, a botnet will be used to launch the DDoS attack. The botmaster will use the command and control server (C&C) to communicate with each of the bots in the botnet, instructing all of the bots to send a slew of webpage requests to the target. The attack could be as simple as repeatedly requesting the website's homepage—draining the capacity of the web server. A botnet can consist of many thousands of bots, with a wide geographical distribution.

■ **Note** DDoS attacks are the most common weapon of choice for hacktivist group, Anonymous.

Active Content Attacks

Active content is the code that runs inside other applications or websites that controls certain kinds of functionality, such as server and client-side website scripting, animated GIFs, weather maps, and even videos. There are a variety of different kinds of active content that can run inside your web browser, such as the following:

- JavaScript
- PHP
- Adobe Flash
- Perl
- HTML5
- Java

As a security manager, you'll need to be aware that each of these capabilities is underpinned by a full programming environment. This means it can be used for a considerable number of purposes than the simple use-cases discussed here. Take Adobe Flash, for example, it is a complete programming environment. This leads to these execution environments having their own inherent vulnerabilities and hence risks.

By running active content from an unknown source, such as a malicious website, it could contain malware, such as a virus, Trojan horse, spyware or ransomware. Most of these technologies can be used to display and interact with a user, however, as a security professional you need to be aware that they are full programming environments and can be used to do an awful lot more than just display forms and pretty pictures. Even Adobe Flash is a complete programming environment—this is why there have been so many Flash vulnerabilities over the years. Furthermore, due to version dependencies and poor enterprise patching support options, these packages are often difficult to patch, leaving the organization vulnerable to exploits that leverage them.

Because of this, each of these programming environments comes with its own inherent risks. If you download active content based on any of these technologies, especially from an unknown (untrusted) source, there is a probability the download could include some kind of malware, such as a Trojan. Most of these technologies have some kind of damage limitation capabilities, however, they are not that great and need the developer to have at least used them properly. By way of an example, Java Applets cannot usually access files on your computer's hard disk; this stops Java Applets from tampering with the data stored on your system.

ActiveX has a bad name for itself and has notoriously been the worst culprit for allowing rogue code to do bad things to your systems. As a result, many organizations have a blanket ban on ActiveX controls downloading and running on users' computers.

ALTERNATE EXECUTION ENVIRONMENTS AND ACTIVE CODE

Unfortunately, there are many hidden and largely uncontrolled environments within your IT systems that pose a major threat. If you look inside the .NET Framework, for example, you'll find a convenient command line C compiler that can be used to build executable programs by any user that needs to. This is yet another attack vector, where malware could be compiled directly on your computer from fragments of legitimate code, thereby ensuring it has its own unique, undetectable signature and cannot be seen by perimeter defenses. If you want to make sure that your systems are as locked down and clean of unnecessary execution environments as possible. You should call in a desktop security expert, since many of these are required by applications. And instead of removing them, you may have to lock them down, limit their activity, and audit their operation from a security operations center.

One of the most common classes of active code malware is the macro virus. These are snippets of code written in Microsoft Office's native scripting language, Visual Basic for Applications (VBA). Macro viruses have been around since the mid 1990s, when VBA itself was first introduced into Microsoft Office. They execute inside of any Microsoft Office application, such Microsoft Word and Microsoft Excel, usually proliferated throughout your environment by infecting documents and spreadsheets which are transmitted without the user's knowledge.

One of the most infamous examples of a macro virus was Melissa. Anyone opening a document infected with Melissa would instantly be infected, allowing the code to the email itself to the top 50 recipients in your address book. This saw Melissa spread faster than any other virus before, taking down email services and entire Internet gateways, with the monumental load it put on infrastructure.

Content Injection Attacks

Content injection can also be referred to as code injection. In recent years, content injection has become the foremost attack vector for hackers. Content injection vulnerabilities are complex and most are introduced through poor programming practices. Often they are introduced by the developer not validating user input correctly, or at all. For example, if a user enters a message into a blog or website, they might place HTML or JavaScript code into the post. When another user opens the blog, their browser automatically downloads the JavaScript, and executes it, leading to some nasty consequences (at the behest of the attacker).

There are two specific forms of these attacks to consider:

1. Cross-site scripting (normally shortened to XSS). There are actually multiple versions of this attack. One such attack is using XSS code to steal cookies from a user's browser. The code injected into the blog message discussed earlier could be used to grab the cookies from the user's browser and send them to an attacker. These could then be used to access websites where the cookie acts as an authenticator.

2. SQL injection. A typical SQL injection attack occurs when users are logging onto a system or application where the database is used to store usernames and passwords. If a website is vulnerable to SQL injection then all the usernames and passwords are at risk. The attacker injects a SQL statement rather than a standard username or password into an input field, which is executed by the database to return a dump of all the usernames, passwords, or even private data.

To mitigate both of these kinds of content injection attacks, developers should ensure that they validate all user input prior to its submission to the database or web server and make sure that only legitimate text has been entered. Read more about SQL Injection prevention at `https://www.owasp.org/index.php/SQL_Injection_Prevention_Cheat_Sheet`.

Threat Vectors

Once you understand the tools that the bad guys use to attack your systems, the next thing to consider is how those malware samples make it onto your computer and take hold. The means by which an infection penetrates your system is known as its *threat vector*. The following list provides some of the most common threat vectors that you need to be aware of; but be warned, this is just a simplified overview. There are actually thousands of specific examples, each of which comprises a set of vulnerabilities that leaves you prone to being exploited.

- **Visiting and interacting with malicious websites.** If you happen to visit a compromised website or one that's been specifically set up by hackers, there is a good chance that the code behind the website is checking your system for vulnerabilities and attempting to download malware. Furthermore, if you download an application from the Internet, unless you can be sure the application is legitimate, you are at risk of picking up an authentic-looking application which contains malware (possibly a virus, worm, rootkit or backdoor). Only download software from trusted sources or vendor websites (as long as you are convinced that the website is the vendor's site—that's another related issues).

■ **Note** The Windows Autoruns feature can be easily exploited by hackers. Systems that have Autoruns enabled will automatically run software from newly inserted removable media, such as CDs, DVDs and USB flash drives. If the Autoruns files on the removable media are malicious, then the user doesn't even have to run an application themselves to become infected. Learn more about how to switch on and off the Autoruns feature at https://technet.microsoft.com/en-au/sysinternals/bb963902.aspx.

- **Malware transmitted to your system as an email attachment.** Email attachments are probably the single most common source of infection these days. How do you know that the document in an email you've been sent doesn't have a macro virus, or the Flash movie doesn't have a virus embedded within it? Also commonly seen is email containing a link to a file stored within a legitimate cloud storage service, such as DropBox or Google Docs, where the target file contains the malware, so it won't be picked up by your anti-malware products until you access it; by then it may be too late.

- **Lack of system hardening.** PCs, Apple Macs, tablets, and mobile phones support multiple forms of communication: Ethernet, wireless and Bluetooth, for example. If you have all these communications services turned on, in theory an attacker could target your system even when you are not using it. For example, if you have wireless turned on, you might end up acting as a wireless access point for others to access your own network. An attacker might break into your device over Bluetooth then jump from your device into the corporate network over the LAN.

Technical Countermeasures

Now that you're suitably frightened by all of these different kind of malware, it's time to look at the technical countermeasures you employ in your organization to protect your assets from attack. In this section we'll look at the following aspects of technical security:

- **Endpoint security systems.** It's commonplace for every computer system you manage, including mobile devices, tablets and laptops, as well as desktop PCs and servers, to have an endpoint security system installed on it. Traditionally, these systems were known as *antivirus products*, but most of these sorts of products have grown unto protection suites that include a number of security controls all working together to protect the host. Endpoint protection suites include malware protection, sometimes a host firewall, as well as features such as device control, application control, rogue device detection, and host-based intrusion prevention. More importantly, these systems require management and must be updated with the latest patches and signatures as soon as they are released, since any lag effectively opens an attack surface that hackers will look to exploit. Most modern enterprise endpoint protection suites also use reputation services to reduce the gap that exists between signature updates, where they continually check files and websites being accessed to see if they have previously been found the be malicious.

■ **Note** Antivirus software does not provide a guarantee you are safe from infection—we've previously mentioned zero-day attacks. Most antivirus products only detect known viruses and malware. A few also provide what's known as *heuristic detection* (behavioral) but these systems are not always as reliable as you might think.

- **Personal firewalls**. Most endpoint security suites these days, especially if they want to remain competitive with the market leaders, come with an embedded personal firewall. It's hard to understand why this trend, especially in the Microsoft Windows marketplace, has occurred, since Windows has shipped with a perfectly good host-based firewall for the last ten years. Either way, whether you decide to use the native Windows firewall or the one supplied with your endpoint security suite, you should make sure that you switch it on and use it to protect your systems from unsolicited incoming connections. This can server s number of purposes, including stopping malware spreading laterally on your network by jumping across hosts.

- **Perimeter controls**. Perimeter controls are used to restrict network traffic flows in and out of your corporate network, such as for email and web browsing. For email protection, you might want your perimeter controls to include malware scanning of all attachments and embedded links prior to delivery to the client. A common architectural choice is to deploy an anti-malware solution that is different from your corporate desktop choice within the Internet gateway, so that you, in effect, have two chances of catching new or mutating viruses. You can also implement spam filters in the perimeter to limit the amount of junk mail that makes it into your internal email system, which in turn limits the users' exposure to potentially harmful content and links. Moreover, some organizations also implement *content filtering* in their Internet gateway, which prevents certain types of attachments coming in, while allowing deep inspection of other content that could be hiding malware, such as within compound documents and compressed folders (Microsoft Office XML files and ZIP files, for example). Website content filtering can scan all web traffic, looking for unsafe downloads and preventing them from getting to the user's computer. It's worth calling out that if a connection is established with a website that insists on encryption, then the encryption shields malware from being detected. In these cases, you need to balance the cost of user security against enterprise security and consider terminating SSL connections in the perimeter to allow your protection mechanisms to check it.

■ **Note**   Content checkers can be used to implement *blacklists* and *whitelists*. Blacklists are lists of websites that users are prohibited from accessing, such as gambling sites or pornography sites. Whitelists are lists of websites that users are permitted to access. Blacklists require that you have the ability to manage the sites that are blocked and continually update when new threats emerge. Whitelists require that all new sites users who want access are added to the list. In a large and dynamic organization, the management overhead of managing both blacklists and whitelists can be prohibitive. This is why vendors have shifted to *reputation services*, where the vendor does the work of identifying malicious or unsuitable sites, based on policy decisions, then all you need to do is manage the policy, not the individual site entries.

- **Import and export controls.** Some organizations, especially those with extensive security requirements such as government agencies, use special system boundary controls known as *import/export controls*. In this case, only users that are permitted to import or export data to the organization's computer systems. This means you would need to deploy a system that can limit access to external interfaces, such as removable media, to authorized and suitably cleared users. It could require special software, complicated configuration and targeted training to be successful (people, processes and technology). Typically, this kind of security control combines an endpoint protection solution with content checking to ensure that anything imported or exported is safe and within the constraints of company policy. For example, for a government department, the import/export control service might prevent any data marked as RESTRICTED from being removed from the corporate network.

- **Intrusion detection and prevention systems (IDS/IPS):** These systems detect attacks through signature matching (much in the way anti-malware products work). Some of them are also capable of detecting anomalous behavior. Intrusion prevention systems detect and prevent attacks, while intrusion detection systems only detect and alert you to the threat. Today, running in IPS mode is most prevalent, since it automatically takes action to remove the threat. Nevertheless, if an IPS is misconfigured, it can stop things from working properly—potentially becoming the source of a denial-of-service attack.

- **Application whitelisting:** Application whitelisting refers to technologies used to prohibit users from executing unauthorized code on computer systems. This is an extremely powerful protection mechanism as it stops users installing extraneous, unmanaged applications on their systems. Furthermore, if malware gets installed on the system, it cannot execute because of the application control policy. The Windows operating system comes with a built-in application whitelisting feature called AppLocker.

■ **Tip**   Learn more about Microsoft's AppLocker at `https://technet.microsoft.com/en-us/library/hh831440(v=ws.11).aspx`.

- **Device whitelisting**: Device whitelisting will prevent users from reading or writing to devices attached to their computer systems (removable media, printers, etc.), unless they are authorized to do so. The system might be configured so that users cannot read or write to USB connected flash drives unless they are selected clerks who have been trained in the company's import and export procedures. Device control can reduce the risk posed by the Autoruns feature in Microsoft Windows.

- **System hardening**: System hardening is the process of locking down your system's configuration. The term is a generic one and can be applied to operating systems, end user applications, middleware, databases, servers, and so forth. It's a great idea to document a hardening approach for your technical teams, so that there is a consistent approach to how systems are locked down and built in the production environment. If possible, system hardening should be built into the system installation procedures and where you can, make this an automated deployment. If the hardening procedure is complicated, human error can sometimes lead to misconfigurations and then a false sense of security, where in reality your systems are still exposed to attack. By way of an example, you could lock down web browsers so that they never permit the downloading of ActiveX controls. This would prevent a selection of exploits that rely on ActiveX being available on the desktop. Every decision you take from a hardening perspective requires a risk management decision, since the removal of functionality such as ActiveX will mean loss of functionality for the end user. Security always comes with some kind of trade off.

SPECIAL TECHNICAL CONTROLS

While it's possible to approach many of the risks with technical controls, there are also other ways to mitigate risks that are not of a technical nature. The following procedural measures will also help you manage technical risks:

- **User awareness**. One of the most important non-technical measures you can introduce into your organization is that of user awareness. There are a number of approaches by which you can begin to instill a culture of more security aware users, including writing clauses into your employment contracts and/or in security operating procedures. You can also run training courses and put up posters, send out email briefing notes and even run a weekly prize for staff who report security issues with your environment or systems. Teach users to be aware of opening attachments in email from unknown senders, to not click links when they don't know the origin, and not to install software they can't guarantee is genuine. If in doubt, they should not be afraid to ask the security team—where you as the security manager can then help, investigate and recommend the best approach.

- **Patching**. We have already looked at why patching is so important, however, it is still surprising how many organizations don't have a good approach to making sure their systems are all up to date. Good practice indicates you should have a patching policy and a team that implements that policy. This includes analyzing all patch notifications from vendors, to see which are most important and ensuring critical ones that affect your security are applied as quickly as possible. It's also worth pointing out that you should create a map of infrastructure services to allow the patching teams to understand the criticality of certain systems and the impact of not patching on time. Using a risk-based heat map is a good way to map your environment.

- **Development standards**. Many organizations develop their own software applications, particularly application that make use of web technologies, either for Internet facing websites or the corporate intranet. However, it's easy for less experienced developers to introduce vulnerabilities into those applications, therefore, for this reason, any organization developing applications should also try and adopt secure coding standards developed by expert organizations, such as the Open Web Application Security Project (OWASP).

To learn more about OWASP, check out the website at `http://www.owasp.org`.

Network Security

Today's business world is very different to that of ten years ago. Modern organizations have staff, contractors, partners, and customers all accessing information, systems and services from a variety of locations, both on site and off site, from mobile environments. Organizations are also moving away from owning all the IT equipment, where renting infrastructure from cloud providers has become commonplace and allowing users to bring their own IT equipment to work has also become popular, branded a *bring your own device* (BYOD). Some staff may be accessing your information from their home office, while customers might interact with you via your consumer website. Even government departments are taking their services online, interacting with citizens in a digital context for tax returns voting and benefits. Furthermore, people are accessing information in different way, using a variety of technologies, such as broadband (via wired and wireless networks), Wi-Fi, 3G, or 4G. Some businesses permit their partners to access your corporate infrastructure via an extranet, which allows them to collaborate on projects, tenders and even R&D. Multiple sites can be connected using an internally accessible Wide Area Network (WAN), with each node on the WAN independently connected to the Internet for staff to access personal or private services, such as social media and banking. In fact, many businesses now have social media platforms for their own staff to collaborate on, such as Microsoft's Yammer, which is hosted in Microsoft's own datacenters. There is such a blurred line between what's corporate and what's private these days that security is no longer considered as a network perimeter problem only, with of security teams now concerned more with controlling data than the network itself. Nevertheless, this does not mean the network should be without security, just that there are now multiple levels of control above the network that are equally as important and that hard boundaries will not work for modern organizations. Security managers will need to understand both the concepts of network security, as well as how other layers of technical security can be applied on top of the network to limit the damage from data traversing your corporate perimeter.

Most network security architectures start with the introduction of a device known as a *firewall*. These are network security devices that isolate and control traffic flows between different networks. Firewalls provide security enforcement based on the traffic flowing through them or the traffic they block, usually based on policies that define what's permitted and what should be blocked.

Figure 10-2 shows how a firewall can be inserted into your corporate network to protect the internal network from the Internet. This firewall will enforce elements of your corporate policy, thus attempting to limit who has access to what. Most firewalls will also provide a comprehensive audit record of all the traffic that passes through them (as well as everything it's blocked and dropped). This audit record can be used to alert security operations teams about potential violations and intrusions that can be further investigated. Some firewalls also act as the endpoint of encrypted connections, known as *virtual private networks* (VPN). VPNs provide the access control mechanism to manage remote access to your infrastructure, such as for home workers and traveling sales staff.

169

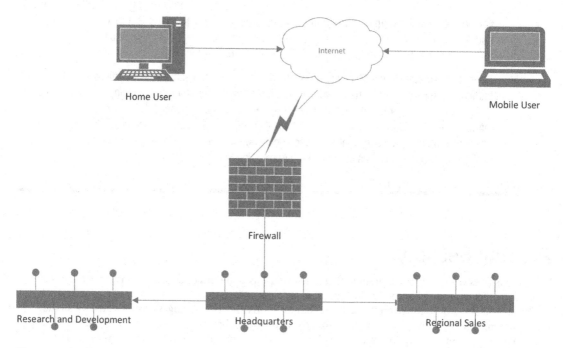

Figure 10-2. *Network diagram showing the position of a simple perimeter firewall*

What Are Firewalls?

Firewalls are used to isolate and control the flow of traffic between networks. Their function is to provide a security control point in the network where administrators choose what can pass and what is blocked. Firewalls assist in providing some protection of a private network by enforcing policies that say that has access to what resources. Firewalls provide a full audit trail of everything they do (blocks and permits) so that you can review what's happened over a period of time. This logging can be used as a feed into an operating center, where they can act on real time alarms, hence managing an incident where an attacker may have been detected at the network layer.

There are a variety of different kinds of firewall on the market. National Institute of Standards and Technology (NIST) categories firewalls in three different ways (http://csrc.nist.gov/publications/nistpubs/800-41-Rev1/sp800-41-rev1.pdf):

- Packet filters

- Stateful inspection

- Proxys

Packet filtering firewalls either permit or deny traffic from passing through its interfaces, based on source and destination addresses, ports, and/or protocols. This is the most basic network protection mechanism for keeping out intruders. No one uses these any more but I've mentioned them just for historical reference.

Stateful inspection (or dynamic packet filtering) firewalls control the *state* of network connections, using this knowledge of who and what is communicating to determine which packets to permit. However, the drawback of using both of these kinds of firewalls is that they have no means of analyzing layer 7 traffic. This means that neither a packet filtering firewall or a stateful inspection firewall can prevent an HTTP-based application attack (this is traffic that will be passed through the other two kinds of firewall unhindered).

Proxy firewalls, which are more commonly referred to as application firewalls, combine all the protection mechanisms of packet filtering and stateful inspection with deep content inspection of application traffic.

UNIFIED THREAT MANAGEMENT

Most recently, vendors have introduced a new category of security products, known as *unified threat management* (UTM) systems—originally introduced by Fortinet, a security company. UTM systems now integrate a variety of network security capabilities that were traditionally provided by separate devices. The value proposition that vendors are extoling on UTM products is that they detect and block all kinds of malicious activity on the network, even integrating endpoint security capabilities with the UTM firewall devices, as well as sandboxes that can profile software activities looking for certain indicators of compromise that denote malware, even if a signature is not available.

In addition to combining all of the typical security capabilities together, the majority of UTM solutions also incorporate sandboxes into the perimeter protection. A sandbox is a specially controlled mirror of the operating systems contained within the environment (not managed by the internal administrators) that the UTM solution can use to execute potential malware samples and then determine what harm it might do. Sandboxes will allow the malware to run, capturing each of the attempts it makes to write to the file system and access the Internet, so that this behavior can further enhance the capabilities of the internal endpoint protection systems to look for this kind of behavior and prohibit it. Sandboxing is one of the key technologies of modern UTM solutions, so you need to be aware of their capabilities, limitations and uses. To learn more about Fortinet's UTM systems and sandbox, take a look at https://www.fortinet.com/solutions/small-business/connected-utm.html.

The Demilitarized Zone (DMZ)

One of the most well-known and implemented network security architecture patterns is that of the demilitarized zone (DMZ). This is a special network segment dedicated to security situated between one network and another, where you would usually trust one of those networks more than the other.

The outer firewall would have its interfaces configured to face the untrusted network, filtering unsolicited traffic and only allowing certain protocols through into the DMZ. The network segment between the two firewalls provides a variety of special security functions, such as content filtering, malware scanning and intrusion prevention, thus trapping any discovered malicious connections or content before they have a chance to reach the internal network. The inner firewall serves to further protect the internal network, potentially limiting access to that network to only the devices in the DMZ. This means that all inbound traffic coming from the untrusted network must first pass through one or more of the special security devices, thus acting as a gatekeeper for all network connections.

Further to providing network security functions, many organizations choose to situate external business services, such as a web server, in the DMZ. This has the added benefit of protecting the web server from a variety of network attacks, since you'll have a number of network security services protecting it.

To illustrate just how powerful a DMZ architecture can be, you might choose to deploy security policies to achieve the outcomes required from the following corporate policy statements:

- External users of the website are forwarded to the external web server, situated within the DMZ. This means that unsolicited connections coming from the Internet can only traverse the outer firewall and be directed to the web server.

- Traffic originating from the external web server can never pass through the inner firewall and enter the internal network.

171

- Internal network users can send emails through the DMZ in both directions.

- Internal network users are permitted to browse to the Internet.

- Internal network users can browse to the external webserver.

- Incoming connection from the Internet are limited to the protocols required for email and web browsing.

VIRTUAL LOCAL AREA NETWORKS (VLANS)

Virtual Local Area Networks (VLANs) are an important security enforcing network capability used to segment networks into smaller security zones. A typical VLAN architecture is used to segment (compartmentalize) your network into virtual networks, with each network's purpose dedicated to one kind of function or the required level of access. By way of illustration, take a company with 350 employees, each with a PC on the internal network connecting to a variety of enterprise servers, providing services such as a corporate intranet, enterprise email, file store, and line of business applications. If each system is plugged into the same network, if a backdoor got installed on one of your PCs, then every other system in your enterprise is at risk. However, if all the database servers are on their own special VLAN, where the only access to that VLAN is offered to front-end application servers (which are also in their own VLAN), then the users compromised computer cannot be used to attack the database directly.

VLANs are often associated with IP subnets, with each device on a given subnet belonging to the same VLAN. VLAN membership on a network switch is often manually configured, thus maintaining complete control over who has access to what.

Using VLANs within your business to segment your internal network is an extremely powerful security control. It is well worth reading up on VLAN architectures and implementation so I've included a link to a great article by Cisco on how they work:

```
http://www.ciscopress.com/articles/article.asp?p=2208697&seqNum=6
```

Network Encryption

Cryptography is covered in Chapter 7; however, it's worth looking at some of the things we can do with encryption within technical security to protect communications traffic. There are four main use cases for cryptography in network security:

- **Confidentiality**. Confidentiality refers to the protection of network traffic from an attacker who may be trying to listen into connections transmitted across your infrastructure. If the connections are protected by encryption, then the attacker can't listen in.

- **Data integrity**. Cryptography is used to detect whether data has been deleted or modified, thus protecting its integrity.

- **Authentication**. Certain kinds of cryptographic systems can be used to support authentication services. This can be used to authenticate both computer systems and users.

- **Non-repudiation**. There are a variety of non-repudiation related capabilities that can be used in network security. Non-repudiation is typically provided using digital signatures.

One significant and pervasive encryption technology that's worth looking at is Transport Layer Security (TLS). Initially designed by Netscape back in 1995, the first implementation of the TLS standard was known as Secure Sockets Layer (SSL). Netscape engineers wanted to be able to secure network connections between users' web browsers and the websites they were accessing. After two iterations of the protocol's design, they arrived at SSL v3 in 1996, which because a standard, ratified by the Internet Engineering Task Force (IETF) as RFC 6101.

■ **Tip** RFC 6101 contains the entire specification of the initial standard for security web browsing, Secure Sockets Layer (SSL). You can read this early RFC at `https://tools.ietf.org/html/rfc6101`.

Due to a number of security flaws and vulnerabilities discovered across the years in implementations of the SSL standard, an evolution of the method for securing web connections was introduced in 1999 called Transport Layer Security (TLS). TLS operates at the application layer of the network, carrying application traffic, such as HTTP (for web browsing) or email. It is designed as a point-to-point protocol so operates between two communicating endpoints.

■ **Caution** One important consideration is that the mechanism used for establishing connections also decides which cryptographic algorithms are to be used by the endpoints. Care should be taken to avoid situations where weak algorithms are selected during this setup phase (as this is still permitted by the IETF standard). Learn more about managing insecure cipher suites here: `https://www.owasp.org/index.php/Transport_Layer_Protection_Cheat_Sheet`

The security services offered by TLS are as follows:

- **Authentication**. Web servers authenticates to the browser using the website's digital certificate, verified using the relevant trusted certificate. If the website has a VeriSign certificate, for example, then the browser will use that certificate to verify the authenticity of the website. This is called *server authentication*. If the authenticity cannot be verified, then a warning is provided to the user to allow them to make a decision as to whether it should be trusted or not. Optionally, it is possible to configure TLS so that the web browser also authenticates itself to the website. This mode of operation is called *client authentication* and is more commonly used in enterprise solutions than commercial solutions.

- **Encryption**. During the authentication phase (session establishment) the encryption algorithm is mutually agreed by the website and browser, and a symmetric encryption key is shared. All traffic to and from the endpoints is then encrypted using this symmetric key.

- **Integrity**. Besides providing encryption, TLS also provides an element of integrity on the data transmitted; hence, any attempts to modify, delete, or insert data are also detected.

SSL ACCELERATION

One additional mode of operation you might come across in the enterprise world is where a VPN is set up using TLS. Just like traditional VPNs, it is possible to use hardware to provide the SSL communication, but in the case of a TLS VPN, they are commonly positioned in front of the web server. These are usually referred to as SSL accelerators, although they do support both SSL and TLS protocols. SSL accelerators, just like VPN concentrators, are dedicated hardware devices and usually come as standalone hardware appliances or as a dedicated card plugged into the server.

The primary reason for using an SSL accelerator is that the SSL session establishment creates a processing overhead on the server during session establishment and the encryption/decryption services, which, in a high-load environment can add a delay into communications. SSL accelerators are fast and efficient and offload the SSL protocol's overhead onto dedicated hardware.

Virtual Private Networks

Virtual private networks (VPNs) are used to create private networks over public networks, such as the Internet. In effect, a VPN will provide a closed community of authorized network users, along with one or more of the following security features:

- Confidentiality and integrity of data

- Network (device) authentication

- User authentication

There are three primary implementation modes that can be used when establishing a VPN:

- Point-to-Point Tunneling Protocol (PPTP)

- Layer 2 Tunneling Protocol (L2TP)

- Internet Protocol Security (IPSec)

VPNs are sometimes referred to as tunneling technologies, which means they provide a secure *tunnel* through a less secure network. For example, you might connect a remote site's network to your primary office network over the Internet, using a VPN between the two sites to provide confidentiality.

Figure 10-3 shows a VPN connection between site 1 and site 2 passing over the intermediary network (this could be the Internet). A VPN concentrator (a device that establishes and manages VPN connections) manages the VPN networks at site 1 and the partner site.

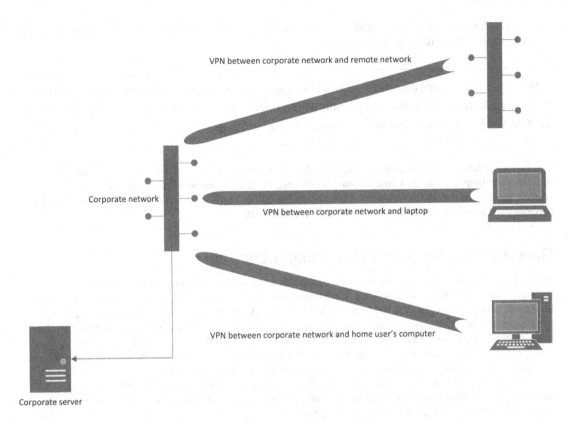

Figure 10-3. VPNs provide a secure point-to-point connection between remote systems

The VPN tunnel may be established using IPSec encryption to secure the traffic between the two VPN concentrators, thus allowing systems operating on the local area networks at site 1 and the partner site to communicate with each other as if they were on the same network.

Wireless Networks

Today, most corporate networks have some kind of wireless access connectivity for roaming users or guests. When a user connects to a wireless access point, they are usually asked to provide a password, in effect acting as the key to unlock the encryption protocol which secures the traffic.

In most cases, users identify the access point's name based on its *service set identifier* (SSID).

■ **Caution**   Open access points, such as those in cafes and shopping malls, can be a security risk. It's easy for attackers to connect to these access points and intercept traffic from any other computer also attached to the same network. Private information transmitted over that network, such as login credentials for a webmail service or bank account, are subsequently at risk.

Hackers have been known to install rogue open access points in public locations, providing open access to Internet as if there were a legitimate provider.

■ **Tip**   If you want to audit the wireless activity of your enterprise users, you should consider looking at Hak5's Wi-Fi Pineapple. This is one of the most powerful Wi-Fi auditing technologies on the market today. Read more about the Wi-Fi___33 Pineapple at `https://www.wifipineapple.com`.

If you connect to a rogue access point, it's highly likely that your data is at risk of being compromised. Attackers can launch what are known as *man-in-the-middle attacks* that break the most secure of TLS session, intercepting traffic to web services, such as your online banking, your email provider and corporate services such as Salesforce, Microsoft Azure, and Amazon's AWS.

Governance Over Network Management

Network management describes the systems, tools and processes needed to operate, administrator, maintain and provision network systems. Information security managers should concern themselves with how those with privileged access to the network devices, such as firewalls and content filters, keep the network secure while changes and upgrades might be occurring. Poor governance can lead to configuration changes occurring on security enforcing functions that may not be fully understood, thus opening up the attack surface to hackers. Similarly, a malicious insider with privileged access to network devices, may change configuration on network devices on purpose to serve a malicious end result.

The security of your business depends on network's integrity remaining intact. This means the architecture and management of configuration needs to be resilient, providing the security manager the assurance that it's sound and without compromise.

Big organizations set up a network management center (NMC) where their entire enterprise can be centrally monitored from. This is most commonly set up as a 24/7 operation, functioning as an extension of the organization's service center and working in conjunction with a *security operations center* (SOC).

The NMC would be required to monitor the status of the network, looking for outages and problems, keeping a watchful eye over the configuration changes that could indicate an attack. Staff working in these sorts of highly trusted roles should be checked for their trustworthiness, potentially being police checked or vetted (if they are government employees or contractors).

The network management staff will be responsible for maintaining all of the network documentation pertaining to configuration, access and architecture, as well as providing governance across all processes and procedures used to manage change requests and implementation.

Make sure that the governance model provides a reporting structure that escalates issues to senior management, so that you can demonstrate you have security policy support for network administration activities.

■ **Tip**   In developing the governance structure and associated processes and procedures, follow the recommendations of a standard such as ISO/IEC 27002, as well as ITIL and ISO 9001.

INTRUSION DETECTION AND PREVENTION

Intrusion Prevention Systems (IPSs) are products that monitor network and/or system activities for malicious activity. The main function of an IPS is to identify abnormal and malicious activity. Many of these products use deep packet inspection in order to identify traffic. Depending on whether it is a prevention system or a detection system, the IPS either prevents or logs the activity. Most modern IPS products can perform both prevention and detection, depending on how they are configured.

IPS systems can be defined in the following four categories:

- **Host Intrusion Prevention System (HIPS)**: These will try to prevent malicious activity. A number of antivirus products can provide this capability. As a simple example of the function, a HIPS product could prevent an unknown outgoing connection initiating from your PC to the Internet. They can also be configured to block attempts to modify critical read-only system files.

- **Host Intrusion Detection System (HIDS)**: These are similar to HIPS products except that they log malicious attempts, but cannot block the activity.

- **Network Intrusion Prevention System (NIPS)**: These devices are hardware solutions that look for certain attack behaviors. They can also prevent attacks, based on predefined signatures. Signatures are usually provided by the supplier but most products allow you to also build custom ones based on your own understanding of threats.

- **Network Intrusion Detection System (NIDS)**: These products can be hardware devices or software programs running on a server, examining all network traffic. As with host-based detection, these report when they detect anomalous behavior, usually based on preconfigured signatures.

Most modern intrusion prevention systems perform both the detection and prevention aspects of this capability. The primary difference between NIDS and NIPS is simply the configuration options you select as a security operations manager. Furthermore, most of the modern security solutions that incorporate NIPS and NIDS into their offerings include additional capabilities with built-in features, such as the following:

- DDoS mitigation

- File emulation

- Geoblocking

- Web application filtering

If you want more information on how NIPS solutions work, take a look at SNORT, an open source product (http://www.snort.org).

■ ■ ■

CHAPTER 11

Digital Evidence and Incident Response

Digital forensics (also referred to as *computer forensics*) is a specialization within the security industry that converges with traditional forensic science. Digital forensics is concerned with the recovery of digital evidence from storage media, computer systems, electronic devices, and social media platforms, incorporating a wide variety of forensic artifacts that can support the efforts of a wider investigation.

Digital forensics has been with us for as long as we've had computer systems, realistically since the first time a computer was involved in some sort of criminal activity. Today, this is a well-established branch of forensic science and is extremely broad in scope (hence the name switch from computer forensics to digital forensics), where investigations are now including analysis of network devices, mobile devices, cloud systems, email (online and in enterprise servers), gaming machines and their associated networks, in-car entertainment systems and GPS devices, as well as all those new devices included in the Internet of Things, such as televisions, radios, and even children's toys. As you can see from this list, it's virtually impossible not to leave a trail of digital breadcrumbs as you go through your daily routine, since every device you interact with is recording information about its use as well as metadata about you that can be useful in a police investigation. I've spoken to a number of law enforcement officers over the years who attest to the fact that every crime now has a digital footprint of some kind that can be help with a prosecution or, indeed, someone's defense.

Digital forensics is such an enormous subject that we'll not be able to go into a lot of detail in just one chapter, however, what's I've done here is so to detail its place from a security management perspective, looking at what it is, what activities are involved in an investigation and what kind of preparation you should undertake to be ready should the need arise.

I've seen many a security guy become so enthralled with this subject that it becomes a calling for them to pursue. The thought of working with the major crime squads from the movies and big-budget TV shows, such as *CSI Cyber*, may seem glamorous and exciting, but the reality of this job is that that there are any number of tedious processes you'll need to follow, meticulously trawling through terabytes of disk data looking for the electronic needle in the digital haystack that could solve the case (or at least give the customer the lead they are looking for). But I'm not trying to put you off choosing digital forensics as a career, since the one common factor throughout the professional digital forensics community is that they all love what they do. Furthermore, I would recommend that you use this chapter as a starting point from which you can further investigate this subject to see if it's for you.

We'll start this this chapter looking broadly at digital forensic science and how it factors into investigations, then we'll look at how to build forensic readiness into your business, including how to operationalize it within the bounds of security management, with a later discussion of how best to build a forensic-readiness plan that underpins your incident response plan. Next we'll take a look at some of the basic disciplines of being a digital forensics investigator then conclude the chapter with a look at how evidence is presented in court, focusing on how to successful give expert witness testimony.

© Tony Campbell 2016
T. Campbell, *Practical Information Security Management*, DOI 10.1007/978-1-4842-1685-9_11

■ **Note** Digital forensics investigations are the purview of only criminal investigations. Businesses are using digital forensic techniques to investigate matters of network attacks, hacking and data breaches, so it becomes a critical disciple that underpins the incident response process.

The Digital Forensic Process

Digital evidence refers to any digital artifact that could be considered useful in an investigation. Artifacts come from a variety of sources, often located in hidden or protected areas of computer systems as opposed to the places directly accessible to normal users. For example, if you delete a document from your hard disk, it doesn't actually get deleted; instead, the file system simply removes the link to where the file is located on the disk. This means the file no longer appears in the standard user interface, but the information still remains on the hard disk unchanged. When using special recovery tools, it's entirely possible to undelete files, returning them to their previous state, even when files are no longer in the system's *recycle bin*. Forensic recovery tools will search through the entire hard disk, ignoring the file system altogether, looking for headers that indicate deleted files are present. As soon as the tool finds an orphaned file, it's straightforward to recover and restore its link. Forensic tools can be used to recover files and folders even allowing entire disk partitions to be recovered from a disk that's been accidentally (or purposely) formatted.

The question is whether this recovered file can be used as evidence. This is where it gets complicated. As long as the proper forensic process has been followed, then the answer is yes; but if the investigator has not followed due process, it can mean that the evidence is tainted and thus inadmissible in court. An entire case can be won or lost on this kind of digital evidence, so understanding the forensic process and following the proper procedures to protect the chain of custody of forensics artifacts is critical to success.

In its simplest form, forensic investigation is a three stage process, as shown in Figure 11-1.

Figure 11-1. *Three stages of the forensic process*

■ **Note** NIST divides this into a four stage process, where the middle box is split into two: examination and analysis. The outcome, however, is the same.

Forensic Acquisition

Forensic acquisition is one of the most crucial steps in the forensic process, because one misstep during these activities can leave evidence tainted and inadmissible. *Acquisition* is the term used to describe the process of obtaining forensic evidence from systems, such as laptops, servers, cell phones, or social media sites. Evidence can be located on hard disks (non-volatile storage) or in memory (volatile storage), so depending on the kind of acquisition you are doing, you will require different processes and different tools.

Acquisition occurs as soon as possible in the investigation, typically as a component on the initial incident management process. In a corporate environment, this would be the job allocated to the incident management team who are responding to the matter. Every activity undertaken during this phase of the forensic process should follow a predefined set of rules. If these rules do not exist as yet, it's time to add them into your incident management process. The incident manager should know how to acquire the data, what tools to use and even how the tools must be deployed to ensure that the evidence remains intact and admissible. Any mistakes made during the forensic acquisition process may be cross examined in court, with the potential to gravely damage a case built around that evidence.

CHAIN OF CUSTODY AND EVIDENTIAL INTEGRITY

Two important aspects of the forensic process are chain of custody and evidence integrity.

Chain of custody is the record of all aspects of the workflows used in handling evidence, from acquisition to presentation in court.

Evidence integrity refers to the ability the investigator has to attest to the authenticity of the evidence, ensuring that throughout the entire forensic process, it remains untainted (unaltered or corrupted) by external influence.

Evidence should be physically sealed in special evidence bags. Some devices with radio transmitters (cell phones and laptops) are best sealed in shielded faraday bags, so that they cannot be remotely wiped by an attacker. Cryptographic signatures are also used to provide original evidence doesn't change as it travels through the chain of custody. The *evidence custodian* signs, dates, and seals the evidence bag, which allows you to see who has handled it at each stage of the investigation.

Write Blockers

Write blockers are special hardware devices that allow forensic acquisition of data from a computer system. The write blocked permits the investigator to make a forensic copy of the original evidence, such as a suspect's hard disk, without the possibility of accidentally damaging the source hard disk. A write blocker passed read commands to the target's hard disk, but actively blocks write commands. Most systems allow read and write commands to flow to and from hard disk in normal operation. The reason a write blocker constrains those write commands from flowing to the target disk is to ensure that an opposing council in a court situation cannot cast doubt over the integrity of the evidence by saying the forensic acquisition process could have introduced unwanted material onto the target disk. Once the original disk has been tampered with in any way, it seriously degrades the weight of the evidence and makes it practically useless as something that could be used for a conviction. This is why it's so important to establish a fully tested and proven forensic acquisition capability, using proven and trusted tools.

Investigation and Analysis

Forensic investigators use evidence collected from the scene of the crime (or incident) to develop a hypothesis of what occurred during the incident, or to locate specific kinds of evidential artifact, such as pornographic images or sales ledgers, that attest to the guilt (or innocence) of a suspect. They use a variety of special forensic analysis tools and techniques to recover data and to help them develop a timeline of events that occurred leading up to the incident.

Timelines are an essential component of forensic analysis. An organization (or a criminal prosecutor) may have trouble understanding the root cause and effect of an incident unless they have a detailed timeline of the events leading up to and including the incident that triggered the investigation. For example, an investigation needs to map a suspect's movements throughout a particular week. It's possible to analyze their cell phone and determine, from GPS records and information sources from mobile phone companies, where that device was located throughout that time period. This evidence can be used to support a case for the suspect being in a certain place at a certain time.

Each of the steps taken during the analysis phase of the investigation must be documented in enough detail so that it's repeatable. Oftentimes the opposing council will hire a digital forensics investigator of their own to check the processes used to find evidence and to look for issues with the processes used to establish guilt.

If evidence is provided in a court situation it will be cross examined by a variety of different kinds of expert witness, such as third-party digital forensic investigators, hardware experts, chain of custody specialists, and even software vendors.

■ **Note**   It's entirely possible that a tool you rely on could be your downfall. If you are in the middle of an investigation and the vendor releases a security patch for the software, if you have no applied that patch prior to starting your analysis, the resultant artifacts presented in court could be contested as the opposing council could legitimately claim that the lack of patching means the evidence could be corrupt. This is why the forensic process is not excluded from your overall approach to information security management and operational security management.

Reporting and Expert Witness Testimony

The last stage of the forensic proves is reporting. All reports must be accurate and without bias and most importantly, should contain only the facts.

When you write a forensic report, you need to be aware that it could potentially end up being submitted in court. The more meticulous you are during your investigation, the more complete your documentation will be and the more valuable it will be in court.

In some cases, the digital forensics investigator may be required to appear in court as an *expert witness*. An expert witness usually has credibility within their profession and has received special training or attained experience in stating their opinion in front of a judge and jury. If you believe someone needs to give evidence in court, you should make sure that they have the knowledge and skills to perform this activity. Training will ensure that the expert witness is well prepared for cross-examination and is prepared to stick to their story, give only the facts and has the strength of character to defend their methods even under severe questioning.

■ **Tip**   For more information on expert witness training take a look at the services offered by company Bond Solon (http://www.bondsolon.com/expert-witness.aspx).

ACPO Principles

In the United Kingdom, The Association of Chief Police Officers (ACPO) of England, Wales, and Northern Ireland, produced a reasonable guide for digital forensic investigations, at least to give you the basic steps you need to go through to keep evidence safe and ensure that it remains admissible in court.

The ACPO guide focuses on four key principles, which are intended to guarantee the integrity of evidence. While there may be nuances that are different across different legal jurisdictions, these are still good practices to follow, especially if you are building digital forensics into your enterprise incident management process.

If you want to read the ACOP guidelines for yourself, take a look at https://www.cps.gov.uk/legal/assets/uploads/files/ACPO_guidelines_computer_evidence[1].pdf; however, I've summarized the four principles for you here.

■ **Note** Investigators must adapt any procedures they use to the standards of evidence and admissibility in their legal jurisdiction. If in doubt, you seek guidance from your local law-enforcement's computer crime squad.

ACPO's First Principle

No action taken by law enforcement agencies or their agents should change data held on a computer or storage media which may subsequently be relied upon in court. (ACPO, 2012)

ACPO's first principle focuses on how you maintain the integrity of digital evidence during the acquisition stage. It looks at how you take a forensic copy of target hard disks, showing that a bit-level image-copy of a disk or set of disks is by far the best approach. A combination of specially designed hardware and software should be used, including write blockers, and in all cases tools should create a cryptographic hash of the acquired image.

■ **Tip** A cryptographic hash is used by legal representatives to attest to the integrity of the data at every stage throughout the chain of custody. No work is ever carried out on the original disk.

ACPO's Second Principle

In circumstances where a person finds it necessary to access original data held on a computer or on storage media, that person must be competent to do so and be able to give evidence explaining the relevance and the implications of their actions. (ACPO, 2012)

Anyone required to give evidence in court should be trained and proven as competent to do so. If you are offered access the original computer or storage media, then you need to be able to stand by your actions and defend your processes and tools in front of a jury or cross-examining barrister. This can be daunting and oftentimes barristers will attack your professionalism and methods to have you expose aspects of your process that could be called into question. Be careful to stick to the facts and remain objective and impartial.

ACPO's Third Principle

An audit trail or other record of all processes applied to computer-based electronic evidence should be created and preserved. An independent third party should be able to examine those processes and achieve the same result. (ACPO, 2012)

For every process undertaken in an investigation, you must be able to provide a complete and incontestable audit trail of all activities, including computer system logs and physical evidence registers, movement orders, packing receipts.

All evidence should be preserved in such a way that another forensic investigator can repeat the same process and arrive at exactly the same result.

■ **Tip** Every single step in an investigation should be fully documented, including any interactions with people, processes, and tools.

ACPO's Fourth Principle

The person in charge of the investigation (the case officer) has overall responsibility for ensuring that the law and these principles are adhered to. (ACPO, 2012)

The fourth ACPO principle is extremely important since it identifies the case offices as the person who is ultimately responsible and accountable for ensuring success of the process. This person needs to be competent (well trained) in investigation techniques and should be credible and prepared to give evidence in court. The case officer should also be aware of the legal frameworks and requirements of courts in the jurisdiction he or she is operating in.

■ **Note** Many investigators are starting to reconsider the validity of this legacy approach to digital forensics since it's almost impossible to extract a forensic image of a cell phone without first changing its configuration. In some cases, the device needs to be *jailbroken*, where the investigator makes changes to the device's hardware configuration to allow them to carry out low-level operations that otherwise they would not be able to do. This is one aspect of digital forensics that is continually being challenged by changing technology and outcomes in court, so it's certainly something to keep watch of.

Forensic Readiness

Forensic readiness a term that you'll hear a lot when you start looking at implementing information security standards in your organization. A forensic readiness plan is the method you use to undertake the necessary steps to acquire examine and report on incidents in a manner this is admissible in court. If you are required (or decide that you should) introduce forensic readiness into your organization, you'll need to examine all aspects of your incident management process, starting with policies and procedures, then moving onto the tools used to prepare for and manage a forensic investigation.

The digital forensics process will become an intrinsic part of your overall incident management process, with the trigger for a forensic acquisition of evidence normally being tested in the early stages of an incident. For example, your security operations center detects strange behavior on a computer in the finance department. The security analyst logs an incident and an incident manager is assigned. When the incident manager assesses the situation, she determines that the computer may contain sensitive corporate financial records, so the investigation may result in the discovery of fraudulent or criminal activity. As a result, she asks the tactical response team to start the forensic acquisition process, ensuring that the computer systems are seized in the most appropriate way, forensic images are taken of all of the hard disks in question, and the investigation can then ensue on those forensic copies. This assures the business that should malfeasance be discovered, due process has been followed and the evidence can lead to a prosecution of the offender.

The key to success in forensic readiness is clearly preparation. NIST has developed an excellent publication that will help security managers integrate the forensic process into an already established incident response process, known as *Special Publication 800-86: Guide to Integrating Forensic Techniques into Incident Response*. You can access this document at `http://nvlpubs.nist.gov/nistpubs/Legacy/SP/nistspecialpublication800-86.pdf`.

Planning

A forensic readiness plan (FRP) is a document that provides your incident management team will all the guidance they need to manage the incident in line with all the requirement of the digital forensics process. A good FRP conforms to your policy and allows you to proactively plan for digital forensics investigations. Furthermore, a FRP should be tested, by means of running exercises and drills to prove the processes work prior to having to use them during a real incident.

The FRP will also identify the kinds of situations where the forensic process must be followed, including documenting all of the anticipated sources of evidence you should consider within your organization— remembering that some evidence may be physical or held in standalone systems, such as electronic door entry records and CCTV, so all aspects of your infrastructure need to be considered. The FRP should contain the following components:

- Clearly stated objectives.

- Designated roles and responsibilities.

- A comprehensive contact list of all persons required for an investigation, including external contacts such as your legal team or law enforcement.

- Processes for acquiring, handling, and storing evidence.

- An escalation matrix that includes who and when to report events to senior management and externally to law enforcement.

There are a variety of standards and codes of practice, pertaining to evidential weight, depending on which legal jurisdiction you operate in. It pays to learn the local rules and consult with your local law enforcement teams to make sure that you are following the correct process for your country or state.

In some cases, your local police force might have a dedicated computer crime squad, so make contact with them, and ask them to verify the forensic processes you have devised. It's unlikely that they won't help you since your having a process that they've endorsed will eventually help them should you become involved in an investigation.

BSI STANDARD BS 10008

In the United Kingdom, the British Standard's Institute (BSI) published a standard numbered BS 10008. This describes the requirements for implementing and operating electronic information management systems, including data processing and information exchange services between computers and storage media. The standard discusses issues of authenticity and integrity of data, helping organizations comply with legal requirements. BS 10008 also covers the process of electronic identity verification, such as the use of electronic signatures and electronic copyright systems. Related to BS 10008 there are three codes of practice published by the BSI. These are referred to collectively as BIP 0008. They provide guidance for the management of electronic documents and show how to ensure that scanned images are accepted as evidence by the courts.

Incident Response and Digital Investigations

When an incident is detected and the incident manager is assigned, this effectively starts your incident response process. An incident is identified when someone or something raises an alert that indicates a violation of company policy or an illegal activity. NIST defines a security incident within Special Publication 800-61 as:

The act of violating an explicit or implied security policy. (NIST, SP 800-61)

An *attack vector* is the means by which an attacker targets a computer system or individual. For example, a hacker might attempt to gain access to a computer system by sending a spam email message to a user, along with a malicious attachment. The attacker is thus attempting to convince the user to open the email and read the attachment, thus executing the malware and infecting the target system. In this case, the attack vector is the spam email, with a blend of social engineering and malware.

Attack vectors are the path an attacker will take to try and exploit vulnerability, so it's the use of these vectors that your security operations team will try to detect, while in turn triggers your incident response process. Once called to action, the first stage of the incident response process is known as *containment*. Your business can significantly benefit from being properly prepared for these kinds of incident, which means your team is more likely to help your business survive during a real attack. By knowing what to do, how to communicate and with whom, a thoroughly tested *incident response plan* (IRP) is the key to a sustainable business, irrespective of what services you provide, what markets you operate, in and how big a target you become.

Security management teams should ensure that the IRP is a primary deliverable of the business's information security management system (ISMS) and is a necessary component part of being certified against standards, such as ISO 27001, PCI-DSS, and COBIT.

■ **Note**   If you don't have a fully tested IRP, when an incident occurs, the ensuing chaos will result in a protracted containment phase, leading to a longer recovery time and hence the resultant business impact (loss of cash, reputation, or lives) will be worse.

The facts relating to each and every incident will undoubtedly be different, but what's important is to test your response plan against a variety of different scenarios, so that your processes are as flexible as possible. This means that your incident response team will be able to think laterally about specific problems and will know, at least at a process levels, what to do throughout the incident's life cycle.

Lastly, regarding the IRP, it's one of those things that needs to be well-understood by all teams and all employees, so that during an incident everyone know what their duties are and what role they play, even if it's as simple as logging out of their computer and shutting it down. When dealing with an incident, well-rehearsed communication and readiness plans ensure that the incident is dealt with effectively and that staff knows who they should and should not discuss the incident with. In a high-profile incident, it pays to prepare the public relations team with pre-canned messages they can tell the media, and one of the very first non-technical aspects of managing any given incident is to work with the executive team or CEO to prepare them for difficult media questioning—this could be on television, on the radio, or during an interview with a journalist which will be published in the paper or online.

Preparation

Your incident management preparations should include defining the methods by which the IRP is communicated to the workforce. The communications plan should be readily available to everyone and it's vital to have both online copies (that are accessed through the corporate Intranet or document management system) and hardcopies that are placed in strategic places throughout your premises so that in the event of systems being down, the plan is still accessible.

As a component of your annual audit of your information security management system, you should review your IRP and update the communication plan, looking for outdates roles, individuals that have left and ensure that you confirm each and every responsible persons' communication methods are up to date, including:

- Phone numbers

- Email addresses

- Work location

- Desk number

- Home address

- Alternative contact information

- The person who is the stand-in if they are unavailable

Corporate policies should indicate how an incident is handled and reported, at least at a high-level, while guidelines and standards should list any necessary reference material needed by incident managers and incident response team members. One aspect of the policy statement that needs to be obvious is the delegation of authority to the Incident Response team. This means that during the incident, the team has special privileges to contain, eradicate, investigate, and restore service, which may involve doing things that, under normal conditions, they may not be permitted to do. This may be because specialist external contractors (forensic investigators) or law enforcement agencies may be brought into the investigation and given special system access to investigate what's gone on. Like your IRP, you should review (maybe during your annual audit) your security policies to make sure that they conform to changes in the law, changes in your organizational governance or court rulings that might affect how you manage incidents. For example, if you open up a new office over a state or national border, you'll need to make sure that you review the legal and law-enforcement implication for your new office and abide by any new rules.

BUSINESS CONTINUITY PLANNING

Business continuity planning (BCP) is another process discipline you'll hear about when you start investigating incident response. It's an aspect of your overall incident preparedness; however, BCP is somewhat different in purpose to that of *disaster recovery planning* (DRP), which you might also have heard of. Let's look at the difference between the two.

Both processes require that you create plans that help you resume business functions if they are affected by an incident. Disaster recovery relates to resuming normal business operation when a system is attacked or fails, such as when you failover a website to a working server, or recover a system from backup storage media. The important aspect of understanding the differences though is that DRP relates to recovery during normal operation. The rest of the business continues to operate, even if it's disrupted for a period of time. BCP is to do with creating the processes and systems for your entire organization to act during an extreme incident. The mode of operations of the business may be insurmountably disrupted, such as during an earthquake or terrorist attack, but critical services that keep the business running are moved to a BCP site (maybe in the cloud) and whatever are deemed critical business functions will continue to work at an acceptable level.

The following four steps will help you build a BCP process:

- Identify the assets that need to be available during the incident

- Design the methods and system you'll need to protect your organization

- Test and validate all of the processes and systems within your plan

- Communicate the details of the plan to all staff

The processes of business continuity planning is closely related to risk management since you are determining the impact of loss of critical systems so that you can quantify the overall value of these systems to the business. This informs your BCP business case when you approach the management for a business continuity budget.

Detection and Analysis

Observing and acting on suspicious activities within the business is a complicated and often overlooked aspect of incident management. If you have no means of detecting an incident, it's possible for an attacker to compromise your systems and maintain access for months. If you don't have adequate means of observing the state of your systems and analyzing their security state, you'll likely only know about the incident when you receive an external trigger, such as confidential information appearing on a hacking website or sensitive details of your business appearing in the media.

Log events are generated by most modern technology so these can be ingested by special monitoring systems known as security information and event managers (SIEMs), which allow security operations teams to monitor the environment from one location (the security operations center). Security events require a level of analysis, either automatic or by a trained analyst to make sense of the information and use it to detect potential threats. If an event or alarm is detected which serves as an indicator of compromise (the industry term for something that could be malicious) then the incident management process can be enacted. The security operations center (SOC) becomes the central early warning system that sifts through hundreds of thousands of log events to look for those indicators of compromise, based on signatures, heuristics, and pre-programed correlation rules that detect attack vectors being used.

There are two methods that investigators can use when investigating an incident, with the choice depending on the circumstances of the event. The first type is known as *static analysis*, which often entails the investigator using special tools to look at what malware is installed on a system and how that malware might work. However, the investigator will not execute the malware to look at its behavior as doing so may be dangerous or destructive. Often specialist investigators will use binary debuggers, such as IDA[1]. Static analysis is also sometimes referred to as *code analysis*. The second form of investigation involves the investigator setting up a special test environment and then running the malware, so that they can record what the malware does and use those results to determine how it operates and what impact it may have on the target machine. These environments are called *sandboxes*. Dynamic analysis is also sometimes called *behavioral analysis*.

VirusTotal (https://www.virustotal.com) is a great online resource that you can use to test malware samples and potentially harmful URLs. The VirusTotal checking systems outputs a file's static properties so can really help the investigator quickly determine some of the basic behavior of the submitted file

---

[1]IDA is a special Windows, Linux, or Mac OS X multiprocessor disassembler and debugger, available from Hex-Rays at https://www.hex-rays.com/products/ida/.

> ■ **Note** Hybrid Analysis is a useful sandboxing technology that, in combination with VirusTotal, provides a very good picture as to whether the sample could be malicious or not. Hybrid Analysis can be found at `https://www.hybrid-analysis.com` with VirusTotal.

Containment and Recovery

Once the analysis phase finishes, the Incident Response Team looks at ways to contain the impact of the incident and resolve it as cleanly and effectively as possible. A well-considered containment plan will help you minimize the incident's impact on the business, but in the rush to contain, for example, a virus outbreak, you need to make sure that you don't lose vital sources of evidence, such as *volatile* memory.

> ■ **Note** There are two kinds of computer system memory that incident investigators need to consider. Non-volatile memory can contain evidence that survives when the power is cut, such as files and folders stored on a hard disk. Volatile memory is where running programs, operating system processes and some user data is stored on a computer system when it's still operational. If the power is removed from the system, anything stored in volatile memory is lost and cannot be recovered. Incident responders need to find ways to preserve volatile data as well as non-volatile data when attempting to contain an incident, so appropriate training and tools are required to ensure that they don't corrupt the evidence and lose vital clues needed to successfully conclude the investigation.

Business recovery is process by which you return the business to normal operations. Most of the time, recovery involves your administrator returning systems to their pre-incident state, such as restoring systems from backups, running scripts or processes that re-establish system access and network access and ensure that the business can move back to the status it was in prior to the attack or realization of the hazard. In cases where multiple desktop systems are affected by malware, such as during a malware or ransomware outbreak, some administrators will perform a clean installation of the standard operating environment (operating system and standard applications) since it's quicker to do this than try to deal with a contaminated system. The rationale is that it's very hard to guarantee the malware has been fully erased (some infections are clever enough to hide multiple copies of themselves and could remain dormant for week or even months without detection). Find the best way to recover from each of your pre-tested incident categories and ensure that you have the technical and process mechanisms in place to allow those recovery processes to work—it's not use saying you'll recover from backups if the backup system hasn't worked for the last couple of months and you don't have a current state SOE to recover to.

Post-Incident Activities

The post-incident activity phase is all about documenting, reporting, and assessing the efficacy of the IRP. The kinds of reports you'll likely need to create include the forensic log of how the incident was handled, through to a closure report which analyses and quantifies the effectiveness of each stage of the IRP. You'll need to consider all aspects of the methods, techniques, methodologies, and findings relating to this incident, remembering that there are multiple stakeholders for these reports so they need to be clear, succinct, and free of unnecessary technical jargon.

Investigating a Malware Outbreak

Data needs to be captured and preserved as early as possible in an investigation, as this avoids what could be considered as critical evidence being corrupted. It's especially important in a malware investigation that volatile data is captured early on in the process before you try to capture other kinds of data, such as the data on hard disks or USB-connected media. One way to handle the capture of volatile data is to dump it to disk, where you force the operating system to store the entire contents of the system's memory in a dump file for later investigation. This is a legitimate way of capturing this kind of data (i.e., it's been used to provide evidence that's been accepted by the courts), however, one drawback is that if you dump the memory to an internal disk you could overwrite deleted files, making later forensic recovery difficult or impossible. As a first responder (i.e., the first investigator to react to the incident) you'll need to quickly assess the situation and make a call as to whether the user is a suspect or not and whether or not there would be evidence on the system disk that the user might have decided to delete when they knew you were coming. Sometimes, in criminal cases, it may be the police are the first people on site, since the crime scene will be off limits until it is secured and other forensic investigations have concluded. So, that police person becomes your first responder, so they need to know how to assess the situation and how to triage multiple incidents linked to the same crime scene. This is an advanced kind of digital forensic investigation, so for the purposes of this book to illustrate how we'd investigate malware, let's use the situation where you work in a business and there has been a malware outbreak. Let's also, for the sake of argument, assume that the service desk told the user to pull the power cord out of the back of their machine, to preserve system state but they lost the volatile memory. So, we start with capturing non-volatile memory. The computer system, for the sake of argument, is a desktop PC running Windows 7 and it's been removed from the network and brought to your lab.

Getting Started

Before you start investigating the system, you'll need to take a forensic copy of the entire hard disk and you'll do your investigation from that. You set up your forensic imaging computer and connect the special write blocker device that makes sure the suspect machine's hard disk is not modified by the copying process. You are now capturing all of the non-volatile data elements you'll need to sift through in your investigation, such as system and user logs, system and user accounts and groups, all of the system's configuration files, along with any stored (cached) passwords, scripts, files, history files (command history and browser history), swap files, dump files, security logs, special temporary files and directory listings. Non-volatile data is collected using traditional *dead-box* forensic processes, where you where disks are removed from the suspect systems then images and recorded in an evidence log for later discovery purposes. So, you've taken out the disk, taken a forensic copy of it, then placed the original disk in an evidence bag, in a locker and recorded what you did, what the serial number and identifying features of the disk are and signed the chain of custody record. Let's now look at how you'd handle a malware sample.

Handling Malware

You'll start by investigating the forensic copy you have taken of the suspect's hard disk. Getting started, you can run a variety of anti-malware tools across the disk, ones that are licensed especially for your laboratory. Your company may use one vendor's antimalware product on its desktop and, if they are particularly careful about their protection, they may also have a second antimalware system in their Internet gateway. However, in the lab, some investigators have another half dozen malware scanning systems that specialize in detecting rootkits, alternative indicators of compromise and even events in event logs that could indicate some kind of attack.

Most modern malware is relatively sophisticated so individual instances can use many techniques to avoid detection. Some hide within the file system masquerading as legitimate files (such as operating system applications) and some hide themselves deeper, such as in alternate data streams. Some malware will be written to specifically exploit known vulnerabilities so that it can avoid detection and close down system protections, such as file recovery or deleting the security logs. Some malware can randomly change its internal code to avoid being detected by signature based antivirus products or Host Intrusion Prevention Systems, also masking the code so that it's very difficult for an investigator to reverse engineer it binary code.

Sandboxes

Investigators will often set up lab environments that simulate the real network, but are self-contained systems that they can quickly rebuild to a known state. These special environments are known as sandboxes since they care self-contained play areas where you can literally destroy the systems in it and no real harm is caused. Sandboxes are helpful as identified malware samples can be executed and observed to see how they operate, which is a method investigators use to fingerprint the malware sample, potentially reverse engineer it to understand the code behind its malicious activates, which can be used for a variety of purposes. It pays to build a sandbox environment in your security operations center so that your incident response team can investigate malware samples in this controlled and safe environment.

■ **Tip**   The most popular malware analysis sandbox technology is the Cuckoo Sandbox (`https://www.cuckoosandbox.org`). The website claims, "You can throw any suspicious file at it and in a matter of seconds Cuckoo will provide you back some detailed results outlining what such file did when executed inside an isolated environment." This is an extremely valuable tool for investigators and malware researchers.

Indicators of Compromise

If the investigator gets to the stage where they have identified some unique behavior of the malware, then it's possible to use this unique pattern to help detect it elsewhere in the environment. To do this, investigators create a special signature that can identify the malware, either from the files it installs or creates on the target system, or by the changes it makes to the operating system, such as modified registry keys, changes to configuration files and modifications to system privileges. One way to do this is to use a common language that is understood by a software tool, so that you can use this as a common way across your enterprise (and even with partners) to share threat information and ensure that all your systems are primed to detect the malware you have just analyzed. A tool, such as FireEye's Redline application comes with a variety of well-known indicators of compromise built into it and also allows you to write your own, which can be exported and shared with anyone who you believe needs it.

You can learn more about Redline on FireEye's website at `https://www.fireeye.com/services/freeware/redline.html`.

Reporting

The last stage of any investigation is writing up the report. This is a document that needs to be clearly written, factually correct and provides a management summary of what was discovered, along with all of the steps that were taken throughout the investigation and all of your findings at each stage.

It is especially important if your incident response leads to a criminal investigation that you accurately record every single action you took and keep this actions log with the chain of custody log.

If you want to learn more about report writing for digital forensics investigations, the SANS Institute provides some excellent resources, templates, and insight into what you need to cover. For more information, take a look at `https://digital-forensics.sans.org/blog/2010/08/25/intro-report-writing-digital-forensics/`.

CHAPTER 12

■ ■ ■

Cloud Computing Security

In the past few years, the IT services industry has seen a remarkable shift from businesses managing the whole of the IT stack within their own datacenters to almost all of their services being shifted to cloud models, where infrastructure, platforms and software are all delivered as-a-service, with the underlying support and maintenance fees shifting into operational expenditure rather than annualized capital expense budgets. However, the information security industry has struggled to keep up with the pace of change, given the lack of detailed technical security standards and guidelines that focus on cloud computing. The entire cloud services industry is still in its infancy, however, the claims being made by some cloud service providers with regards to the strength of their security capabilities is leading customer to make decisions to shift into these environments without understanding all the risks. In this chapter we'll take a look at some of the basic technologies of virtualization, the systems that power cloud platforms, then look at what cloud computing is and how security should be considered if you are moving to the cloud.

The basis of cloud computing technology is that of virtualization, where systems can be logically divided up into multiple virtual hosts that are then provided to customers. The units of virtualization—that is, what's provided—are based on what it is the customer needs, starting with infrastructure (the basic computer processing capability), the platform (the computer system plus the operating system), or the business application (the software).

Cloud Computing 101

First thing's first, let's start with some terminology. The term *subscriber* is used to describe any entity that consumes a cloud service. Subscribers come in a variety of guises, including:

- End users, who are the actual users of the cloud service
- Server systems, which an organization might use a cloud provider to provide its email system

The *cloud service provider* might provide a service to a single subscriber tenant, known as a *private cloud*. Private clouds are usually provided by large enterprises or governments to multiple internal teams, using all the technology a public cloud service would use, but retaining complete control over all aspects of the service for the purposes of security. A private cloud with multiple tenants can also be called a *community cloud*. A *public cloud* service is the kind of service model run by providers, such as Amazon and Microsoft, where many customers use their infrastructure services, but for all intents and purposes it appears as an extension of their enterprise. For these kinds of service, the security of the underlying systems is vitally important to the cloud service provide, since a breach will see them potentially lose lots of customers and face irreparable reputational damage, however, you should be aware that the configuration of the individual instances of each service are still the responsibility of the subscriber, thus you'll still need to manage these as if they were installed in your own datacenter.

© Tony Campbell 2016

T. Campbell, *Practical Information Security Management*, DOI 10.1007/978-1-4842-1685-9_12

Services are logically grouped into cloud service models, represented as logical layers in a stack. The service models are shown in Figure 12-1.

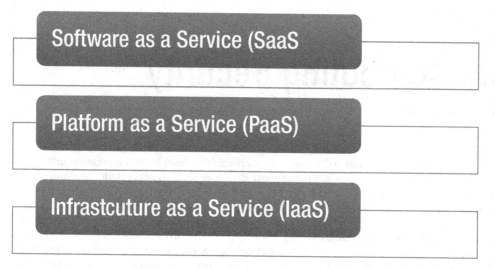

Figure 12-1. Cloud computing as-a-service model

In Figure 12-1, right at the top of the stack, you see *Software as a Service* (SaaS). This is the service model where the cloud service provider offers software to the subscriber via a network, usually accessed through a browser or application programming interface. The subscriber has no control over the underlying operating system, infrastructure, such as network or storage, and simply pays for access. Good examples of SaaS applications include SalesForce (https://www.salesforce.com), Google Apps (https://apps.google.com), and Microsoft Office 365 (https://www.microsoftstore.com).

Moving down the stack, the next layer to examine is *Platform as a Service* (PaaS). This is where the subscriber is provided with the environment for self-managed software to run, such as, operating systems over a network rather than being loaded directly onto a local computer. The subscriber doesn't directly manage the underlying infrastructure, including, network, servers, operating systems or storage, but has control over the deployed applications, such as a webserver or web application platform. Examples include Amazon's Simple Storage Service S3 (https://aws.amazon.com/s3), Microsoft's Azure Storage (https://azure.microsoft.com/en-us/services/storage) and Force.com (https://www.salesforce.com/platform/products/force).

Finally, at the bottom of the stack lies *Infrastructure as a Service* (IaaS). You might have noticed that as you move down the stack, the subscriber has increasingly more control over what's running on the cloud service. IaaS is the provision of a full computer infrastructure, for example, a computing platform where you can deploy your own operating system, management software, and application, configured however you want them. The subscriber has no control over the underlying hardware, but has full control of everything above that, including storage, deployed applications and even limited control over selected networking components (depending on the service that's been provisioned). Amazon's Elastic Compute Cloud (EC2) is a great example, where the subscriber has access to server resources where they can install whatever they want (https://aws.amazon.com/ec2/).

As a security manager, your ability to influence your organization's choices on what kinds of cloud services they buy is critical. The higher up the stack you go, the more you lose control and visibility of what's happening under the cloud interface. The security of SaaS services is almost exclusively in the hands of the provider, so you need to ensure that you have a strong contract that stipulates their security obligations and if you are unhappy with any aspect of the service being provided, challenge it and see if there is any way to address those concerns. Communicating these threats to your management will at least allow them to make a balance, risk-based decision on placing their trust (and corporate data) in the hands of the cloud provider.

Cloud Security

When you start to look at cloud security, be aware that you'll have less the further up the stack you go. SaaS offerings, at the top of the stack, mean you have no control or influence over how the software service is hosted or configured, aside from what you have provided to you by the vendor. The vendor, in this case, is fully responsible for all aspects of security, from the physical protection of the datacenter, through to the network, operating systems, storage, and even the personnel working on their development team. As a result, you will not be able to perform the audits and configuration checks that you were once able to, when the software was hosted in your own datacenter. Now you are relying on the service provider to manage the patching, configuration, and administration of the systems, without necessarily telling you when they have upgraded, what they've patched, or how they are handing the security clearance or police checks of their staff.

For security managers who are used to being involved in all aspects of the organization's security architecture and management of information risk, this may well sound like a scary prospect. And it is. Nevertheless, there are a few things that cloud service providers can do to help allay your fears.

Start by asking if they have any security certifications or accreditations for their services, such as ISO 27001, ISO 38500, or COBIT. Once you have confirmed the cloud service provider has the kind of certification you believe they should have, ask for evidence related to both the scope of the certification, its expiry date, and any caveats that may be relevant for the service you are subscribing to.

■ **Note** If the cloud service provider is a member of the Cloud Security Alliance, they take their commitment to security seriously by actively participating in the CSA Security, Trust & Assurance Registry (STAR) scheme.

Next, you need to check how their services have been architected and if needs be call in a specialist security architect to assess how robust the service provider's security model is. Check that your information won't be put at risk by practices that might be cheaper for the service provider but not secure enough for the sensitivity of your data. Like all security evaluations, you need to know the value of the data you are entrusting to the provider and make your own decision as to whether the risk is acceptable or not. What systems are used for data separation between tenants, looking at all levels of the technology stack, from the physical hardware, through to the network, operating systems and if you're taking a SaaS application, you also need to consider how they provide individual instances of the application to each customer.

■ **Note** If your data is highly sensitive and keeping it out of prying eyes is essential, consider using encryption for both the communication channels and when the information is at rest on the cloud service provider's disks. If you cannot guarantee the security to an adequate level to suit your risk appetite, then you should make a call as to either accept a higher level of risk and maybe trade off using insurance, or choose not to move to the cloud.

One commonly used method for choosing the best cloud service provider is to create a *review, retention, and deletion* (RRD) policy then present it to the cloud provider as requirements tender to see if they have the means to deal with all the controls you require for protecting the different types of data in use by your business.

I would advise treating any acquisition of cloud services as a competitive tendering process, since there is an abundance of choice. Ask questions about their life cycle management for all aspects of the hardware stack, such as how they will support your exit strategy, should you wish to leave their service. You also need your own plans as to how you would continue doing business if the cloud service provider went out of business, which would be part of your wider business continuity strategy.

You also need to ask the provider where your data is physically stored. Many cloud service providers keep service costs as low as possible by locating their datacenters in low-cost countries, where labor, electricity and other overheads are less expensive. If this is the case, then you need to be satisfied that your data is now offshore and potentially unrecoverable if something goes missing, given your own legal system won't be effective in another country. Most of the larger service providers have multiple regional datacenters around the world, which are used to failover services from one zone to another should a business continuity event affect your local zone. So, even if you have contracted them to only use the local datacenter for your service, you may have no choice if a fire or flood affects the cloud provider's local datacenter, since they care about more than just one customer and their own survival depends on their remaining available.

■ **Tip** Dig a little deeper before you sign up for any cloud service. Some providers have what's called a *layered supply chain*. This means that while their trading entity might appear as a local service, they may subcontract an aspect of their service to an offshore third-party company, hence negating any safeguards that you may have thought you had by using a local company.

ISO/IEC 27017:2015

As you might expect, a standard has been published by ISO relating to cloud services: ISO/IEC 27017:2015 — Information technology — Security techniques — Code of practice for information security controls based on ISO/IEC 27002. This standard can be used to help you decide which security controls are applicable to the cloud services you might be looking to consume, with the controls based on ISO/IEC 27001 and ISO/IEC 27002, so it's complimentary for your overall information security management system (ISMS), allowing you to extend your ISMS to cover cloud services.

ISO/IEC 27017 suggests that both the cloud service provider and its customers (i.e., you) should follow the standard to ensure that you can translate the controls you build into your consumption of cloud services into controls that the service provider must be able to demonstrate. This ensures that the provision of cloud services remains practical while putting the onus for security at each layer of the technology stack onto both parties where appropriate.

Cloud Security Challenges

Moving your business into the cloud has been seen by many as the nirvana of IT Service provision, where someone else takes care of all those pesky IR problems and provides all your computing capabilities as a utility, much in the way you get water, gas and electricity. But there is one overarching difference with IT that makes it practically impossible to consider it a utility: IT services are complex and vary depending on context. Moreover, there is so much that can go wrong with IT systems, especially given the bugs and issues we see with even the most mature systems, such as Microsoft's server platform and Apple's OSX operating system. They all have bugs and they all need patching.

Starting at the bottom of the stack, with IaaS, the benefits obtained down here are simple and are the closet you'll get to utility computing: you don't own the datacenter or the hardware and the networking interconnects, Internet uplinks and datacenter services, such as heating, ventilation and air conditioning are the service provider's responsibility, as are the service levels—that is, if they say commit to a 99.999% uptime service level, that's what they need to provide and service penalties can apply for downtime that exceeds those targets. If you have installed a series of servers and systems within the IaaS environment, you'll need to manage those systems as if they were in your own datacenter. From this perspective, there are no positive gains other than not owning the datacenter, so if you are using to hiring an IT service company to manage your systems, they won't need to run the tin, but they will need to continue servicing all of your systems as they have always done. In fact, from the executives' perspective, not a lot will have changed, other than you pay one provider for using their facility rather than having separate bills for your equipment, electricity, and so forth. If your goal for shifting to the cloud is to ditch the local IT support team, you'll have to go up the stack to at least the PaaS level.

This is where it gets interesting from a security perspective, since you'll still have to deliver on all of the same security controls you used to provide when your kit resided in your own datacenter, except for the physical protection of the facility, which you entirely give over to the service provider in the hope that they have good processes for physical access management, fire suppression, intruder alarms, CCTV, security guards, fences, secure loading areas, and so forth. You'll be providing the same old endpoint protection systems, intrusion prevention systems, firewalls, content filters, event management systems and you'll still have to undertake incident management in exactly the same way as you have before. The main difference, if physical access is needed or you need to investigate a breach from a physical perspective, you'll need to access someone else's datacenter rather than having a fully audited access control system that provide access to only your own trusted staff. Who knows who the service provider allows access to your physical systems? That's for you to find out, if they'll tell you.

Now that you are sharing infrastructure with other datacenter tenants, there are a variety of new physical threats you'll need to consider, such as another company's engineers having access to your servers. What kinds of protection mechanisms stop them from putting removable media in your servers and stealing your data? In your own datacenter, this is not so much of an issue, but you'll now need to consider a whole new level of physical threat that you never had to consider before. Sounds good, right? This is why the concept of it being cheaper is a fallacy. It's certainly simpler to have a monthly fee for hosting that comes out of your operational budget, but it may turn out to be more expensive rather than less expensive, but that's the price you are paying for convenience. You'll need to factor all of these new threats into your service design and ensure that you have adequate physical security controls to protect your servers any form of physical tampering, whether it's malicious or accidental. Your entire business could be shut down by someone accidentally cutting the power to one of your server racks, but how would you trace the fault, especially if the datacenter is at the other side of the country, or the planet in some cases.

Further to all these issues, as soon as you open access to your servers up to the Internet, either for your own staff to access business application or for customers to access your external storefront services, you are susceptible to the same threats you would have been exposed to when you owned the datacenter. Nothing has changed. The cloud provider, at least at the IaaS level, won't protect you at all—their job is to protect the availability of their datacenter service, down at that IaaS level, but they'll take no responsibility for your poor management or bad configuration, and won't help you in the case of a cyberattack. You will still need to build that protected edge zone on your perimeter to protect your core business, such as a good old fashioned DMZ that provides filtering and antimalware services.

The nature of this divided responsibility between you and the provider is certainly prone to failure, especially if you assume that the cloud provider expects you to provide it. What I mean by this is, if you breach the terms of the service contract, the provider might actually reduce your service level or even switch it off if you're not protecting yourself from a denial of service attack—they can't risk all their customers being affected by your bad configuration on their Internet uplink. It pays to really understand where the line of divided responsibility lies and ensure that you work closely with the service provider to iron out any contractual wrinkles. It's possible to negotiate the terms of an individual contract, especially if they are keen to have you as a customer, so don't cave in to their standard contract demands, since there are many providers coming to market that may be more flexible and accommodating of your needs.

Another area of contention relates to the provider having the right to change how the back end service works—that is, where your service is provided from. By way of example, say you took on the service and the datacenter was located in Los Angeles. When you signed up, they assured you that all your information remained within the United States, so you concern about data sovereignty was allayed. Nevertheless, two years in and their business is booming, so they open up another node of their business in Europe, providing a failover node for the Los Angeles datacenter where all their clients will have even better guarantees of uptime and are protected against a massive business continuity event, such as an earthquake. Sounds great, doesn't it? So, they run a test and fail the whole datacenter over to Europe and you don't even notice. But all your data, in fact, your entire business, has now been mirrored into a legal jurisdiction where you have absolutely no ability to recover it or legal recourse if your IP goes missing (or ends up in someone else's hands). You have just lost your data sovereignty, which, especially for a government service, may be an extremely serious problem. This kind of dynamic moving of entire virtual datacenters will undoubtedly be a problem for many years to come, since cloud services providers need this kind of scale and continuity to assure their PaaS and SaaS customers the levels of availability they need. And there is no great solution other than working closely with your provider and having good contractual oversight and legal teams that work with the provider to get the guarantees you will have notification and enough notice to leave their service if it no longer suits you.

So, that's IaaS, but what about as you go up the stack and start consuming either platform or software as a service? The sliding scale of control versus utility means that the higher you go up the stack, you lose direct control over configuration and your need to manage the service diminishes, but you gain utility. Furthermore, you will lose visibility of logs, meaning that your SOC service may suffer in not being able to continue monitor systems when they are moved to the cloud. By this I mean that, for example, if you decide you are going to use Salesforce.com as your customer relationship management (CRM) system, you don't need to manage the physical tin or datacenter, you don't need to worry about operating systems, databases, or secure Internet gateways, but you do need to trust that the provider (Salesforce.com) will do all of that well enough to make sure that your instance of the CRM is private to just your users. If you have a valuable customer database, it's Salesforce.com's job to make sure that it's as protected as it can be, where you will hope they will treat every customer with the same level of rigor, big or small. From their point of view, a breach of even a small client would significantly damage their reputation, so they will hopefully be doing security management really well. But the advice I would offer here is simple: ask them. Find out how they do all those things you used to do yourself, such as containerization of databases and application instances, intrusion protection and denial of service attacks. This is where you can ask for certifications, such as ISO 27001, to check that they've been independently audited, and most importantly look at the scope of the audit to make sure that it covers all the areas they claim are protected by their security systems. They may claim ISO 27001 certification in the marketing material, but if the scope is just datacenter management and the operating systems and middleware are not included, or personnel security is omitted, then you need to know this when making your risk-balanced case to your board for moving to the cloud.

Cloud Security Architectures

I cannot stress enough how important it is to understand the shared risk model for building your cloud solutions. Before the cloud, security was entirely your responsibility; but now, as you move to PaaS and SaaS models, the contract is what assures the security controls that you have no direct control over. The Cloud Standards Customer Council, created a set of principles that help customers evaluate the maturity of a service provider's offerings. These are as follows:

- **Ensure that effective GRC processes exist**. Cloud service providers need to ensure that they comply with at least one or more of the usual cybersecurity standards, such as COBIT, ISO 20000, or even ITIL (for service management) depending on the type of workload they are managing.

- **Audit operational and business processes.** Ensure that the cloud service provider conforms to the ISO 27000 series of standards—as many of them as possible is best. If possible have them provide you the processes and procedures used to manage security outcomes.

- **Manage people, roles, and identities.** You should ensure that the cloud service provider is capable of supporting federated identities and single sign-on using a variety of the most respected architecture standards, such as, SAML 2.0, OAuth 2.0, WS-Federation, OpenID Connect, and SCIM.

- **Ensure the proper protection of data and information.** Make sure that the cloud service provider can support standards that protect information confidentiality (such as HTTPS, SFTP, and VPN) using IPSec or SSL and encryption at rest or in backups.

- **Enforce privacy policies:** Depending on which legal jurisdiction the cloud service provider operates in, they should be able to demonstrate and attest to how they uphold your privacy needs.

- **Assess the security provisions for cloud apps.** The cloud service provider should be capable of supporting all the technologies and techniques required to protect your applications in the cloud. This means they need to provide the same technologies you would normally use in your own datacenter, such as firewalls, VPNs, IPSs, and DoS countermeasures.

- **Ensure that cloud networks and connections are secure.** You could insist that your cloud service provider supports the ISO/IEC 27033 standard and 27001 certifications (and ISO 27002 controls) for implementing network security controls.

- **Evaluate security controls on physical infrastructure and facilities.** You should make sure that your cloud service provider is capable of being ISO 27001 certified and especially look for compliance against the ISO 27002 standard for information systems security as there are a variety of physical security controls that they should be using to secure their datacenters.

- **Manage security terms in the cloud SLA.** There are no current standards that support real-time assessments of security terms in cloud service level agreements; however, you can use ISO 27002 certification and ISO 27017 when it's finally published.

- **Understand the security requirements of the exit process.** There are no current standards that support the exit process for customers leaving service providers. However, you should discuss this in detail with the provider prior to taking on their service, because you want to avoid the issues associated with service lock-in.

The technology stack in a cloud implementation is extremely complicated and can be very difficult to assure, especially from a security perspective. Really, this is a massive subject area and in each provider's architecture, you'll find different ways to deal with threats. What you need to consider, from a security management perspective, is that there are a few fundamental aspects of secure cloud computing services that you should look at from the outset:

- **Access control:** Build a solution that extends your identity and access management capabilities from your on premise systems into the cloud, operating as an access control broker for third-party public cloud services, especially if there is no integration between your local directory and the end system. To address this, new systems, known as *cloud access security brokers* (CASBs), have been developed to provide policy enforcement, which situate between cloud service users and providers to manage access request. They offer services, such as authentication, single sign-on, credential mapping, profiling, encryption, tokenization, comprehensive logging, and alerting, and their security offering can be further bolstered with malware detection and intrusion prevention.

- **Firewalls and IPS**: When you build systems in the cloud, you still need to provide the same network security controls you would in a locally installed environment. Most cloud service providers, such as Azure and Amazon Web Services provide virtual security appliances you can configure to meet the requirements of your security architectures, with rulesets, profiles and hack prevention modules all working in concert to protect your hybrid environment. You should also include intrusion prevention systems in your cloud installation to alert on and block any attempts at hacking your systems. In reality, you are no less exposed in the cloud as you would be in your own local data center, so you need to replicate every one of the security systems you'd expect to locally in the cloud.

- **Testing**: When you finish building your cloud solution, thoroughly test against every one of the security requirements your enterprise architecture team stipulated for this service. By conducting comprehensive security testing prior to switching over to live production, it ensures that you catch non-compliances and can rectify them prior to opening up the attack surface. If you can't meet a particular security requirement, or the controls prove to not mitigate enough of the risk, you can make a risk-balanced decision on how to proceed. Penetration testing of more complex systems, especially if they are handling sensitive business data, will give you an extra level of assurance that your information will remain secure once you go live.

■ **Note**   Most cloud service providers' security efforts are put into protecting the shared infrastructure they sell rather than any individual customer instance. In effect, they provide customers with an open connection to the Internet and a walled perimeter around the rest of their service, but don't concern themselves with the security of your own internal systems.

API Security: An Old Threat with New Targets

Many customers dive right into using cloud services with the anticipation that the cloud service provider will be better at security than what's possible to achieve themselves. However, all the same old threats are still present, such as hackers trying to steal your data or take down your systems, with threat actors, such as criminals, nation-state actors, and rogue insiders still having the potential to harm your business. However, there is one old aspect of software architectures that brings a new kind of threat to cloud systems: accessing cloud application programming interfaces (APIs). Many of the standard functions used to manage a cloud service instance, such as provisioning new systems and monitoring what's running are done using special APIs.

APIs have to be able to control access and assure that they cannot be exploited to attack other tenants in their infrastructure from one tenant's access. If they were to allow attackers to bypass controls or tamper with security policies, then they'd be providing a direct interface for attackers to manipulate their systems and potentially access a vast number of their customers' data. As part of your up-front assurance process, prior to taking on a new cloud service, ask the provider which APIs are used to manage their systems and find out what levels of programming assurance have been undertaken to check their security. Clearly, APIs are one of the most attacked threat vectors within cloud service provider environments, so they should have undertaken an extensive penetration testing and vulnerability testing exercise on each interface in the not too distant past, but ask them about ongoing assurance to see how they manage change and how security testing is completed prior to each new version of the software interface.

Virtualization

Virtualization is the dividing up a host system's computer resources—its CPU, memory, and disk space—into smaller, self-sufficient computer systems, known as *virtual machines* (VMs).

Each VM thinks it is an independent system and the operating system, for all intents and purposes, works as if it is its physical counterpart. VMs rely on the host system's processor, where a system known as the hypervisor governs the provision of resources to the guest VM, which provides isolation from the other guest VMs.

One of the design tenets of a hypervisor is that any one VM cannot directly affect the operation of any other host VM, even if one of those hosts is attacked or crashes. This means that the hypervisor doesn't allow the hosts to directly access system resources; instead, it provides a virtual interface to what appear to be physical hardware resources, so that they can never directly affect the host.

There are two kinds of hypervisors you should know about: *Type 1* and *Type 2*. A Type 1 hypervisor, also known as a *bare-metal hypervisor,* is installed directly onto the physical hardware (no other operating system is present). Each guest operating system subsequently runs on the hypervisor. A Type 2 hypervisor, also called a *hosted hypervisor*, requires an operating system to be installed on the host, which it then installs on top of (such as Windows or Linux). Each of the guest VMs then runs within the hypervisor as they do with bare-metal hypervisors.

■ **Note** The differentiation between Type 1 and Type 2 hypervisors is really moot. Type 1 hypervisors, such as VMWare's ESXi, have been built on a special customized Linux kernel, so in effect, they are all Type 2 systems.

From a security standpoint, the virtualization hypervisor maintains the separation between each of the VM guest instances. However, the configuration and administration of the guest VMs needs to be tightly controlled, since the majority of hypervisor systems can be set up to allow information and services to be shared between VMs. In some cases, this may be desirable, but in most cases of cloud computing, each host will be for a different customer where the must be absolute separation between them.

VMware is probably the best known of the virtualization vendors, followed by Microsoft. VMWare publishes a variety of system and application hardening guides that show engineers how to lock down their systems. The following security principles are incorporated into most of these hardening guides. They make a good checklist for a security manager to use when auditing the use of virtualization in the enterprise.

- **Apply patches**. Virtual machines need to be patched, just like normal computer systems.

- **Minimize the attack surface**. When you install any computer system, you should disable unnecessary services, ports, and protocols to reduce the number of components that could be hacked.

- **Harden the hypervisor and the VMs**. Both the hypervisor and the VMs are targets. Don't focus on one and forget the other.

- **Disconnect unauthorized devices from VMs**. VMs are capable of presenting virtual hardware interfaces, such as for USB connected devices. If you don't need these, disable them in the hypervisor.

- **Use a trusted time source**. This makes sure that your systems are all synchronized and the audit systems on each of the hypervisors and VMs report events that have an accurate time (needed for forensic purposes), make sure that all systems use a trusted, authoritative time source.

- **Decommission unnecessary VMs.** Prevents VM sprawl by deleting VMs that are no longer needed. If you need to keep them for a period of time, because of corporate policy, and then have your administrators remove them from the active list of systems and store them somewhere safe, where they no longer contribute to the attack surface.

- **Isolate management traffic.** All the network traffic pertaining to systems management should be isolated from the end-user VM traffic, to ensure that no one on the end-user access network can attack your management systems.

- **Compartmentalize your network.** Subdividing your network like you would in a physical network architecture will bolster your overall security capability. Just because you use virtual systems doesn't mean you should follow different architecture principles.

- **Protect management servers.** Again, as you would in a physical architecture, you should isolate your management servers since they would be the most valuable target to compromise in an attack.

Application Virtualization

Application virtualization is a special kind of virtualization software used to encapsulate applications and separate them from the operating system they run on. A virtualized application is not really installed on the operating system, the way you would normally install an application, but it still runs as if it were installed locally. All of the system calls are actually handled by the application virtualization system, therefore the application is executing in its own sandbox. What this means is, the administrator can, based on the security policy (for example), enforce how the application behaves on the operating system, and can simulate any interface to any kind of operating system, even if the native operating system would not normally run the application. For example, an old application built for Windows XP could now run as a virtualized application on a Windows 10 platform where it would not normally be able to be installed and run.

You might use application virtualization to build a user application that doesn't install or write any files directly on the operating system. This could be used where applications leave messy temporary files all over the hard disk, especially if that data could contain sensitive information. By virtualizing it, you can maintain better control of what the application does and how it's used.

■ **Note** PortableApps.com has a software virtualization solution that allows users to run software on a PC without installing it. It is an open source, free virtualization platform and can be installed on any portable storage device. The beauty of this solution is that all of the application files are installed on the removable device (even Windows registry settings) and when the device is unplugged it leaves no trace of the application on the host system.

Virtual Desktop Infrastructure

Virtual desktop infrastructure (VDI) is a desktop virtualization capability for managing user environments (PC operating systems) on a server-based virtual machine. Users access the desktop service from a terminal system, over the network using some kind of remote display protocol.

Access is usually provided using a client system installed either on an existing workstation or on a specialized terminal, known as a *thin client*. These days, remote desktop capabilities are even available on tablets, such as iPads and Android systems. Thin client means a system where its functionality is limited to just providing access to the server (thus providing minimal hardware support and a display system). These are cheaper than PCs since they have less processing needs, limited memory requirements and don't need a lot of local storage.

Thin client systems are useful in security architectures because they can help prevent data loss, since all user data resides within the datacenter rather than on the end system. If the client device is stolen, for example, there is no risk of data loss as the client is simply acting as a viewer for the system stored somewhere else. Thin clients often lack hardware interfaces so can also reduce the direct hardware attack surface simply through the omission of those interfaces.

References and More Reading

Since cloud services are a relatively new concern for security managers, besides being a massive subject area in their own right, we've not got enough time in this book to go into a lot of detail. Instead of trying to cram too much into this chapter, I've compiled a variety of references here that will be useful to help get you started.

The Cloud Security Alliance

The Cloud Security Alliance (CSA) was established, in their own words, "to promote the use of best practices for providing security assurance within cloud computing, and provide education on the uses of cloud computing to help secure all other forms of computing." It's a membership organization, where individuals, corporations and other interested groups come together to set standards and best practice for all aspects of cloud security. You can find out more about the CSA on their website at https://cloudsecurityalliance.org.

Amazon Web Services

Amazon has established the largest of the cloud service systems in its Amazon Web Services (AWS) capability. Amazon, as you might expect, has created an exceptionally rich and capable security platform, and AWS claims that, "as an AWS customer, you will benefit from a data center and network architecture built to meet the requirements of the most security-sensitive organizations." Amazon publishes a variety of useful reference architectures and how-to guides on building secure solutions, and you can read more at https://aws.amazon.com/security/.

ISO/IEC 27017:2015

ISO created a standard that focuses on the provision and supply of cloud services that neatly fits in the 27000 series of standards. ISO/IEC 27017:2015 provides a series of guidelines for information security controls over and above what are provided in ISO/IEC 27001 and ISO/IEC 27002, by putting those controls in context as well as providing additional controls with implementation guidance that specifically relate to cloud services. Read more here: http://www.iso.org/iso/catalogue_detail?csnumber=43757.

NIST

The National Institute of Standards and Technology (NIST) publishes a plethora of useful security related documentation and standards. A few good cloud security documents have been published over the past few years. Two of the most useful are:

- Special Publication 500-291 v2: NIST Cloud Computing Standards Roadmap (`https://www.nist.gov/sites/default/files/documents/itl/cloud/NIST_SP-500-291_Version-2_2013_June18_FINAL.pdf`)

- NIST Special Publication 500-292, NIST Cloud Computing Reference Architecture, September 2011 (`http://www.nist.gov/customcf/get_pdf.cfm?pub_id=909505`)

Australian Signals Directorate

Australia's defense agency that handles electronic security has a variety of good publications on cloud security. For more information, visit this webpage: `http://www.asd.gov.au/publications/protect/cloud_computing_security_considerations.htm`.

CHAPTER 13

■ ■ ■

Industrial Control Systems

SCADA networks potentially vulnerable to disruption of service, process redirection, or manipulation of operational data that could result in public safety concerns and/or serious disruptions to the nation's critical infrastructure. Action is required by all organizations, government or commercial, to secure their SCADA networks as part of the effort to adequately protect the nation's critical infrastructure. (US Department of Energy)

Securing industrial control systems has become a major global concern. This is why I've included a chapter of its own in our journey through the information security management world. Threats that might only result in digital impacts in the business enterprise, such as loss of information or services, have real, physical impacts in the connected world of industrial control systems. This was highlighted by the infamous Stuxnet worm, which targeted the programmable logic controllers (PLCs) that lay at the heart of the centrifuges used by the Iranian government to separate and enrich uranium for their nuclear weapons research and development program. The Stuxnet story, which we'll look at a little later in this chapter, was the incident that made the world take note of the reality of cyberwarfare. Prior to this, cyberwarfare was speculation, since government capabilities hadn't at that stage been demonstrated in the wild. Researchers determined that the Stuxnet worm, comprising three sophisticated attack modules, was the progeny of a US-Israeli collaboration, where it was seen as a global security measure to slow the development of nuclear weapons in Iran. We'll cover more aspects of cyberwarfare and its implications later in this chapter.

What Is an ICS?

Something that you might have wondered about is why the term *industrial control systems* (ICS) is used instead of *supervisory control and data acquisition* (SCADA). SCADA systems are actually just a subset of ISC and constitute one single category of a special kind of control system. The fact that there are different types of ICS technologies on the market means it's important to consider the target of the attack and the outcomes (impacts of successful attack) as much as it is the technology.

By considering the threats and impacts of loss of confidentiality, integrity, and availability across a variety of different ICS technologies, where the systems support large-scale automated processes, such as those used for controlling the cooling rods at nuclear reactors, flow and control valves for water supplies and the electricity grid, or even the safety systems in diamond mines, you can see the full impact of attacks on confidentiality, integrity and availability. You'll find that many of the attacks hypothesized in the ICS world are not related to confidentiality at all. In fact, if you look at the Stuxnet story, you'll see that the primary intent was to disrupt production through attacking the controllers' integrity, thus rendering the role of the centrifuge useless and slowing Iran's overall development nuclear program.

ICS therefore categorizes real-time industrial process control systems which monitor and control remote or local industrial equipment, such as motors, valves, pumps, and relays. ICS are used in a wide

© Tony Campbell 2016
T. Campbell, *Practical Information Security Management*, DOI 10.1007/978-1-4842-1685-9_13

range of applications, such as chemical plant processes, oil and gas pipelines, electrical generation and transmission equipment, manufacturing facilities, water purification, and even burglar alarms.

Another kind of ICS to look at is that of the building management system (BMS). BMSs control and monitor a building's mechanical and electrical equipment, such as its ventilation, lighting, power systems, fire and smoke monitoring and security systems. Again, considering the impact of compromise of a BMS, it doesn't take an Orwellian-level of creativity to postulate certain damaging outcome of tampering with the systems. But just in case you can't, an attacker starts a fire, overwhelms the fire suppressant system to allow the fire to spread and locks shut all the doors. The outcome: catastrophic loss of life, systems, and information.

What's Changed in Regards to ICS Risks?

If we look back in history, ICS technologies had little resemblance to what we'd call traditional IT systems. They were isolated systems running proprietary control protocols, built on specialized hardware and software. However, there was always a significant overhead of managing these devices, considering the dangerous and often remote locations they were installed in, so manufacturers, at the behest of CIOs and executives, have increasingly looked to connect these systems to networks to allow them to be remotely managed, patched, and diagnosed for issues. Just image, if you have a control system at the bottom of the sea controlling some aspect of an oil platform, then it's costly to send out a team of technicians if something goes wrong. You really only want to send them once—with a high degree of certainty that they'll fix the problem. If they have a bunch of diagnostics from the old device, know exactly what's gone wrong and know what they need to do to fix it, the they'll make sure that they have the right components, tools and knowledge before they leave headquarters. This is a much better outcome for all concerned. However, this connectivity comes at a price. Low-cost Internet Protocol (IP) devices are now replacing all of these proprietary solutions, which is increasing the possibility of them being susceptible to the same security vulnerabilities and incidents that the rest of our enterprise systems are susceptible to. However, much like the issues with the rest of the world's Internet of Things (IoT), manufacturers have not had to consider security issues or secure development practices before, so systems are getting installed in production environments with the same old issues we'd been dealing with for decades—buffer overruns, open ports and protocols and data integrity issues.

THE INTERNET OF THINGS

The Internet of Things (IoT) is the term that describes the devices that are now coming onto the Internet that were once stand-alone. The race to get all sorts of products online has well and truly started, with everything from cars to fridges and clothing coming online and sending data to manufacturer's servers. There is the estimation that by 2020, we'll see as many as 200 billion devices connected to the Internet. However, in the race to get connected, most of these manufacturers are shortcutting the design process and almost completely ignoring the security risks. We've seen some amazing hacks over the past few years, such as on remotely managed pacemakers and cars. Jeep hit the news in 2016 when researchers were able to remotely take over a car, applying the brakes from a distance of a few miles away, from the comfort of their lab. Another team of researchers discovered that a medical device (a pacemaker) could be attacked over Wi-Fi, where the attackers proved they could change patient details, and most worryingly, modify the frequency and intensity of the shocks the device provided.

The primary issue with IoT devices is that many of these companies have never built connected software platforms before. This results in them not understanding the cyberthreat environment and hence ignoring it in the first iteration of their products. In 2016, security journalist Brian Krebs' website was taken offline by the largest recorded denial-of-service attack in history. The interesting aspect of this story was that the bots, which were situated all over the world, were mainly IoT devices that contained simple vulnerabilities that allowed them to be hijacked by the botnet owner. As more and more unprotected IoT devices come online, this problem will only get worse. It's fair to speculate that this foreshadows a troubling time ahead for the Internet where this kind of crime-as-a-service has the potential to take down even the largest and most protected of websites.

ICS Architectures

Most modern industrial control systems usually have a three-tiered architecture. The human-machine interface (HMI) provides the administrative and user access points used by operators and managers. They might be workstations, tablets, or proprietary web interfaces running on any number of different kinds of operating system. More often than now, they are using some kind of Microsoft Windows platform, but some have been known to run on Linux or even OS X. Web interfaces, as you might have guessed, can run on any platform, and present a whole new set of issues that we'll look at shortly.

HMI systems are connected to the ICS server over a network of some kind—usually a LAN. The LAN could have a direct connection to the corporate network, which typically then has onward Internet connectivity for standard user access to web services and email.

The ICS server connects to the remote sites where the control systems do their work. Wide area networks can be built on a variety of different technologies, such as satellite communications, wireless, 3G/4G/5G or more standard Internet WAN technologies, such as ADSL. Older ICS solutions may also use proprietary networking protocols to achieve the same result as these WAN technologies, but increasing demand from customers has forced ICS manufacturers to look for cheaper and less proprietary ways to operate. However, there are plenty of legacy ICS solution still on operation today and, whilst it may seem archaic for us technology people to be dealing with this kind of ancient technology, there is an old engineering adage that goes something like this, "If it's not broken , don't fix it." Some ICS systems even use telephony modem technology to chat between systems, control points, and managers. These days, the SCADA management servers are more often than not based on modern operating systems, such as Microsoft Windows Server or one of a number of variants of Linux.

The control technology itself—the system the company uses on site to interface with a physical process—could be as simple as a rotary actuator, motor, valve, or sensor, or a complex system for monitoring the nuclear enrichment process for weapons-grade uranium. For now, the detail of what the system does is not important, what you need to understand is its purpose so you can determine what telemetry information is sent back to the SCADA server and what inputs it takes to control all of the necessary devices it's supervising. The two main categories of equipment companies install at remote sites are *programmable logic controllers* (PLC) and *remote terminal units* (RTU). PLCs are more sophisticated than RTUs and have the ability to be programmed using special ICS languages. The PLCs and RTUs are connected to a variety of physical interfaces, such as temperature, pressure or light sensors, electrical relays, pneumatic valves, and stepper motors. PLCs and RTUs almost always use proprietary operating systems, given the specific nature of the work they do and the fact they are entirely embedded (built on the hardware) in the engineering process. Some of the more complex ICS technologies can have thousands of physical endpoints, where each one will require a level of management and maintenance during its lifetime.

Figure 13-1 shows how a typical network topology for an ICS network would be configured. Starting at the bottom of the picture, the administrators or system managers would log into the SCADA servers via a standard PC or tablet. In typical network topologies, a firewall would protect the SCADA server network from unauthorized access at the network and application layer by only permitting the users, ports, and protocols required to connect from the computer systems to the SCADA server to traverse the firewall. These firewalls are not special ICS firewalls in any way; instead, they are standard network devices that you'd find in the corporate environment.

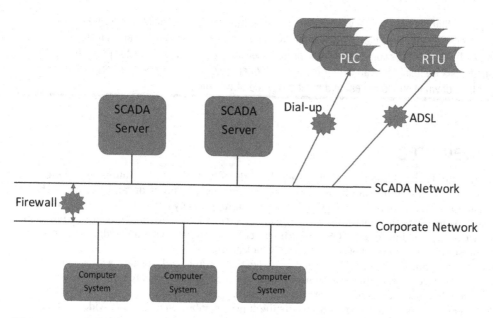

Figure 13-1. *Abstract layered ICS network topology*

Once the administrator connects to the SCADA server, they will access a management interface that presents them with feedback from the RTUs and PLCs and allows them to diagnose and manage the end systems being controlled on the remote sites. There may be additional network connectivity provided between the SCADA server network and the remote RTUs and PLCs. It's not shown in the diagram, but each of the RTUs and PLCs will then interface with a physical system to control and aspect of the industrial process in question.

ICS system architectures should therefore be conceptualized as consisting three distinct layers:

- **The IT Layer**: Comprising networks, operating systems and applications, such as the SCADA server and the manager's application interface. Importantly, from a security management perspective, an attack will normally target this layer of the architecture first because it's the most accessible to the threat actor. If one of the authorized computer systems on the corporate network is compromised, then it's not hard to monitor the SCADA server and look for vulnerabilities.

- **The ICS Layer**: Controllers, such as the PLCs and RTUs reside within this layer. The controllers are used to manipulate the physical devices used in the industrial process. If these are attacked they can negatively alter the outcomes of the industrial process, hence causing failures or reductions in productivity.

- **The Physical Layer**: Comprising the physical devices connected to the controllers, such as values, electrical drives, and rotary actuators. It is the manipulation of the control devices and its impact on the physical systems, where damage to systems is the impact. In some cases, the physical damage can endanger lives or destroy a business's productivity or reputation.

From a cybersecurity standpoint, systems on the IT Layer are concerned with the whole range of traditional security threats—that is, attacks that are impacting the confidentiality, integrity, and availability of data. There is, however, a fourth impact consideration for ICS systems, that of physical damage. Most attacks on ICS systems are focused on damage or disruption to a manufacturing or distribution process, again demonstrated well in the Stuxnet story. So, before we continue, let's look at Stuxnet.

STUXNET

Stuxnet is one of the most infamous and sophisticated attacks on an industrial control system, sparking controversy and foreshadowing the age of cyberwar (in the press, at least). In 2010, investigators were looking into an issue with the Iranian government's nuclear enrichment capability and inadvertently stumbled upon a new Microsoft Windows worm that was designed to target the specific Siemens industrial software and equipment being used for this process. It appeared to affect target only systems in Iran, specifically targeting the enrichment manufacturing program for making weapons-grade uranium. It is believed that the malware was introduced to their remote network when a worker plugged an infected USB memory stick into one of their HMI workstations. The worm spread rapidly across their network, connecting to network shares and leveraging a variety of unknown Windows vulnerabilities. However, the thing that piqued the interest of security researchers was the nature of the highly sophisticated payload, which seemingly had been to serve one purpose: to attack Siemens PLCs.

As soon as the Stuxnet worm made it onto the PLC, it audited its surroundings, testing for the presence of Vacon or Fararo Paya frequency converter drives—these are essential components in the operational running of the enrichment centrifuges. The malware then used two different exploits to damage the internal rotors:

- It increased the internal pressure
- It made the rotors spin too fast

It was the second attack that was the most successful, accelerating the rotors to damaging speeds. But that's not the clever part—the reason security researchers attributed this attack to a foreign nation state was the method Stuxnet used to cover its tracks. Before launching its attack, it captured valid baselines operational information, which it then replayed during the attack, so the systems reported that they were working correctly, while the malware accelerated the rotors to critical speeds.

Stuxnet was a highly sophisticated cyberweapon. Since its initial discovery in 2010, there have been new variants of the worm discovered elsewhere around the world. Furthermore, security researchers have determined that the original development was carried out as a collaboration between the United States and Israeli governments (no surprises there).

Stuxnet heralded the new age of cyberwarfare, perfectly demonstrating how kinetic effects can be derived using nothing but a well-crafted cyberweapon.

ICS Security

Defending ICS systems isn't easy. They are subject to a variety of problems that most IT systems are not, some of which are due to the physical interfaces they control coupled with the remote locations some of these systems can be situated in. Most control systems are built to have a lifespans of 10 to 20 years, which means there is a vast quantity of what you might term legacy equipment out there to protect. Moreover, individual systems could be decades old, running on extremely old versions of operating systems, such as Windows NT or even Windows 98, where there are no supported patches or maintenance agreements. In effect, this means that if a vulnerability is discovered in one of these old systems, the vendor (in this case Microsoft) will never produce a patch—so the system will remain at risk until it is decommissioned.

Industrial control systems have always tended to sit on proprietary equipment. This means their operating systems and communication protocols were almost certainly designed with performance and safety requirements in mind, rather than security requirements.

For this reason, security aspects of design will typically be lacking, especially when contrasted with modern industry best practice. The majority of control systems have a connection out to an external network or some kind, usually for maintenance and monitoring purposes—think of the typical control room in a power station or hydro-electric dam. However, these systems are often installed with default passwords, insecure protocols, or weak cryptographic systems, leaving them open to attack. In today's world, where everyone in the enterprise has an expectation of being on the Internet, once separated HMI systems are now connected to the corporate network, which in turn has an upstream connection to the Internet. Now, what was once a physically secure system, has a direct attack vector from anywhere in the world. Maintenance is also an issue. Most control systems will not be maintained in the way we maintain enterprise IT systems. It may be impossible to take one of these systems offline, so patching them, where they need a reboot, might not be practical. Furthermore, there is a tendency to adopt the "if it isn't broken, don't fix it" attitude. It's hard to convince a system owner who has never seen his systems hacked or taken offline due to a vulnerability that the best thing they could do is upgrade it to some new and un-proven version of the system. It's rare to find test systems that are exact copies of the production environment, so this mean team may be suggesting they roll out an update to a production system without any real-world testing. If it crashes the production systems, it could have catastrophic consequences, with the potential for an unrecoverable system and even the loss of life. A lot of systems won't have proven backup solutions, so yet again, this risk of messing up the production environment is a higher risk to the business than not patching it.

Best Practices

As an information security manager, there are a few things you should consider for your security program. If in doubt call in the experts, since these issues will not be resolved easily, but for now you can consider the following:

- Establish a network protection strategy based on the principle of segmentation and defense-in-depth. Don't have a flat network where all ICS components can communicate with each other indiscriminately. Identify systems that serve critical functions or contain sensitive information, and implement additional levels of protection where necessary.

- Identify all connections to ICS systems and disconnect any unnecessary connections to the ICS network.

- Harden ICS servers by removing or disabling unnecessary services and only permit known services, or applications, into and out of the ICS system. Evaluate and strengthen the security of any remaining connections in and out of the ICS network.

- If possible, investigate the use of application whitelisting since ICS systems are one of the easiest platforms to switch this security control on. This is because it rarely changes and once the whitelist is enforced, malware will not be able to execute.

- Establish strong controls over any data coming into the system either over a communications channel or on media, such as a USB memory stick.

- Consider AV scanning and content checking in the architecture.

- Design the system so that components can be taken offline for maintenance, including application patching. Establish effective configuration management processes.

- Implement internal and external intrusion detection systems and establish 24/7 incident monitoring, especially focusing on communication between components that normally don't talk to each other. Monitor the integrity of operating system configuration files and applications.

You can also refer to ISA/IEC-62443 to get more information, which is a series of standards focusing on ICS security. However, ICS security is really a massive subject in its own right, now seen as a massive international risk area, with specialist roles and positions being recruited for every day.

If this is a subject you need to find more out about, there is plenty of reading material that you can access freely on the Internet, such as the US Department of Energy's *21-Step Guide to Improving ICS Security*, which is at `http://energy.gov/sites/prod/files/oeprod/DocumentsandMedia/21_Steps_-_SCADA.pdf`. The best advice is to take nothing for granted, ensure that you consider all the risks in your risk assessment, and where possible, call in the experts.

CHAPTER 14

■ ■ ■

Secure Systems Development

This chapter introduces the concepts associated with change in your production systems, be that through the implementation of infrastructure projects, integration projects, or software development projects. We'll take a look at the solutions development life cycle and how adopting a secure development process can considerably reduce the number of vulnerabilities left in systems once they transition from development into production.

We will look at the following areas of the solutions development life cycle to see exactly where and at what stage security needs to get involved and how you should engage with the appropriate project team members:

- Security requirements specification

- Product assessment and selection

- Security issues associated with commercial off-the-shelf (CoTS) software packages

- Business processes related to secure development

- Environments (development, test, and production)

- Software and system acceptance processes (passing products through an assurance process prior to transition into a production environment)

- Managing security outcomes in the change process

- Risk reduction strategies

■ **Note** This chapter will not make you a developer or an infrastructure engineer. However, what this chapter will teach you, as an information security manager, is just enough on the solutions development life cycle to help you explain security to teams of designers, architects, and software developers. They need to be aware as to how they build security into all aspects of their design life cycle, so that security requirements are front loaded into the project, cogent test plans are developed early in the design life cycle and an overall assurance plan is adhered to all the way through to deployment.

Next we'll look at how bad practices in software and systems development can introduce security vulnerabilities into our organizations that can have disastrous consequences. You'll learn how the solutions development life cycle must be augmented with a step that includes elicitation of security requirements, both in the design and testing phases. By adopting a security centric approach to development, vendors, outsourcers, and in-sourced teams can help reduce the number of security vulnerabilities in their finished products.

© Tony Campbell 2016
T. Campbell, *Practical Information Security Management*, DOI 10.1007/978-1-4842-1685-9_14

We'll round off this chapter with an overview of the audit and review process, and consider the improvements in your change control and configuration management processes that will ensure that you always take security into account.

Secure Development

The information security manager's role in systems and software development is key. You will be required to ensure that the output from any development projects running in your organization (or outsourced to a third-party development company) is secure, whether they are creating a new line-of-business application or a new infrastructure capability. "But I'm not a developer," I hear you shout. I've also heard new information security managers say, "What do I know about configuring a network switch or Windows Domain Controller?" The simple answer is that no one expects you to be a developer or know as much about Windows Domain Controllers are the SMEs in your infrastructure teams, however, you need to have enough knowledge to work with those guys to determine what changes may need to be introduced to make them secure.

If you are lucky enough to have introduced a full organizational program of security, then you'll probably have some architect-types you can call on to help you express some of those complex security requirements that need to filter into development projects. If not, you should really seek a champion in the development team that can become the security go-to guy, who takes advice and guidance from you on your assurance plan, but has the skills to look at the detail of how systems and code are constructed and can help find the pesky defects in release packages that end up as vulnerabilities in your production systems.

■ **Warning** Secure Development is a gigantic topic, worthy of many books all of its own. This can become a career path in itself, testing applications and code for weaknesses and vulnerabilities. It's extremely well paid and code analysts are in high demand, but you need to be very focused and niche. As the information security manager, try not to get into the weeds too much in this area. Outsource code reviews to analysts and stick to your assurance plan, otherwise this will consume you. Nevertheless, if you are interested in this and want to learn more, this article on the Open Web Application Security Project (OWASP) website is a decent place to start (`https://www.owasp.org/index.php/Static_Code_Analysis`).

Microsoft Security Development Life Cycle

In 2004, Microsoft was tired of being targeted by hackers and tired of the bad press the media gave them for continually developing and releasing buggy code full of security vulnerabilities. In response, Redmond decided to get serious about security, announcing the introduction of the Security Development Lifecycle (SDL), a company-wide initiative where developers and program managers were mandated they use SDL in every project. This was a massive investment for Microsoft but they were hailed by the security industry at large as pioneering this initiative which has become the common methodology now used by practically every Microsoft development company worth its salt. The SDL is based on three concepts:

- Education
- Continuous process improvement
- Accountability

Microsoft now prides itself of the level of education and training it provides its technical job roles within software development groups and considers this training critical to their success as a company. They also provide continual refresher training and are great at reacting to changes in technology and the threat landscape when new technologies or threats appear.

The SDL doesn't tell developers what code to put in their systems, instead teaching them about security, based on a "cause and effect" paradigm, so that the developer can see from the security point of view where weaknesses might lie. This continuous process of improvement ensures that applications are always being fixed, and vulnerabilities are being found faster and earlier in the development life cycle; hence, fewer vulnerabilities are making it out into the wild. Finally, accountability is key, because all staff in development roles need to perform their duties and adhere to the SDL, which is tightly monitored and controlled. Data is collected from development teams and training outcomes are tailored to ensure that new threats and defects are understood and stamped out across their entire development ecosystem.

For more information on Microsoft's SDL, you can research the end-to-end process on Microsoft's Security Development Lifecycle portal on their website (https://www.microsoft.com/en-us/SDL).

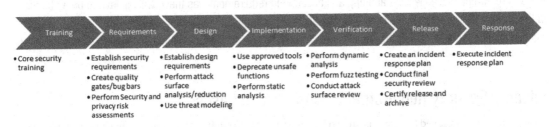

Figure 14-1. *Microsoft's SDL incorporates seven stages of development, starting with training*

Security Requirements Specification

If your company embarks on a new software development project or infrastructure design project, the first thing they should do, if they follow any kind of development methodology, is create a set of requirements that specify what the developers will deliver.

The complete set of requirements will ones that affect the user (user requirements), ones that relate to the technical integration of and inner workings of the system, specifying how the application runs and operates within the context of the operating system, network, and so forth, known as *system requirements*. Also, if you're lucky enough to work in a company or organization that gets security, they will have already developed a set of non-functional security requirements that will be incorporated into your project.

The information security manager's role in development is to ensure that the security requirements have been incorporated into the development program of work, starting with ensuring that they have at least specified some requirements relating to your needs.

Furthermore, like any other set of requirements, it's vitally important that the security and assurance requirements are captured and agreed with all stakeholders at the beginning of the development life cycle so that they are embedded in every aspect of the project as it progresses, including being in the budget estimations for development time to build the application and in the test plan for explicit checking they have been met.

Invariably, good requirements management will significantly reduce the amount of rework needed down the line f defect or vulnerabilities are discovered that could have been fixed by simply engineering it into the system from the get go. It's typically a lot harder and more complicated to add security into a system at the end of the development life cycle. This invariably pushes the costs up considerably—one of the reasons why security often gets a bad name.

So, the information security manager needs to continually ensure that all the security and assurance requirements have been built into the application, including making sure that testing is incorporated into the release cycle, alongside the typical vulnerability testing and penetration testing that you see in many systems releases. The information security manager must ensure that security trade-offs and methods are well considered and prohibit developers or project managers from trading out security requirements due to cost or complexity without ensuring that the underlying reasons (risks) are understood by all stakeholders (customers and suppliers).

Finally, the information security manager must assure the development processes end-to-end. This will ensure that you influence developers to adopt a defensive approach to coding at all times and imbue them with enough knowledge and curiosity to include appropriate methods for backup and restoration of data in their designs.

■ **Note** The information security manager should pay attention to legal requirements, communications protocol requirements, as well as auditing and accounting requirements, as these will all have to be embedded in the product or system to make sure that it's secure and compliant. If in doubt, consult with auditors or read the compliance regulations your business is governed by to see if they provide any insight into what's required.

Eliciting Security Requirements with Misuse Cases

A method often employed by systems and software architects to elicit requirements is based on a UML (Universal Modeling Language) construct, known as a *use case*. A use case is used to depict a desired behavior or process flow of a system, where users interact with processes and other systems, and pass data in order to complete a task. Tasks are usually written as a single high-level function, such as *change the wheel on a car* or *order a burger from the drive through*. The developer will take these diagrams and use them to create software systems and functions that replicate those use cases.

The problem in our world of information security is that security analysts are focused on what systems should *not* do rather than what they should do, so the concept of misuse cases was conceived by two Norwegian computer scientists, Guttorm Sindre and Andreas Opdahl, in their groundbreaking paper, "Eliciting Security Requirements with Misuse Cases" (Springer-Verlag London, 2004).

> *Use cases have become increasingly common during requirements engineering, but they offer limited support for eliciting security threats and requirements. At the same time, the importance of security is growing with the rise of phenomena such as e-commerce and nomadic and geographically distributed work. This paper presents a systematic approach to eliciting security requirements based on use cases, with emphasis on description and method guidelines. The approach extends traditional use cases to also cover misuse, and is potentially useful for several other types of extra-functional requirements beyond security.*

—Guttorm Sindre and Andreas L. Opdahl

■ **Note** If you are interested in learning more about security requirements analysis, the Software Engineering Institute, along with Carnegie Mellon University has developed the Security Quality Requirements Engineering (SQUARE) process for helping organizations build security, including the all-important privacy requirements, into the early stages of the development life cycle. For more information on SQUARE, check out their website at http://www.cert.org/cybersecurity-engineering/products-services/square.cfm?.

System and Product Assessment

Any new system will need to go through a series of acceptance trials prior to moving into a production environment or being released for general sale. The process proves that the product or system is fit for purpose and typically involves comprehensive testing from a variety of different standpoints, such as user acceptance, system and factory acceptance, and security accreditation.

Irrespective as to whether the new system is a commercial product, such as a shrink wrapped software product like Microsoft Office bought from an external vendor, or one you've built in-house by your own developers, you still need to go through an acceptance process to ensure that the product is fit for the purpose for which you bought it.

When you design system and product acceptance tests, the product or system being tested should be considered in terms of its effect on the underlying infrastructure as well as its capabilities. For example, it may be that you have bought a great word processor and it seems to do everything your users want, but if it requires that the user is logged in as an administrator to run it, it's probably not going to work in an enterprise environment.

In each case, assurance needs to be considered in terms of confidentiality, availability and integrity and each test must check at least one (or more) of these tenets. This is the same as the fundamental risk management process that you learned about earlier in this book; and it is best carried out by the information security manager's team.

Some organizations maintain test environments, known as *sandboxes*, where they subject their systems and products to rigorous penetration testing and vulnerability scanning and have their security team analyses the results. The amount of rigor you take in any one particular test should be derived from the risk assessment you undertook way back at the stage when you were deciding to introduce some kind of change into your environment.

COMMERCIAL OFF-THE-SHELF PRODUCT SECURITY

Products that you procure from an external vendor are colloquially known in the IT industry as commercial off-the-shelf (or CoTS) products. They need to be handled with care by your security team as they come from an external vendor where you have no say in how the develop software and no initial trust that their development practices are as robust as those that Microsoft suggest they should have if they use the SDL. So, how do you get to a point where you can trust a software vendor and feel assured that they have done their job properly and developed their solutions using defensive coding practices?

The most dangerous threat you must consider when selecting a CoTS product is that of rogue code hidden within the application. This kind of malicious function could undermine your security since it's already trusted and you've installed it on your platform and have users using it. What if it's your word processor or email system that is stealing information in the background and mailing it to your competitor? Unlikely if you are a real estate agent, but much more likely if you are a government intelligence organization and are in the sights of another nation state. As usual, the decision comes down to being risk based.

If you trust the vendor and use reputable sources, using checksums when downloading software from the Internet, for example, then the threat is lessened. If you bought Microsoft Office and it contained rogue code, it would almost certainly be discovered by the security community at large and Microsoft's reputation would be in tatters. This is why it's as important for Microsoft as a vendor to create secure untainted code as it is for us to use their products and have faith that they are doing a good job.

Lastly, make sure that you use legitimate, licensed copies of software, since pirate software is often modified to contain malicious code.

Secure Development Business Processes

The users need a system that does x. So, the developers set about coding a system that does x. Sometime, the better developers will say, "hold on just a minute, we've not even written these requirements down and checked them." That's a good developer, hang onto her.

The reality is that software development will significantly benefit from contact with aspects of the business that could be impacted by the introduction of the new system or product. Brand new business applications often arrive on the users' desktops as nothing more than mere reflections of what the developer thought the user wanted, given a couple of high-level discussions. However, without consultation with the user community, including usability testing with new interface ideas, workflow checking and security requirements analysis from the beginning of the development cycle, you'll never be sure you've delivered the application that the business really wants.

The software development process works particularly well when trade-offs are required, where certain requirements may need to be dropped because of cost or timeframe. Security requirements are also often traded off against expediency to market, which can lead to business data being placed at significant risk. In project management terms, the job of dealing with these trade-offs is known as *stakeholder management*, which is a powerful tool that should be used for managing both user and security requirements.

The information security manager's role in all of this is to maintain contact with the development team, retaining an executive role on the project board, providing input and guidance to the technical development team to ensure that security policy, security requirements, and any security standards or guidelines are understood and adhered to. You will also need to make sure that test plans include security testing, both from a security requirements perspective and a penetration testing perspective.

Change Control

The majority of businesses have a decent approach to managing change within their environments. The underlying service management approach to managing this kind of change, be it business process change, infrastructure change or application change, is known simply as *change management*. If you use a framework to manage services, such as the IT Infrastructure Library (ITIL), change management will be a fundamental process that sits at the heart of everything you do.

If you look at the typical change cycle, the beginning of this process has the requestor submit an outline of the request to all stakeholders for review and approval, along with the justification as to why it is needed. The benefits, risks, costs, implementation plan, test plans, and so forth are considered by the official *change advisory board* (CAB), a group that represents security, sales, business, and technical areas of the organization. The role of the information security manager in this context is to ensure that all risks and vulnerabilities introduced by the change process have sufficient mitigation strategies, security fixes, and testing plans (including penetration testing and vulnerability testing plans). If the change approval board approves a change, then they have the authority to specify any number of conditions that must be met prior to the change being implemented.

Once a *change* has been fully developed, regression testing in a representative test environment should show the CAB that the production environment should not be adversely affected when it's installed. Test should be incorporated into the documentation that accompanies the change, along with instructions for installing it, configuring it, backing it out if it fails, and whether the introduction of the change required a service interruption. This package is referred to as a *service design package* in most cases, especially if the organization uses ITIL as its service management methodology.

Acceptance Processes

The process of developing applications is followed by the *release process*, which dictates various milestones that need to be achieved before the application can move from one environment to the next (development to test to production).

A paper trail (or electronic form trail) should be created that accompanies the service design package, which must include all the documentation that the service management team needs to run it. This includes any updates to procedures or work instructions that are required because of this change. Once the service design package and all associated release documentation has been checked and validated by the test team, rigorous testing can begin.

The testers should now follow the deployment instructions created by the change instigator or developer, installing the application or system update in a preconfigured, production representative environment that is good enough to check whether the change will adversely affect any of the existing production systems or services.

Testing ensures both that all of the requirements (user, system and security have been met) as well as assures that the production system isn't broken by the introduction of the new product. Any defects found during testing need to go back to the developer for remediation prior to the testers giving the change the seal of approval for transition into the production environment.

Security testing should occur at this stage. The test report that accompanies the change should include details of all the tests that were carried out and should clearly state whether or not the system passed or failed to deliver on each individual requirements. If a new version of the product is released from development to the test team, at the test team's discretion (based on what tests were previously carried out and what the change was) the testing may have to start again. Finally, when the application has passed enough tests and it is deemed acceptable, it moves onto the next stage of the release process.

Some projects life cycles introduce what's called *user acceptance* stage at this stage. This may mean real users will be drafted into run typical workflow tests on the system (on the test network) to make sure that it does what they need. If the system is then accepted, the product can be deployed. The service design package is then given to the system administrators who manage the production environment to deploy it.

Managing Multiple Environments

From a security standpoint, it's advisable to separate your production environment from the location where your developers create product updates and system changes are experimented with, as well as where the testers run their scripts prior to product release.

The primary reason for having your production environment separated from your development and test environments is to protect your live users from malware, bugs, or inadvertent adverse changes that creep into the development process. Without exception, new systems will contain defects and these are usually caught during the testing and validation stages of the development. By separating the environments out in this way, your developers should build new solutions on a system that is physically isolated from your test and live environments, provided as a representative platform that they can entirely destroy without affecting your core business. If you build your development environment on virtualized servers, for example, then it's very easy to rollback or rebuild it to a good state if things do go wrong.

The test environment should be used to deploy a newly built service design package and should be as close in its construction to the production system as possible (cost permitting). Just like the development system, this test environment is still not directly connected to the production system so that any catastrophic system change or security concern doesn't affect your core business. Test systems are often subject to heavy load testing and security penetration testing so the performance of systems may be adversely affected to see how much load they can take. This is not something you would want to occur in a live environment. The test system should be configured to be as close in construction to the production system as possible and, if cost permits, the network topology should also be replicated.

I've also seen some businesses run an additional staging environment that is entirely representative of the user environment - in every way. This is very costly, but allows some flexibility in how you construct your test environment. Some testing may require additional administrative accounts be created and additional tools be installed, especially when doing load testing or penetration testing, so by its nature the test environment is not entirely like production, which may be cause for concern. The pre-production environment, on the other hand, is completely live-like. It is often the last check before a package is transported onto the live systems, and as a cost saving measure, it can double up as the business continuity system, if needs be, so that users can switch to using it as their primary workhorse should the production system be crippled by a disaster.

Obviously, the more environments you have to manage, the more it will cost you and the more you will need to patch and update them. This can leads to you requiring more system administrators, more processes and procedures and greater complexity, therefore the decision on the number of environments is one for senior members of your business and customers and usually security is but one factor in the decision making process. However, as the information security manager, you need to make sure that your voice is heard when these things are being discussed as security is a major consideration.

THE ROLE OF ACCREDITATION (GOVERNMENT SYSTEMS)

Some businesses and government bodies, such as military and intelligence organizations, use people known as *accreditors* to ensure that the systems deployed meet the goals and objectives of the security policy. The accreditor is the customer touch-point for all aspects of systems meeting security policy and can decide upon whether or not the system is fit for purpose from a security perspective. The job of the accreditor is to accredit the system through the process known as *accreditation*. Accreditation is typically granted when systems have been through and passed all aspects of penetration and vulnerability testing, and have shown that they meet all aspects of the security requirements. Where there are non-compliances on the system, the accreditor makes a judgment as to whether these are acceptable or not. Accreditation is granted or denied based on this decision. It's worth noting that accreditation is performed by someone who is not the senior risk owner. The senior risk owner can override accreditation decisions, but it's the job of accreditation to present those risks to the risk owner, so that the decisions made are based on the truth.

Accreditation can also apply in private sector industries, such as finance, where companies gain accreditation from external bodies, such as the PCI-DSS auditor, to check a business is capable of handling financial transactions. There is a code of conduct they must follow and an approach to systems' security they must adopt, both of which are checked by audits and then the business gains accreditation only when the external body is content that everything is being handled properly. Accreditation in the private sector may include the signing off on requirements being met from the ISO/IEC 2700x series of standards, or PCI-DSS for the financial sector, COBIT, or HIPAA.

The final point to highlight is that accreditation is not a one-off process, conducted only at the beginning of a system's life. Accreditation is a *state of being* that stays with the system through its life and monitors all aspects of change to a system, including the authorization off major modifications and upgrades to the components. New threats in the hacking community can change the system's risk profile, and in turn, affect a system's accreditation status.

Working with Outsourcers

Outsourcing software development and service management is extremely common. This practice has more recently been regarded as risky, as it introduces new threats that were not considered in the early days of the Internet gold rush. The introduction of malicious code, either inadvertently or purposely is not unheard of, and it's been proven extremely difficult to manage the coding practices of organizations that operate thousands of miles away on Indian subcontinent. Threats of loss of IPR are of grave concern and if the theft occurs in a country where your own law enforcement organizations have no jurisdiction, recovery may be neigh on impossible. You need to be able to fully trust your outsourcer to deliver what you need, so when engaging them, tight contracts and tight specification will be the only way to reduce risk. Unambiguous requirements and discussions with the coders will help build that trust. Finally, you look for a mature organization that has proven its development prowess to be of high enough quality, maybe using Carnegie Mellon University's Capability Maturity Model (CMM) accreditation—the scale runs from 1 to 5, with 5 being the most mature. Where possible, CMM level 5 should be your target.

REDUCE RISK THROUGH ESCROW

If source code is written or provided by another organization, your security is dependent on that developer for support, updates, and security patches. There are plenty of documented examples of outsourcing relationships going wrong, especially if the developer goes out of business.

One solution to mitigate this risk is to use an escrow service. Between your company and the supplier company you agree to set up an escrow service, where a trusted third party organization, such as a legal firm, holds copies of the source code and documentation. If the contract is breached or if the developer goes out of business, then the terms of the escrow agreement states that the rights to the source code revert to your organization. In this way, if the developers do go out of business, then you can contract someone else to maintain the code.

Finding Covert Channels and Embedded Malware

Code analysis can be automated using special scanning tools, such as Hewlett Packard's Fortify Static Code Analyzer. Take a look at the documentation at http://www8.hp.com/au/en/software-solutions/static-code-analysis-sast/.

By testing software from a user's perspective (trying to break it using the standard user interface) can also help identify covert channels that could be built into the software inadvertently (or on purpose). A covert channel is function of the software that allows users to bypass built in security controls. For example, within your corporate email solution you might have a system that controls attachments using digital rights management (DRM). However, the calendaring solution, such as the one build into Microsoft Exchange, allows users to add attachments to meeting requests. By sharing the meeting request, it could bypass the DRM security function. Your testing needs to look for these loopholes in the security controls you think will be protecting your systems and information as it's often the simplest aspects of legitimate functionality such as this that leave your organization open to attack.

If you expect to test all aspects of a software application from both a system and user perspective, you'll soon see that it's extremely labor intensive and time consuming. Often you will be analyzing traffic on the network between software clients and servers, looking for simple issues such as passwords and being sent in clear text across the network, or other sensitive information potentially being sent unencrypted. This would leave it open to interception.

Security Patching Considerations

Due to the immense complexity of most software applications, they almost certainly contain bugs. Even with the most rigorous testing processes and quality assurance methods employed by the most trusted developers, unwanted behaviors between complex components of the system exist. This complexity of code is what makes it impossible to test every combination of every line of programming interacting with every other. Bugs have varying impacts depending on the severity of what's been found, from incorrect values being reported to a user to a process suddenly operating with the wrong level of privilege. One way or another all bugs will have some impact on confidentially, integrity or availability of your systems (and information); therefore they need to be eradicated.

When bugs are detected or reported to the vendor there is a short lag before the development team can crank out the fix. During this time, it is very unusual for the company to broadcast the fact that there is a vulnerability; however, if it's a critical security problem, from a trusted vendor like Microsoft, then the time to produce the fix is fairly fast. Nevertheless, rolling out patches to your production systems should only happen once you've tested the patch on your reference systems. You should treat security patches and other critical functionality patches as normal changes, and make sure that their deployment follows your proper change control process, albeit fast tracked if they are priority critical fixes.

The process for evaluating your exposure to the vulnerability needs to be fast, determining whether or not it's critical to you. For example, a critical patch for Microsoft's RDP protocol might be vitally important for some users but if you don't use this remote desktop protocol it's of no significance. As soon as a vulnerability is announced to the open market, hackers will be downloading the code for the patch, reverse engineering it and using it to determine how the hack might work. This is why the detect patch cycle is likened to the arms race, as both sides are trying to outwit each other.

Security Testing

This section covers the testing, audit and review of IT systems, including vulnerability analysis and penetration testing. We'll cover the importance of reporting, testing, and reviewing systems to look at how these reports should be structured and presented to stakeholders. Furthermore, we'll look at highlighting the differences between computer-related processes and those that are considered clerical, with the intention of making sure that you see the need, and reason why, both kinds are useful. Next, we'll analyze techniques that can be used for monitoring system and network access, including the role of audit trails, logs, and intrusion detection systems. Finally, we'll complete this area of study with a look at some of the techniques that can be used in the recovery of information from these audit logs.

Testing Strategies

Consider the scenario where your software development group has created a new application for your finance team. They have been coding for four months and now have what they believe is a useful tool that they would like to roll out to the whole company. However, as the information security manager, you are concerned that there may be problems with this code. You need assurance that the new software is secure and won't cause a security risk that is deemed unacceptable by the management. Therefore, once this new software package has been created, and prior to rolling it out, there is much value in having it properly tested prior to deployment. This kind of security testing provides your management with the required level of confidence that this new system doesn't introduce vulnerabilities into your infrastructure that could leave your company exposed.

So, how do you go about testing such a system? There are various methods that can be employed, with the most common being a hybrid regime, comprising aspects of all available methodologies. This provides a holistic approach to evaluating the security posture of your new application, ensuring the most common coding errors and mistakes are eradicated before it's rolled out to end users. Testing from a business perspective allows you to test what a typical user might be able to exploit in the software. This kind of testing can include running through various workflows that mimic how a typical user would use the software. You can then instruct your tester to perform ad-hoc testing where he uses his initiative to attempt to break the system, using only the interfaces that are available to the user. In support of this, you would perform vulnerability analysis, code reviews and targeted penetration testing, all of which we'll cover in more detail shortly.

TEST SCHEDULES

Maintenance of your testing regime is essential to ensure that you both update your testing as the application evolves, and you perform repeat testing, based on the knowledge of new vulnerabilities and methods that may have been unknown when you last performed the application testing process. The frequency of testing applications is determined based on the frequency of updates to the code base, what the extent of the updates are, and if supporting environments have changed. For example, even if your code base has not changed over the last 12 months, the underlying Java Runtime Environment (JRE) might have changed, forcing your IT support team to update your Windows 10 tablet PCs. As a result, the supporting infrastructure in the Java modules may have introduced some unknown vulnerability that a repeat test might find. On a similar vein, vulnerabilities in the current Java Runtime Environment might have been discovered that now leave your application exposed, even though 12 months ago that vulnerability was unknown to you. Therefore, you need to update the JRE and retest the application to ensure that it still works.

Testing frequency should be defined in policy and detailed in your operational security plan. This will cover all aspects of your system, including bespoke solutions, infrastructure components, configuration, access control systems, and can even include testing physical security and administrative processes.

Vulnerability and Penetration Testing

Vulnerability testing is the process of identifying vulnerabilities within a system. This could be a software system, a physical system, or even a mechanical system, and the testing can be targeted to focus on components that might be technical, physical, or even administrative in their nature. A vulnerability test is very like a risk assessment, where assets being tested are indexed, value is assigned to them, vulnerabilities are then identified in terms of explicit issues or potential threats, concluding with a list of mitigations which could be employed to reduce the potential of exploitation. Automated tools exist for testing vulnerabilities in applications and infrastructure components, looking for typical issues with components, such as the potential for buffer overruns, SQL injection attacks and cross site scripting attacks. Depending on the level of assurance you require, you might want to conduct code level analysis of your bespoke application and in many cases outsource the vulnerability analysis to a third-party company that specializes in this kind of assessment. Tools such as Nexpose, Nessus, and OpenVAS are great places to start in terms of covering all the basic vulnerabilities that software systems can contain.

Penetration Testing

As you know, a penetration test is a simulated attack whereby the testers use all the tools of the hacking trade to attempt to break into your systems. When you roll out a new piece of software or create a new infrastructure system, a penetration test should be conducted on that system, to see if any discovered vulnerabilities can actually be exploited. Unlike vulnerability analysis, which identifies the problems in your system, the penetration test will determine whether those vulnerabilities can actually be exploited. This quantifies the risk to management and allows them to make investment decisions on whether additional money should be spent on further securing the system.

The other benefit of penetration testing over simple vulnerability testing is that it can be conducted from either a black-box or white-box perspective. The difference between these two kinds of testing is based on the amount of prior knowledge the testing team is given by the system owners. With black-box testing, the penetration testing team is given no information (or very little) about the system they have to attempt to hack. This way you are testing whether a bad guy would have the necessary tools and skills to break into your systems. On the other hand, white-box testing is carried out from an internal perspective where the test team gets full access to accounts, documentation and other resources that makes their life easier. White box testing helps you deduce what might be possible should you be attacked by someone who has inside knowledge. Both kinds of penetration testing approaches are useful and both proffer up useful risk assessment metrics for you to evaluate. Most importantly though, you can determine from the penetration testing report which countermeasures would be the most important to implement within your environment.

Code Analysis

Code analysis is a form of security assurance, where an expert security-aware developer—someone who understands the programming language and its nuances from a security perspective—casts their eyes over the code to look for common problems or issues that could lead to a vulnerability being delivered into the final production version of the application.

There are also tools that can be used to help the analyst locate common mistakes in source code, such as buffer overruns and SQL Injection points, which should always be eradicated during early development.

Code analysis is one of the most fundamental checks you can undertake in a computer system, which is why it requires a great deal of expertise, not only in the programming language used to build the application, but in understanding the weaknesses and inherent vulnerabilities that could be introduced by the developer. Even if your expert uses tools to find the obvious flaws, they should be nothing more than the first pass by the expert review team, who should then use the tool output as the place to start their investigations.

It's worth noting that scripting engines such as PowerShell, Python, Lua, and VBS also introduce security concerns of their own and which are found in many locations within your infrastructure. Microsoft systems are built on a strong foundation of PowerShell, an extremely powerful scripting language used to manipulate low level operating system functions. However, if it's not properly controlled, PowerShell can become the hacker's best friends as it really can do anything. You need to properly control scripts, user privileges to run such scripts and execute scripts using these kinds of execution environments, as they become vulnerable unless properly locked down.

Most outsourcing penetration testing companies offer code analysis as part of their service portfolio and you'll find, especially in government security contexts, accreditation authorities will require an independent code analysis be undertaken as part of a wider assurance plan for all new systems being deployed into the production environment.

■ **Note** If you work in a company that employs Microsoft system or application developers, you're in luck. Microsoft has released a series of useful tools you can use to improve and test code using static analysis. For example, Code Analysis for C/C++ is a static code analyzer that's built right into Visual Studio Team System Development Edition and Visual Studio Team Suite. It detects and corrects code defects, systematically working through your source code, function by function, looking for patterns of incorrect code that could indicate a vulnerability.

Test Reporting

The test and review process has to be followed up with accurate and comprehensive reporting. The report has to be as honest and direct as possible, ensuring that all findings, no matter how small or seemingly without risk they are.

Any attempt to hide or downplay the significance of vulnerabilities discovered in testing will leave you wide open to exploitation so this needs to be avoided at all costs.

The report must be balanced in terms of having both deep technical content and summaries that management can understand. A traffic light system is often used to describe the impact and the likelihood of a vulnerability being exploited, so allowing the system owner to make decisions on the priorities of the fixes needed to improve the system's security. The final point to note on a test report is that it needs to be protected in terms of its distribution. The report contains details of vulnerabilities in your systems, as well as the methods used to exploit those vulnerabilities. As such, it is the perfect blueprint for a hacker to plan their attack on your systems. Many organizations mark their test reports with the highest classification of data they can handle, as well as treating it as strictly need-to-know.

Verification

Verification is when you check that the original design specification has been met and whether the processes for design and development have been properly followed by your development teams. In terms of software assurance and systems security testing, you will be checking that the security requirements you specified at the beginning of the project have been met.

These requirements might come from a specific risk assessment, or might come from your secure coding guidelines, laid out by the development team leader for instructing your junior developers how to avoid security pitfalls in their code. All aspects of the check stage of the design life cycle should be tested at this point, and the results should inform you as to whether the requirements have been met and whether the requirements are legitimate in the first place. For example, if a coder introduces a SQL injection vulnerability into his application by not properly verifying input from the user, this is a coding bug which would be eradicated. However, if the team continually introduces a XSS error into a web application that requires the use of an open source piece of forum software, then the fundamental requirement might need changing. If a process you have created for your developers to follow is almost always being circumvented, then it should be re-evaluated to see if the process itself is flawed.

The term *verification linkage* refers to the need for rigorous system testing that covers both the computer system and any proposed clerical processes that support the business function being delivered. This confirms that assumptions and requirements built into the computer system can actually be achieved in live operation. User instructions, system operating procedures, administrative processes, and so forth, are all types of clerical or administrative processes that could involve the use of the new or updated computer system. Where a computer system has an impact on clerical process, the testing must be end-to-end. This kind of testing usually involves real users. An example might be that a user can link an envelope she's just printed to its matching letter that was produced on a different printer.

Auditing

As your IT systems run and perform their functions, each component of the infrastructure should account for its actions. For example, as the Windows operating system boots up, it records the starting of all of its system processes and starts logging users' activity in the Windows security event log. The analysis of this information is known as *auditing*, which can be leveraged to provide both detective and preventative security controls in your overall enterprise computing environment.

Accounting records are created by most system components, in both Unix and Windows environments, and contain a good source of information to describe who, what, where and when something occurred, such as the source and destination IP address, usernames and the time the function triggered. Most event logs a lot more information than just these fundamental entries, however, it's these few items of information that are critical to an investigation since without knowing the who, what and when of the event, the rest of the information will be useless.

As discussed in Chapter 10, security information and event management (SIEM) systems are often installed to manage the vast quantity of events produced in normal enterprise networks. Most of these, with only a few exceptions, will normalize the events from each source into a standard format, making it easier to mine the data and produce reports.

The collection of events often becomes an onerous task especially in massive organizations where the amount of data demands vast amounts of storage. In most cases, many hundreds of thousands of events are generated over just a few hours, meaning it's incredibly hard to detect the needle in the haystack that indicates an attack.

The basic principles to follow when creating an effective auditing solution are:

- Collect data from each endpoint on your network (computers and network devices).

- Only collect security relevant events.

- Normalize the data, thus allowing you to search across multiple sources in a single query.

- Generate alerts based on rules that indicate a security incident or breach.

- Use trained and experienced security analysts to monitor the SIEM and investigate breaches.

- Have robust and rehearsed procedures for managing audit information as digital evidence.

- Make sure that you synchronize all of your systems with an accurate time source since this will be essential in your analysis.

When you embark on building an auditing infrastructure, remember that this capability will fast become the focal point for all future cybersecurity investigations. Keeping data for up to six months might be necessary to provide the right level of historical data mining to satisfy your regulators or corporate policy, so plan for a large amount of storage to deal with that quantity of data.

Log Analysis

Log analysis is a complex and skilled task, often undertaken by teams of analysts in your security operations center (SOC). Auditors may be employed by your organization to undertake these investigative activities, so you'll need to make sure that your audit analysts have all the skills, training, and experience to undertake the investigations and forensic analysis to needed to get the best results.

Often logs are used as a component of the collection of forensic evidence needed in investigating crime. The need for expert training, especially when you consider digital forensic investigations, is essential, since one badly executed process could see the evidence being dismissed in a court of law. Auditors need to know how to properly investigate an incident and present the evidence in a forensically sound way, especially wearing the hat of the expert witness.

The integrity of the investigation and data must be sound throughout the entire investigation, therefore the investigator must follow the processes in a way that align with the legal handing of digital forensics data in your local legal jurisdiction. This is known as maintaining the *chain of custody* and often makes or breaks a criminal case. Badly handled information or weak reporting can discredit the expert witness, therefore adequate training and practice is required for anyone who might have to take the stand. As part of the analysis phase, auditors look for patterns of behavior that indicate an attack. Events are correlated with other events coming from different system components to find patterns that indicate an attack. One of the primary activities of SOC analysts is to develop the triggers and thresholds that show when something needs to be further investigated.

Intrusion Detection and Prevention

We talked about *intrusion detection systems* (or IDS) and *intrusion prevention systems* (IPS) in Chapter 10, however, it is worthwhile briefly recapping here. IDS emerged from research labs quite a number of years ago, but it has now been largely superseded by IPS, which perform all the same functions as an IDS, but augment it with proactive measures that can also stop at attack. Intrusion prevention systems have two methods of operation:

- Anomaly-based
- Rules-based

Anomaly-based systems create a baseline of your network activity over a learning period, then report on any deviations outside the norm. Rule-based systems match traffic patterns with known attack signatures and base their decision-making on matching these signatures to real network traffic. Most contemporary intrusion prevention systems can perform both kind of protection, however, they are also notorious for triggering on false positive detections, especially during the learning phase of them being introduced into a new environment; therefore, you need to properly manage their introduction and ensure that you don't overreact during this time. The prevention aspects of your solution should only be activated (switch from IDS to IPS) when you are confident that the learning phase is over and most of the triggers are reporting real attacks rather than false positives.

Index

© Tony Campbell 2016
T. Campbell, *Practical Information Security Management*, DOI 10.1007/978-1-4842-1685-9

Get the eBook for only $4.99!

Why limit yourself?

Now you can take the weightless companion with you wherever you go and access your content on your PC, phone, tablet, or reader.

Since you've purchased this print book, we are happy to offer you the eBook for just $4.99.

Convenient and fully searchable, the PDF version enables you to easily find and copy code—or perform examples by quickly toggling between instructions and applications.

To learn more, go to http://www.apress.com/us/shop/companion or contact support@apress.com.

Printed in the United States
By Bookmasters